# THE ROPE OF GOD

# THE ROPE
# OF GOD

## JAMES T. SIEGEL

*Ann Arbor*
THE UNIVERSITY OF MICHIGAN PRESS

Published by the University of Michigan Press 2000
First published by the University of California Press 1969
All rights reserved
Published in the United States of America by
The University of Michigan Press
Manufactured in the United States of America
♾ Printed on acid-free paper

2003     2002     2001     2000     4     3     2     1

Library of Congress Cataloging-in-Publication Data

Siegel, James T., 1937–
        The rope of God / James T. Siegel.
            p. cm.
        Originally published: Berkeley : University of California Press,
        Includes bibliographical references and index.
        ISBN 0-472-08682-0 (pbk. : alk. paper)
        1. Aceh (Indonesia). 2. Islam—Indonesia. I. Title.

    DS646.15.A8 S53        2000
    306'.09598—dc21                                    00-37742

to the memory of
Anne Siegel

# PREFACE TO THE NEW EDITION

Aceh is the name of a Sumatran province of Indonesia, once an important sultanate. It is the subject of *The Rope of God*. Before I went to Sumatra in 1962 I had read the ethnography of Aceh by Snouck Hurgronje. Dutch forces invaded Aceh in 1873, but it took nearly forty years for it to be considered "pacified." I wanted to see how a people could defy a great Western power for so long. Acehnese dug up canon from the time their sultanate was powerful more than two centuries earlier and did battle. Dutch victory is usually credited to Snouck Hurgronje. Snouck was an Islamacist who, like a few other westerners, had disguised himself as a Muslim to live in Mecca, forbidden to unbelievers, and who had first written compelling accounts of life in that holy city. He made a masterly study of the political situation in Aceh seen in its widest cultural setting.

Having read Snouck's book I wanted to go to Aceh. I was impressed, as anyone should be who reads that masterful interpretation of culture and politics. Nonetheless I wanted to show that Snouck was mistaken. Snouck after all had been a very important figure in the colonization of the Indies. In the era of decolonization, I was confident he had to be wrong. I had no doubts about my own political sentiments, all the more so since they were shared by everyone I respected. I looked for evidence of any kind that would contradict Snouck. I did not then know that people who had political inclinations different from my own could be not only accurate in their facts but correct in their interpretation. I never succeeded in showing that Snouck was mistaken, but I think I did show that he never suspected what would happen next. That was because he underestimated the strength of certain forces that he had actually noticed. I stumbled on the evidence of this force, the power of reformist, modernizing Islam, and spent my time showing its origins, its appeal, its effects, and its embeddedness in Acehnese society of the 1960s. *The Rope of God* was my answer to Snouck.

Later, what happened to Snouck happened to me. And not much later. In 1965 and 1966 in the wake of the presumed coup through which Suharto replaced Sukarno as president of the Indonesian Republic, there were massacres of "Communists" throughout Indonesia. In 1969 I went back to Aceh to see what had happened. I was appalled to hear the gleeful accounts of those with whom I had lived, whom I respected and of whom I was very fond. The joy with which they told of murder was unbearable to me. There were not many who could be suspected of Communism in Aceh, but it was the boast of Acehnese that all were murdered and none were kept as prisoners.

The massacre of Communists was of course a political event. But the people I knew well and the ones I came to know later who did the actual killing and who, before that, joined in the demand for the elimination of Communists were not political types before 1965. I did not know where to look for the sources of this horror. Perhaps the obvious assumption was that I had merely misread the violence inherent in Acehnese society manifested in resistance to colonial power. When I returned to Aceh in 1969, however, I found that the actors in 1969 were first of all Indonesian army officers who had to go to great lengths to arouse Acehnese to action. Those aroused were mainly high school students.[1] What are not accounted for in *The Rope of God* are the forces that are associated with the nation and that expressed themselves in 1965–66. Though the study accounts for the effects of colonialism in the construction of Acehnese society, it does not take account of the relation between Aceh and Indonesia, a relation that I now believe to be very close.

I have not changed the text of *The Rope of God* for this edition, but I have included two new essays in a final section titled "Aceh Viewed in 1978 and 1999." The first essay, which appeared in *Glyph* 3 (1978):18–31, was written shortly after the book was published and concerns curing rites and domestic politics. It deepens the description of the place of women and, I believe, elucidates elements that underlie political life on the larger scene.

In addition, I now think that the dynamics of both constructive and lethal impulses are to be found in the complex way in which Aceh is connected to national society and culture. The second essay in this new edition, "Possessed," focuses on the present day demand for an independent Aceh in order to develop this argument.

Finally, I want to thank Webb Keane for his efforts in seeing that this book was republished and for his comments on the appended new essay.

July 1999

[1] A description of the events can be found in the epilogue to Siegel, *Shadow and Sound: The Historical Thought of a Sumatran People* (Chicago: University of Chicago Press, 1979).

# ACKNOWLEDGMENTS

Sandra Siegel's contribution to this book is apparent in Chapter 7, but it extends much beyond that. It is because what she saw while we were in Atjeh differed so greatly from what I saw that I wrote this book. Clifford Geertz taught me most of what I know about anthropology and about Indonesia. I am also indebted to him for supporting this work through its various stages. Ben Anderson has shaped the way I think about Atjeh; every chapter reflects his influence. Any anthropologist interested in religion today must be aware of the work of Victor Turner. My debt to him will be apparent to anyone who has read "Betwixt and Between: The Liminal Period in *Rites de Passage*." Chandra Jayawardena commented on the manuscript in detail, exposing many of its weaknesses and prompting me to rewrite it when I had thought it nearly finished. Michael Rogin and Gerald Berreman have been encouraging and helpful throughout. They, along with May Diaz and Oliver Wolters, read an early version of the manuscript and made many useful suggestions, and Lance Castles saved me from some embarrassing errors. It is with nostalgia that I thank Teungku Abdul Rachman Mas, his wife, Tjut Po Mariah, and her mother, Tjut Po Fatimah, for their generosity. I cannot list all of those who helped me in Indonesia, although I must mention Madjid Ibrahim and Muzakir Walad as well as M. Amin Aziz, without whose help I could not have worked in Atjeh. Let me also thank the officials of the Governor of Atjeh's Office and the Indonesian

Army who extended me many courtesies. I hope that my appreciation and respect for the people we know in Atjeh are apparent in what follows.

The Foreign Area Fellowship Program generously supported this study both in Indonesia and on our return to America. The Institute for International Studies of the University of California, Berkeley, also furnished support for nine months of writing while an earlier version of the manuscript was being prepared as a Ph.D. dissertation for the Department of Anthropology of the University. The Cornell Southeast Asia Program supported me for a summer and provided secretarial services as well as the best possible conditions in which to write about Indonesia.

# NOTE ON FOREIGN WORDS AND NAMES

Neither Indonesian nor Atjehnese words have a plural form, and I have not therefore added an s to these when using them in the plural.

*Alem* is derived from the singular form of the Arabic word for *ulama*. In Atjehnese, however, both *alem* and *ulama* can be either singular or plural. To the Atjehnese, *alem* designates a person less learned in Islam than an *ulama*.

A glossary of all Indonesian and Atjehnese words that appear more than once in the text can be found on page 285. Wherever possible, I have changed the names of all people and places.

# CONTENTS

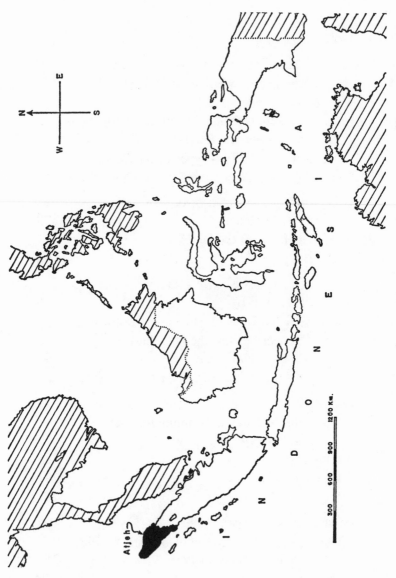

MAP 1. Southeast Asia, showing in particular Indonesia and Atjeh. Redrawn from a map in the *Atlas Nasional Tentang Indonesia dan Seluruh Dunia* (Bandung: Ganaco, 1960).

# INTRODUCTION

Van Gennep (1960) has spoken of transition within society. Perhaps only in those societies we call tribal, however, can we describe social structure and feel that we have used the same terms by which men describe the course of their lives. In peasant and industrial societies the idiom of experience is, often, no longer that of society. Movement from one status to another is thought of in terms that obscure the social nature of the experience. In this essay I have tried to trace the development of an idiom of experience and to relate it to the changing structure of society.

Victor Turner has shown how, in tribal societies, men come to know the nature of society and of themselves in rites of passage. Following van Gennep, he has explicated the middle period in rites of passage, the time during which initiands are no longer what they were before the ceremony began and have not yet become what they will be when the ceremony is over (1967: 93 ff.). Having no social role, the initiands are not persons. Since society and person are thought of in the same idiom, they are often spoken of as though they were dead. Their understanding of society depends partly on the fact that not being persons they are outside of society and therefore have a standpoint from which to view it.

When interior experience and social roles are no longer understood in the same terms, however, rites of passage no longer provide a standpoint from which to view society. Men are men and, as such, are describable in terms of their nature apart from the society to which they belong. At the same time they are aware of social position as influencing their valuation of themselves. There is tension between social position and interior experience in defining moral worth. Attempts to resolve this tension take various forms, such as escape from the world or social reform. In some periods of history, men do not try to resolve the tension at all; rather they strive to achieve momentarily a state which is a pure expression of interior nature, apart from the world, by which both the world and the self can be known.

In no case is there a permanent solution. Interior experience and social relationship are different orders of reality. Attempts that seem to reconcile them by promising social reform, for instance, are actually attempts to transcend structure altogether. Each mode of resolution is in fact the creation of a standpoint analogous to the middle period in rites of passage, by which the world and the self are understood, although the tension between them is in effect perpetuated.

From the point of view of those who were born into one sphere of society and find themselves in another, attempts at reconciling religious worth and social position not only explain their own experience but also conceptualize linkages between social spheres which previously had been discrete. Although no permanent resolution is reached, at any moment the attempt to resolve self and society demonstrates that experience of all social spheres is explicable in a single frame of reference and that society is, therefore, unitary.

One can recognize a progression in the forms of these attempts at resolution which is due both to changing social structure and to increasing awareness of interior nature as something different from the world. I have tried to trace this progression in one society by looking first at the genesis of the distinction between the world and human nature and then at changes in social structure and religious aspirations.

By accident I came to study a place, Atjeh, on the northern tip of Sumatra (see Map 1), where in the nineteenth century men had radically conflicting ideas about the nature of their society. While political ideologies claimed to describe the proper relations between groups, religious teachings advocated the unity of men regardless of the groups to which they belonged. Religious scholars thought that the unity of men was a possibility inherent in man's nature and was the final point of their passage out of the family and the village. From the views of the religious scholars came ideas of interior experience which, in the twentieth century, men used to interpret social roles as well. I have tried to describe nineteenth-century Atjehnese society in order that we may understand the genesis of Atjehnese ideas about experience. I have then gone on to describe the religious revival of the 1930s, when the ideas of the religious scholars became popularly accepted, and have continued by outlining the roles of men in contemporary

Atjeh, showing how religious ideas today inform social awareness. Hopefully, the sharpened consciousness of the Atjehnese of themselves and their society,
expressed through religious goals, can thus be understood.

The history of Atjeh is told largely in terms of
Islam and trade. Before it was unified into a single
state, Atjeh was the site of several different kingdoms.
Marco Polo visited one of these, Perlak, in 1292,
giving us the first evidence of an Islamic sultanate in
Southeast Asia. Another early kingdom, Pasai, has
been described as "an important centre for the dif-
fusion of Islam in the Indian Archipelago" (Th. W.
Juynboll—[P. Voorhoeve], 1960). The exact dates
of Pasai are not known, although it endured into
the fifteenth century. By the early sixteenth century, the various kingdoms had been unified under
Sultan Ali Mughayat Shah (d. 1530?) of Atjeh
(Djajadiningrat, 1910).

Atjeh reached its political greatness in the early
seventeenth century under Sultan Iskandar Muda
(1607–1636). Through his navy he controlled the
ports of Atjeh, forcing all trade to pass through his
own harbor and exacting tolls. During his reign Atjeh
had political influence on both sides of the Strait of
Malacca and, indeed, nearly succeeded in taking Malacca from the Portugese. The destruction of most of
the Atjehnese fleet during the final raid on Malacca
must have been a major cause of the political decline
that began after the death of Iskandar Muda. Although there were periods of resurgence, Atjeh never

achieved the same political importance again.

The sultans of Atjeh probably never controlled the chieftains of the interior. With the decline of the power of the sultanate, the chieftains began to trade in their own ports, no longer respecting the monopoly of the sultan. In the nineteenth century disputes between local chieftains and officers of the sultan over trading rights led to charges of piracy by foreign traders (Anderson, 1840; and Tarling, 1963: 183 ff.). These charges were the immediate cause of a lengthy colonial war between the Dutch and the Atjehnese. In the early nineteenth century the Dutch had pledged to the English not to extend their control of the societies of Sumatra to Atjeh. At the same time, however, they were responsible for keeping the waters of the Strait and the Indian Ocean surrounding Atjeh free of piracy. They felt they could not do this without some control over Atjeh itself. A new treaty between the Dutch and the English in 1871 released them from their pledge not to become sovereign over Atjeh. After negotiations between the Dutch and the Atjehnese failed, the Dutch declared war, and hostilities began in 1873. Because the war had no formal conclusion, it is not possible to say precisely when it ended. By 1910, however, the Dutch had broken most organized resistance, although it was necessary for them to maintain military government until 1918.[1]

Dutch policy for settling the colonial war and maintaining peace is discussed later on. Here it is only

[1] For a concise summary of the issues of the Atjehnese War and a description of its course, see D. G. E. Hall (1958: 495 ff.).

necessary to note that the end of Dutch rule at the time of the Japanese occupation did not mean the end of Dutch policies. The Japanese continued the Dutch practice of ruling through the traditional chieftains, although they also strengthened the religious scholars whom the Dutch had considered rivals of the chieftains.[2]

The Dutch did not return to Atjeh after the war. The coming of independence, however, marked the end of the rule of the chieftains. Siding with the Dutch, they were overthrown by rival forces led by members of the modernist Islamic youth groups which had emerged in the 1930s. From the end of 1945 until the transfer of sovereignty from the Dutch to the Indonesians in 1949, Atjeh was governed chiefly by Daud Beureuèh, the leader of the Islamic modernist movement.

In 1949 Atjeh became part of the province of North Sumatra. The replacement of Atjehnese in governmental positions by other Indonesians, coupled with Atjehnese dissatisfaction with the kind of nation Indonesia was becoming, precipitated a rebellion which began in 1953. The rebellion was led by Daud Beureuèh, and although it was largely settled by 1957, it continued until 1961, when Daud Beureuèh finally reached an agreement with the central government. Today Atjeh is again a province of Indonesia. It now has a population of about two million, 90 percent of which is ethnically Atjehnese.

[2] An admirable history of the Japanese occupation has been written by A. J. Piekaar (1949).

# PART I
## ATJEH IN THE
## NINETEENTH CENTURY

# ATJEHNESE TRADE AND THE POSITION OF THE *ULEEBELANG*

ISLAM AND ADAT

In 1873, the Dutch expedition sent to pacify Atjeh was driven into the sea. The Dutch returned six months later and with great effort captured Kotaradja, the Atjehnese capital (now called Banda Atjeh). This was the beginning of the Atjehnese War, the longest and costliest in the history of the Netherlands East Indies. As part of the Dutch effort to conclude the war, the famous Islamicist, Christian Snouck Hurgronje, was sent to Atjeh. The ethnography he wrote, *The Achehnese* (1906), is one of the most incisive accounts of any Indonesian people. He pointed out that while the Atjehnese chieftains, the *uleebelang*, were in theory officers of the sultanate, in practice they were independent. He suggested that the Dutch concentrate their efforts on bringing the *uleebelang* under control, supporting those who pledged allegiance to the Dutch. Recognizing that the leadership of the war had passed into the hands of the religious scholars, the *ulama*, he advocated suppressing them by force and confining their activities to "religious" matters.[1] His advice was followed and, after several years of intensive effort, the war was ended.

Snouck was correct in pointing out the political independence of the *uleebelang*, although he miscon-

[1] For an outstanding analysis of Snouck's policies, see Harry Benda, *The Crescent and the Rising Sun* (1958), Chapter One.

ceived its basis, as I hope to demonstrate. Snouck
saw the *uleebelang* as paratypes of European lords,
tied to peasants through rights to land; he thought
of them as deriving their power from revenues raised
through fines levied in the settlement of disputes and
the control of land. He saw their position threatened
by the *ulama* who, constantly urging reform in accordance with Islamic law, wished, he thought, to
eliminate the *uleebelang*'s source of income. Snouck
saw the *ulama* as alien agitators, disrupting the natural arrangements of Atjehnese society. The conflict
between *uleebelang* and *ulama* was to him simply one
more example of the conflict between Islamic law,
*hukum*, and indigenous custom, *adat*, found in all
Islamic lands. He wanted the natural harmony between lords and peasants restored and felt thus that
the *ulama* must be removed from politics.

Snouck's distinction between *adat* and Islam implied that there were close political and cultural
connections between villagers and lords expressed
through *adat* and disrupted by Islam. Actually, the
*uleebelang* were similar to the chieftains on the West
coast of Malaya that Gullick has described (1958:
65 ff.). They had few ties with villagers whom they
supposedly ruled. Their revenues came not from the
administration of the law but from their control of
the market. They used their profits to support a body
of retainers who were the real source of their power.
Dependent on trade rather than on their subjects for
revenues, they formed a class isolated from village

life, in conflict with the sultan, and occasionally at odds with the *ulama*. Atjeh was not a society bifurcated into Islamic and customary elements, but one divided into four groups—*uleebelang, ulama*, peasants, and the sultan and his group—each of which had its own view of the nature of Islam and *adat*.

Among these groups, however, the *ulama* had a special place. Only they were born into a sphere of life—the village—which they had to leave in order to achieve their status. Chieftains, sultans, and peasants were all, in theory, born to their places. *Ulama*, however, had to leave the village, where relationships were governed by kinship, in order to unite as Muslims in the religious schools. The experience of two radically different kinds of life made them stress the qualities common to all men regardless of social identifications. They saw their own life in the religious schools as a manifestation of common human nature. Their views expressed not only their place in Atjehnese society but also their passage from village to religious school. Their ability to express the nature of passage from the village linked them, on occasion, to villagers with a strength that the *uleebelang* seldom achieved in their relationship with their subjects.

The *ulama*'s view of the nature of man and society, stressing the qualities of men and not their social roles, was only occasionally popularly accepted in the nineteenth century. Not till the 1930s did it become the basis of men's awareness of their society. In the first part of this study I want to trace the social sources of the *ulama*'s ideas in the nineteenth century in order to understand their meaning and their popular acceptance in the twentieth.

## THE REGIONS OF ATJEH

The Atjehnese divide Atjeh into four regions— Atjeh proper, Pidie, the East (Timo), and the West (Barat) (see Map 2). These divisions correspond to ecological realities. Atjeh proper, the area in which the sultan had his capital, is at the very tip of Sumatra. It is bisected lengthwise by the Atjeh River and is flanked by mountains. In the narrow river valley people live chiefly by growing rice, although some Atjehnese tend cattle on the mountain slopes. The sultan's capital was situated near the mouth of the river.

Pidie, on the coast to the east and south of Atjeh proper, was the site of an independent kingdom until it was conquered by the sultan of Atjeh in the sixteenth century. Pidie was the greatest rice-producing area of Atjeh. Here, in a broad plain ringed by mountains and intersected by three rivers flowing into the Strait of Malacca, is a very old (300 years?) irrigation system. Pidie, with an area of only 4,000 square kilometers, was broken up into principalities which were nominally subject to the sultan.

Most of the rest of Atjeh, the West and the East, was settled by people from Pidie and Atjeh proper. These were the areas of the pepper gardens, Atjeh's most important product until the 1920s. Here the local principalities ran perpendicular to the coast and had rivers for their axis, rather than being fragmented

MAP 2. Atjeh. Redrawn from a map in *Atjeh* by H. C. Zentgraff (Batavia: Koninklijk Drukkerij De Unie, n.d.).

as Pidie was. In the East and the West, the coasts
tend to be either marshy or mountainous, with few
of the fertile plain areas that are found in Pidie. These
regions were considerably less populated than Pidie
or the Atjeh River valley: according to the 1930 cen-
sus, the rice areas of Pidie, for example, had 132 persons per square kilometer, as opposed to approximately 35 persons per square kilometer in the East
(Dept. van Economische Zaken, 1935: 156). Generally, settlement follows the rim of Sumatra, pene-
trating inland where rivers permit access. The mountains are mostly unpopulated except around the great
volcanic lake, Laut Tawar, where the Gajo live, and
the region to the south of them which is the home of
the Alas people.

## ATJEHNESE TRADE

In the nineteenth century the chieftains, the *uleebelang*, controlled the flow of goods in and out of Atjeh. Their major source of income was the duty they
were able to collect by virtue of their control of traffic
through the areas they governed. Moreover, their
connections with the outside world made it possible
for Atjehnese products to reach distant markets and
for foreign goods to enter Atjeh. The extent of
Atjehnese trade was striking. For centuries Atjeh was
known as one of the important pepper producers of
the archipelago. In addition, areca nut was sent from
Atjeh to Penang, off the coast of Malaya, and was
then shipped on to China and Burma, as well as to
the Malabar and Coromandel coasts and to Bengal

(Anderson, 1840: 163); various other less significant products were also exported.

In return for the commodities it exported, Atjeh
imported many necessities. Cloth, for instance, was
the most valuable import. Although the Atjehnese
made both silk and cotton fabrics from their own
fibers, imported cloth was used for everyday clothing. According to the ethnographer Jacobs (1894:
77), imported fabrics were cheaper than Atjehnese
manufactures. Anderson (1840: 239) listed the cargo of a Chinese junk which sailed from Penang to
Atjeh. Of its $7,600 (Spanish) worth of goods,
$2,000 was cloth. Among the other items were
25,000 Chinese needles, 55 hoes, 700 frying pans,
28,186 pieces of coarse China ware, 16 dozen knives,
2 catties of silk thread, 20 muskets, 10 cannisters of
gunpowder, 105 catties of sugar candy, 1 picul of
iron nails, 29 piculs and 6 catties of dates, and 57
pieces of lutestring. Jacobs pointed out that almost
all of the spices used daily in cooking were imported,
and Snouck (1906: I, 30) mentions that the stock
fish (*eungkot keumamaih*) eaten in areas distant from
the sea, was also imported (from the Maldives).

Atjeh as a whole was a rice-deficit area because the
pepper planters did not ordinarily grow rice (Tolsen,
1880: 37–50). Pidie, however, had rice surpluses
which it sent both to the pepper areas and to Penang
(Veth, 1873: 44; and Anderson, 1840: 222 ff.).
These surpluses were so great that when trade was
halted during the war with the Dutch, the people of
Pidie only planted every other year and still had an

excess that was left to rot (Encyclopaedisch Bureau, 1916: 13–14). Rice, in fact, was the most valuable Atjehnese export sent to Penang for four of the years between 1810 and 1823, ranking only below pepper and areca nut in the other years (Anderson, 1840: 222 ff.).

As the preceding comments have indicated, a large part of Atjehnese trade was carried on with Penang.[2] The traders were Chinese, Atjehnese, and British. In 1840 John Anderson reported that there was a well-established "direct commercial intercourse between the several ports [of Atjeh] and Bengal, Madras, and Bombay and latterly with Singapore and Malacca" (p. 159). There were also American ships participating in this trade, Arab vessels landing pilgrims from Mecca as well as "salt, dates and Surat piece goods," Portuguese ships from Macao and Goa, "Parsee vessels from Surat and Bombay," and French ships (Anderson, 1840: 159 ff.).

The role of the *uleebelang* in this trade was essential to their political position and cultural views. They operated on the borders of their *nanggrou* (the name used in some places to designate the areas governed by the *uleebelang*) rather than trying to control events within it. As I shall try to show, they were not representative of their areas; they did not symbolize the unity of the *nanggrou*. The rights of the *uleebelang* were concerned primarily with trade.

[2] Atjehnese trade with Penang extends back to the late eighteenth century (Puvanarajah, 1960: 2; and Khoo Hock Cheng, 1959: 4).

Their rights over land tenure were insignificant. Although they were responsible for the administration of the Islamic law within their *nanggrou*, they violated this duty for personal gain. As might be expected, the position of the *uleebelang* differed in the pepper- and rice-growing areas, and hence we shall look at them separately.

The pepper regions were always frontier areas. New parts of Atjeh were continually being opened up as a result of expanding production and shifts in patterns of trade in the archipelago. Pepper was one of the products of Pasai on the East coast in the fourteenth century and of Pidie in the fifteenth. For the greater part of Atjeh's history, the West coast has produced the bulk of the pepper. W. L. Ritter who visited Atjeh estimated the production of the West coast at between 150,000 and 200,000 piculs a year (a picul is equivalent to about 137 pounds) (Ritter, 1838–1839: I). After the founding of Singapore in 1819, however, the center of production moved gradually to the East coast (Kreemer, 1922: II, 7 ff.).

Pepper requires four years to mature, during which time the growers must be supported. The financial arrangements for the founding of new pepper-growing settlements tell us a great deal about the nature of the pepper states. The *uleebelang* provided the capital in most cases, at least on the East coast in the nineteenth century; they in turn were financed by merchants from Penang, most of whom were Chinese.

A garden was begun when a person with capital (*pangkai*), the *peutuha pangkai*, agreed to furnish

advances for the support of planters until the pepper
could ripen. The agreement was not made with the
planters themselves, but with an intermediary, known
as the *peutuha seunubok* (*seunubok* means garden).
The *peutuha seunubok* chose the ground and then
brought together the workers (*aneuk seunubok*, literally, children of the garden). The boundaries of
the garden were established on three sides with one
side left open; the owner of the garden had the right
to extend the enterprise on the unbounded side. The
land was cleared and the felled trees burned. Often
in the first year rice was planted. Then *dadap*, the
trees which shade the garden and around which the
pepper vines twine themselves, were planted. When
possible, the *dadap* shoots were bought from established gardens. An irrigation channel was dug, usually at the expense of the *uleebelang*. A year and a half
after the start of the garden, the pepper itself was
planted. Throughout this period the *peutuha pangkai*
supplied the provisions for the workers, but the *aneuk
seunubok* were obligated to repay the advances during the fourth or fifth year of the project, depending
on the region. In return for providing the capital,
the *peutuha pangkai* was entitled to collect a fixed
amount of the crop annually so long as the garden
was in production (about twenty years). The *peutuha
pangkai* also had the right to buy the rest of the crop
at the market price. The garden, however, was the
property of the *aneuk seunubok*, the workers, not of
the entrepreneur, and they had the right to sell it, although the obligation to furnish the *peutuha pangkai*

with his share of the crop was passed on to the new owners.[3]

Each garden had one to ten men (Kruijt, 1877: 78), usually from Pidie and probably from the same village. Initially they returned home each year "after the pepper harvest with the money they earned— home to wife and children" (Kruijt, 1877: 63). After a few years, however, many chose to settle permanently in the East, and they brought their families to live with them; in spite of this, they still relied on connections with their kinsmen and fellow villagers in Pidie, for at harvest time additional hands were needed for drying and shipping, and relatives and friends were called upon for temporary help (Kruijt, 1877: 78).

In virgin areas, the *peutuha pangkai* became the *uleebelang*, although he often had another title, such as radja or imam. The formation of these states was described by Ritter (1838–1839: II, 2–3): "If the enterprise is successful and the product lives up to expectations there will be a *gampong* [village] in a spot where a few years before there was nothing but

---

[3] At various times the garden was appraised. If it appeared neglected, the workers had to make up the difference between what the garden should have yielded and what it actually did yield. The workers paid this penalty from their share of the harvest.

There were various other arrangements between workers and the *peutuha pangkai*, although the one outlined above was most common. Sometimes the whole crop was divided equally between workers and entrepreneurs. In this case the workers were supported for three years and only had to pay back half of the advances (Encyclopaedisch Bureau, 1913: 73–95).

wilderness. . . . The perimeters become slowly extended and in this way another state is formed which, if the volume of trade is sufficient, gets a great name, blossoms, and establishes other *gampong* in the area. Finally it becomes independent of the prince of the land." The new radja, when he had the money, usually got a letter patent or edict of appointment (*sarakata*) from the sultan legitimizing his position. So long as he was able, however, he did not give the sultan the share of the export and import duties that the sultan claimed (Veth, 1873: 42).

The *uleebelang* tried to retain the right to act as the sole *peutuha pangkai* in their areas until the Dutch interfered (Encyclopaedisch Bureau, 1913: 151). It does not seem likely, however, that they could have financed the rapid expansion of pepper cultivation that took place on the East coast without the help of Chinese merchants from Penang. Kruijt noted that along a 100-kilometer stretch of coast there was only one settlement (out of about twelve) more than forty years old (1877: 62). Given that there was no return on the *peutuha pangkai*'s investment for four years, it is hard to see how most of the production in a *nanggrou* could have been financed by a single source and still have expanded so rapidly without outside help. Kruijt described the relationship between the *uleebelang* and the Chinese: "The Atjehnese chiefs and traders (both types are almost always united in one person) are eager, flashy, and ostentatious, and therefore are always in debt to the

merchants (chiefly Chinese in Pinang [sic]). They
pledge delivery of pepper and other products at a
fixed price as settlement of their debts. It is easy to
see that these agreements are always to the advantage
of the much cleverer Chinese who provide their debtors with renewed advances of thousands of dollars to
continue holding them in their power" (1877: 55).
The *uleebelang* may have been extravagant, but it is
easier to see the advances as loans to be used for the
expansion of gardens rather than for personal consumption. If this was the case, it solves the problem
of the source of capital for the continual building of
new gardens, at least in the nineteenth century. Certainly, the *uleebelang* must have been anxious to expand pepper production, particularly in view of the
double returns they received as *peutuha pangkai* and
as *uleebelang* collecting import and export duties.[4]

The relations between the Chinese merchants and
the *uleebelang* are important because they illustrate
the commercial role of the *uleebelang*. The Chinese

---

[4] The difference in the marketing of pepper between East- and
West-coast ports is another clue to the role of the Chinese in financing pepper expansion. In the West, the pepper was sent to Penang
and sold there. When it left the West-coast ports, it was still the
property of West-coast dealers. In the East, pepper leaving the
ports was already the property of the Penang dealers, undoubtedly because of the indebtedness of the *uleebelang* (Kreemer,
1917: 154). This indicates that the *uleebelang* on the West coast
were not indebted to the Penang merchants, as, indeed, we should
have expected, since pepper growing developed there centuries
before it flourished in the East. The cause of the indebtedness of
the *uleebelang* on the East coast was not, then, their ostentatious
standard of living but their need for capital for expansion.

were not only money lenders; they were also the buyers of pepper.[5] The *uleebelang*, in exporting the pepper from Atjeh, linked growers and buyers. They were political figures because they were first of all commercial figures.

The relations between subjects and rulers in these states were all within the framework of commerce. As I have said before, the rights of the *uleebelang* focused on trade. There were apparently no obligations of a citizen as such; the only contacts between *uleebelang* and subject were at the points where commodities changed hands. There was no head tax, no property tax, no corvée labor.

There was, however, a distinction between the rights of the *peutuha pangkai* and those of the *uleebelang*. The rights of *peutuha pangkai* have already been mentioned; they are called *adat peutuha*. The rights of the *uleebelang* are called *wasè*. The *wasè uleebelang* proper is export duties. There was also the *wasè djalan*, a tax levied on the use of roads paid by planters who had to pass through *nanggrou* other than their own in order to get their pepper to the harbor. According to a report of the Encyclopaedisch Bureau (1913: 91), this was often a "substantial sum." In return for the payment, the *uleebelang* was supposed to maintain the trade routes and keep peace. But, according to the report, "it frequently happened that the chiefs absolved themselves of these

[5] In fact, the radja (*uleebelang*) of Idi, the leading port in the East, leased his right to collect duties to a Chinese firm in Penang for $50,000 (Spanish) a year (Kruijt, 1877: 186).

obligations" (while presumably still collecting the tax). The *wasè lueng* was a tax levied for use of irrigation channels built by the *uleebelang*. If someone other than the *uleebelang* built the channels, that person collected the *wasè lueng*. Some growers built their own irrigation channels to avoid this impost, especially since those built by the *uleebelang* were often inadequate (Encyclopaedisch Bureau, 1913: 76).[6]

The intermediary between the growers and the supplier of capital, the *peutuha seunubok*, also received a fixed share of the pepper yield. All shares were distributed by the *uleebelang* after he bought the pepper at the harbor. "It frequently happened that the *peutuha* and other right holders never got their shares, or only part of them, and then only after long periods of time" (Encyclopaedisch Bureau, 1913: 91).

The rice-growing areas were for the most part much older than the pepper areas. But it would be a mistake to see the political situation in Pidie as essentially different from that in the East. Pidie was no more self-sufficient economically than the pepper areas were. Here, just as in the pepper areas, the *uleebelang* lived off taxes they imposed on trade. Here, too, they were entrepreneurs who tried to control all of the trade in their areas. The only difference between the two regions was the kind of goods pro-

---

[6] There was also a *wasè tanoh,* a tax on land, but it was not frequently imposed. According to the Encyclopaedisch Bureau (1913: 93), it was "paid to the original owner of the land in a few areas."

duced and exported. Originally Pidie was a center of
pepper; in fact, in the sixteenth century it was one
of the two most important pepper areas in North Sumatra (Das Gupta, 1962: 37–49). Later, however,
pepper was replaced by other products—particularly
rice, but also areca nut and coconut.[7]

The plain of Pidie is watered by three major rivers
and several smaller streams that fork off from them.
Each year, the *uleebelang* built stone obstructions at
the foot of the hills to divert a portion of the river
waters into irrigation channels. On the plain itself,
these channels branched off into smaller ones. The

[7] So far as we can measure it, the volume of trade in Pidie
was not quite as large as that in the pepper areas. In 1913, for example, the port of Sigli collected f1.12 annually in import, export, and excise duties for each person in its hinterland, as opposed to f1.51 collected in Idi and Lho Seumawè, the two most
important ports in the East, for each person in their combined
hinterlands. The reasons for this difference are, first, that rice
from Pidie was going by rail to the East in 1913 and did not
pass through Sigli, and, second, that some of the people included in the population of Sigli were actually growing pepper
in the East. There probably was a difference in the volume of
trade in the two areas, but in both there was a substantial dependence upon trade, and the *uleebelang* derived most of their revenues from their share in this trade.

The population figures used in calculating the index of duties
collected per person are actually for 1917, the first year in which
there was an accurate estimate of population (Kreemer, 1922: II,
215–216). The tax figures are taken from the Encyclopaedisch
Bureau volume on the Buitenbezittingen (1916: 217). I chose to
cite the figures for 1913, because it was the first year in which the
war with the Dutch could be said to be over and the last before
the disruptions of trade owing to World War I. The hinterland
of Sigli includes the subdivisions of Sigli and Meureudu (Lam
Meulo was not a separate subdivision at that time). The hinterlands of Lho Seumawè and Idi include the subdivisions of Lho
Seumawè, Idi, Takengon, Bireuen, and Lho Sukun.

water had to be diverted from the rivers near the hills because further downstream, near the Strait of Malacca, the rivers had worn ravines up to thirty feet deep, making the water inaccessible.

It might be thought that the *uleebelang*'s control of the irrigation system would have been a major source of power and revenue. This, however, was not the case. In fact, there was no attempt to coordinate water usage over the whole plain or even to control the drainage of a single river.[8] This is because there was sufficient water, and although the people closest to the hill received the water first, there was an excess, owing to the heavy rains, that drained into the Strait and was used by those downstream.

The irrelevance of irrigation to political matters can be seen by comparing the boundaries of states with the courses of the irrigation channels. There is not a single state which follows the course of a single channel. In fact, the boundaries of the states, as well as those the confederacies into which they were loosely linked, show no relationship at all to the irrigation system. It might be expected that states sharing a single channel would have cooperated in building a water diverter, but this was not so. Whoever wanted water first built the diverter, and repairs were made on the same basis. Conflicts sometimes occurred over the division of water between two channels, but because there was an abundance of water,

---

[8] There was an *uleebelang* with the title Bentara Blang (*blang* means rice fields), but there is no evidence that this was ever more than a title.

these conflicts seldom resulted in a serious disruption of agriculture.[9]

Like the pepper gardens, the rice fields themselves were not subject to duties. Mere ownership or tenure of land did not entail the payment of rent or taxes. Nor did one have to be a resident of a particular *nanggrou* in order to own land there. It was only when commodities were exchanged that duties were levied.[10]

Rice lands were fully alienable. The *uleebelang* owned more rice fields than his subjects; moreover, they were his own private property, and not part of the *nanggrou*.[11] At his death they were supposedly divided among his heirs as part of his estate. In practice, his successor, usually his oldest son, retained the fields and supported his brothers and sisters. (The estate was often divided after the death of the successor, but this practice created tremendous confusion and was one of the causes of the interminable wars

[9] Unless otherwise noted, all statements in this section are common knowledge. Statements from my informants about this period are not completely reliable since they concern events that took place before my informants were born. I have marked statements of this nature with an asterisk.

[10] Marsden seems to contradict this when he reported in 1811 that "a measure of rice is paid to the feudal lord for every measure of paddee [seed] sown, which is about the 20th part of the produce of the land" (p. 317). This was neither rent nor taxes, however, but payment for use of the irrigation channel which belonged to the *nanggrou*.

[11] As I have mentioned earlier, *nanggrou* is the term for the area of an *uleebelang*. It was not used everywhere in Atjeh, but it is the only word available for an entity that otherwise would be nameless.

among heirs and their factions that took place prior
to the Pax Neerlandica.)

Fields were worked by their owners, with women
doing the sowing, weeding, and husking and men
doing the ploughing and harvesting and taking care
of irrigation.* The *uleebelang* did not work his own
fields, nor did his retainers. Through a contractual
arrangement, known as a *mawaih*, he leased his fields
to workers in return for half the yield. Ordinarily,
there was no corvée, but a few *uleebelang* could, if
they were "powerful enough, . . . get the work done
by feudal service" (Snouck Hurgronje, 1906: I,
290).

It is not possible to say how much of the total rice
area *uleebelang* owned. In many cases, they did try
to confiscate rice land (Snouck Hurgronje, 1906: I,
117), but it seems clear that they never succeeded in
becoming major landlords until after the Dutch con-
quest.* By the 1940s their control of rice land
reached its peak, with the *uleebelang* of Pidie owning
between a third and a half of the rice fields depending on the particular *nanggrou*, but even then the
Atjehnese were mostly freeholders.*

The other important exports of Pidie, areca nut
and, in the twentieth century, coconut, were grown
either along village paths or in small gardens owned
mostly by *uleebelang*. These products were taxed
only when they entered the market.

Control of the markets was, indeed, the major
source of revenue for the *uleebelang* in all areas of
Atjeh. The regulations of the *nanggrou* differed from

one to another, but generally there was a levy of 5 to 10 percent of the value of all goods entering the markets. Some commodities had a fixed toll rather than a percentage, but nearly everything was taxed.

The most heavily trafficked markets were those at the mouths of navigable rivers, rivers being the principal means of access to the interior. These were not the only markets, however. Jacobs noted that in Atjeh proper each of the subdivisions of a *nanggrou*, the *mukim*, had a market, and that markets were also found in villages that were more than half a day's journey from the *mukim* centers (Jacobs, 1894: 68). Tolsen reported that "the more important villages have markets consisting of an open space or short road flanked by rows of shops under a single roof" (1880:47).

Given that a network of markets did exist, who were the traders and what was the pattern of trade? The anonymous writers of the Encyclopaedisch Bureau noted that "the Atjehnese is at bottom no trader, his chief occupation remaining agriculture. Trade only concerns him as it touches the products of his own labor for which he himself has no more use. . . . One cannot speak of a class of professional Atjehnese traders" (Encyclopaedisch Bureau, 1916: 211). On the other hand, some Dutchmen did notice a group of Atjehnese traders, the *uleebelang*. Kruijt, quoted above, said that "chiefs and traders are united in the same person." And a former Resident of Atjeh, J. Jongejans, said, "trade is in the blood of many

Atjehnese, especially the Chiefs and the better situated" (Jongejans, [1939]: 227).

Possibly all are right. There probably was very little trade between *nanggrou* since, given the difference between the pepper and the rice areas, most *nanggrou* produced the same things. The great bulk of trade must have been between the *nanggrou* and non-Atjehnese regions. Fishermen sold their catch to the interior, but the highlands depended mostly on dried fish from the Maldives. Some pottery was locally made, but there were also imported wares. The absence of trade between *nanggrou* is perhaps the reason that there were no rotating markets in Atjeh before the Dutch introduced them (Encyclopaedisch Bureau, 1916: 212). Trade must have consisted of the gathering of products at local markets and then shipping them out of Atjeh. The gathering of products most probably was the work of the Atjehnese who "at bottom [were] no traders" and only sold the "products of [their] own labor," while it is quite likely that external trade was carried on by the *uleebelang* who had acquaintances abroad. The *uleebelang*, then, were the focus of trade, gathering products from within their areas and reselling them to the outside world.

THE STRUCTURE OF THE *Nanggrou*:
THE NATURE OF POWER

What did the *uleebelang* do with the money he collected? First, he supported his dependents. These included officials in charge of the market (the *sjah-bandar peukan*) and their deputies (the *hariah*); there was usually a clerk (*krani*), who was able to write in Arabic script; and there was also a judge (*kali* or *kadi*). In addition, there were the *imeum*, the heads of the subdivisions of the *nanggrou*, and the *uleebelang* also had a deputy (*banta*), usually a younger brother. There was also a *panglima prang*, a person skilled in fighting with lances, who led the *uleebelang*'s forces in battle.

The most important of the dependents were the *uleebelang*'s followers, usually known as *rakan* (titles varied regionally). The *rakan* lived in or near the house of the *uleebelang*, and were fed and clothed by him. Often the yield from some of the *uleebelang*'s rice fields was set aside for them. Upon the *rakan* depended the might of the *uleebelang*; without them, he was powerless to enforce his prerogatives. According to Snouck, "If he [the *uleebelang*] has a considerable following at his command, no one will dare challenge his authority . . ." (Snouck Hurgronje, 1957: 50).

The role of the *uleebelang*'s dependents has been described by Snouck in the following passage:

The Achehnese has been accustomed for centuries to a considerable degree of independence in the management of his own affairs. He pays but little heed to the uleebelang or other authorities in matters pertaining to his family and gampong [village], and is wont to show a certain impatience of control more akin to license than to servility. Yet he approaches the representatives of territorial authority with deep submission.

The Achehnese are, comparatively speaking, among the least well mannered of the inhabitants of the Archipelago, yet in their behaviour towards their chiefs they pay regard to sundry formalities. If a man be sitting on the roadside as the uleebelang and his retinue pass by and omits to ask *meu'ah* or forgiveness for his presence, he may feel sure at the least of a beating from the rakans by way of correction. Both the chiefs and all the members of their retinue are as a rule very free with such sharp admonitions towards persons of low degree. The ordinary Achehnese, who is prone at the smallest insult to draw his *reunchong* [dagger] or *sikin* [knife] on his equals, shows no rancour against ill-treatment on the part of the uleebelang and his folk or even the imeum. *He fears them, and it is his natural impulse to bow to superior power alone, but to this he submits unconditionally.*

Impossible as it is for the uleebelang to exercise despotic power, they loom before the individual as irresistible forces, even though he has the support of his *kawom* [kindred] to rely upon. The uleebelang has a powerful and numerous *kawom* united to him through interest and otherwise; he has also his various rakans, who though taken as a whole they would not be likely to make an imposing impression on a European, constitute a formidable force in the eyes of each kawom and gampong.

. . . [The uleebelang] as a rule inspire mistrust rather than hope.[12]

It seems impossible that a political system based on fear, on the threat of force, could have existed in

[12] Snouck Hurgronje (1906: I, 118–119); emphasis supplied.

the nineteenth century. But the Atjehnese situation is difficult to understand only if we think of the *uleebelang* as rulers. Actually they did little governing, and life in the *nanggrou* could not have been onerous for villagers simply because the *uleebelang* did not concern themselves to any extent with the affairs of their residents. If we think of the *uleebelang* as essentially concerned with trade, operating on the borders of the *nanggrou* to control the flow of commodities in and out of it, with no extensive ties between them and villagers, a political system based mainly on force and with weak legitimacy is understandable.

Snouck claimed that the *uleebelang* derived their income from the maladministration of the *sjariat* Islam and *adat* (Islamic law and custom), and therefore interfered substantially in the internal affairs of their districts. He pointed out that disputes which could not be settled in the village were brought before their courts and were adjudicated with the help of the *kadi*. The *kadi* were the tools of the *uleebelang* and the only persons who benefited from the settlement of such disputes were the *uleebelang* themselves. Fines were imposed, property confiscated, and punishments administered, all to the sole profit of the *uleebelang*. "These chiefs," said Snouck, "hold it before them as their principal aim to get as much cash as possible for themselves, and take but little pains with cases, however weighty, from which there is little profit to be made." The fact remains, however, that the settlement of disputes was for the most part out of the hands of the *uleebelang*. As Snouck himself has added, "It is only in the direst necessity that their mediation is sought" (Snouck Hurgronje, 1906: I, 102).

Occasionally the *uleebelang* tried to get the residents of the *nanggrou* to perform certain services for them, such as working their fields, as I have mentioned, or building fences around their houses. Their success depended entirely upon their ability to coerce their subjects through the threat of punishment by the *rakan*, and only the most powerful *uleebelang* could do this. Consequently, such work was not a regular feature of life in the *nanggrou*.

The *nanggrou* were, politically speaking, friable. Wherever a resource afforded sufficient surplus to support a group of dependents, a new state appeared. Pidie had many more states in proportion to its size than the East because of the advanced development of rice growing and hence denser population. However, as the pepper settlements developed and expanded in the East, sections of them broke away and became independent. The *peutuha seunubok* (garden chiefs) became village heads and, if the expansion was extensive enough, independent chieftains (Encyclopaedisch Bureau, 1913: 64 ff.). "Independent" in this context meant not recognizing within the area the rights of the original *uleebelang* such as the *wasè lueng*. But so long as the pepper passed through a port in control of the old ruler, he presumably collected the appropriate tolls. The point is that there were natural limits to an *uleebelang*'s power based on the use of personal dependents. Extraordinary rulers sometimes effected consolidations of areas, but the general tendency was for subordinate chieftains to break away when they acquired their own dependents.

# 2 THE SULTANATE AND ATJEHNESE NATIONALISM

We have seen that the residents of a *nanggrou* stood in no particular relationship to the *uleebelang* either through personal ties (*rakan* excepted) or by virtue of living in their *nanggrou*. Men did not identify themselves by their membership in a particular *nanggrou* (whereas *gampong*, village, was a central term of identification). One can speak only of "residents" of a *nanggrou*, never of "citizens" or of any other form of group identification.

Without feudal, ethnic, or national ties between them and the residents of their *nanggrou*, and with their dependence on trade, the *uleebelang* seem to have been purely economic figures. Yet there was a connection between them and their villagers that was more than either the functional tie of trade or the supremacy they maintained by fear. While all *uleebelang* relied primarily on the support of their *rakan* for their power, the *uleebelang* as such were an accepted part of the Atjehnese scene. For instance, the *ulama*, whom Snouck called the great rivals of the *uleebelang*, returned control of *nanggrou* they liberated from the Dutch to the *uleebelang* (Ismail Jakub, 1960: 101–102). And one never hears of attempts to institute any other kind of political leadership in Atjeh.[1] Dutch scholars emphasized descent as a fac-

[1] One exception is the small amount of land directly controlled by the sultan as *wakaf*. The *mukim* may also have been the result of attempts by the sultan to limit the power of the *uleebelang*.

tor distinguishing the *uleebelang*. *Uleebelang* did, in
fact, keep more complete geneaologies than villagers,
but descent alone did not entitle them to their position as it did the nobility of the unilineal Minangkabau, for instance. Descent was important insofar
as it linked *uleebelang* with the original holders of the
letters patent (*sarakata*) issued by the sultan.

The *uleebelang* regularized their position through
their relationship with the sultanate. Yet this relationship was always anomalous. Beginning in the seventeenth century, the sultan demanded a portion of
the duties collected by the *uleebelang*. For only a
short period of time, however, did the *uleebelang*
ever pay these duties. Yet they continually returned
to the sultan for letters patent which would proclaim
them *uleebelang* of their *nanggrou*. Through these
letters patent they hoped to make themselves part of
Atjehnese tradition and so make sense of a social
position which otherwise would leave them somewhere between pirates and merchants.

To understand the relationship between the *uleebelang* and the sultan it is necessary to say something
about the sultanate. Through the control of a powerful navy, the Sultan Iskandar Muda (1607–1636)
was able to prevent all trading in Atjeh except in
the port of Atjeh itself (Braddell, 1851*b*: 19).
Through the collection of duties and through his own

---

Another exception is the village of Tiro where *ulama* were given
full political control (Snouck Hurgronje, 1906: I, 178). One
hears of no other such case in Atjeh, nor even of any similar
attempt by *ulama*.

participation in trade, the sultan became enormously rich and powerful.[2] Although the sultanate itself had existed for many centuries, it achieved its greatest strength in the seventeenth; this is also the period that possibly marks the beginning of the tradition of Atjeh as an Islamic state.

The capital of Atjeh, known as Bandar Atjeh Dar-es-Salaam, was a cosmopolitan place.[3] There were separate compounds for each foreign group, including, among others, Indians (mostly Gujeratis), Arabs, Turks, Chinese, Abyssinians, Persians, and people from Pegu. There were a great many mosques, presumably one in each compound where appropriate, and a Great Mosque. The sultan's palace was set in grounds two miles across and surrounded by a moat. There were two market places, and there were a number of schools where students were taught Arabic writing among other subjects. The city was one of the largest in Indonesia in the seventeenth century, having seven to eight thousand houses.

Various officers of the sultan were responsible for the administration of the city. There were the *orang kaja* (literally, rich men) who presided over the

[2] Atjeh was so powerful that in 1619 a Frenchman, François Pyrard, reported: "All those who go to the Indies and other places beyond the Cape of Good Hope, when they desire to go to Sumatra, only say that they are going to Achin, for that town and port conveys the whole name and reputation of the island, as is done on Java Major with Bantam, so that talk is only of these two kings." (Quoted in Schrieke, 1955: 43–44.)

[3] Das Gupta (1962) has described Atjeh at the height of its power, and the following information has been taken from his account.

courts, patrolled the city at night, and presumably
outfitted the sultan's galleys. They were formed into
three companies which took turns "guarding" the palace, unarmed, under the eyes of the sultan's slaves.

Each gate of the palace was guarded by 150 slaves.
They were not allowed to leave the palace grounds
and were forbidden to talk to anyone. Inside the palace grounds there were, in addition to the slaves, 150
eunuchs, 3,000 women (some of whom formed the
sultan's bodyguard), and various artisans.

The sultan also had an army made up of soldiers
from the provinces who were raised and trained by
officials called *uleebelang*. *Uleebelang* means, in fact,
military chief; in the seventeenth century there is no
mention of *uleebelang* acting as local chiefs. The
army was supplemented by the palace guard. There
were also religious courts presided over by the *kadi*.

It is easy to conceive of Bandar Atjeh Dar-es-
Salaam as the kind of medieval Islamic city that
Grunebaum (1955) has described. According to
Grunebaum, such a city was not an organic cultural
whole but a multi-ethnic society. Each group lived
according to its own customs, in its own section of the
city, and with its own internal order. Groups met only
tangentially in the market and at the Great Mosque.
The ruler was not the symbol of their overriding unity
but the regulator of their intercourse in the market
and the protector of Islam, the religion of most of the
groups.

Islam, with its emphasis on society rather than pol-
ity, provided a framework based on universal law

rather than ethnic identity. The state was not a Southeast Asian divine kingship with the palace the center of the world surrounded by concentric rings of decreasing holiness. Rather the sultan was the protector of the law, and the state existed so that the law could be administered. Neither the palace nor the sultan was of intrinsic significance.

Islam was, indeed, the ideology of the sultanate. The *Adat Atjeh* (written in the nineteenth century but based on older works) claims that the first sultan converted Atjeh to Islam and makes this the basis of succession to the throne. "This is the Geneaology of all the Kings who have reigned in Acheen," begins the translation by Braddell. "On Friday the 1st of Ramazan, in the year of the flight of the Holy Prophet of God, Sultan Juhan Shah came from the windward and converted the people of Acheen to the Mahomedan faith." The Annals continue with a list of his descendants (Braddell, 1850: 728).

One section of the *Adat Atjeh* begins with an explication of the word Rajah based on the Arabic letters of its Arabic spelling. Ra is Rahmat, or mercy. Alif is "the mercy of God to Kings—so that all the inhabitants of the earth fear them; from the mercy of God to Kings the people recognize and acknowledge all their actions." Aliph (the letter ا ) is upright, and so "Kings become the Lieutenants of God on earth and He bestows his favor on them. 2nd (it signifies) the exaltation of the commands of God and that all precepts given shall be made known. 3rd (it signifies that) Kings ought to elevate and

guard their actions according to the wishes of God."
Jim, the last letter, means among other things that
the king "ought to make all his actions excellent in
order to follow the commands of God, and render
His name great" (Braddell, 1851*a*: 26).

The power of the sultan never extended very far
into the interior, primarily because he was too concerned with the ports. What incursions the sultan did
make into the interior were probably not for the purpose of governing but for the purpose of limiting the
power of chieftains. This he tried to do by balancing
the chieftains off against one another—the same technique that he apparently used with his officials in administering the city of Bandar Atjeh. Snouck, for one,
has seen the creation of the *mukim* (the name of an
area served by a single mosque, and which later became a subdivision of the *nanggrou* in Pidie and Atjeh
proper) as an attempt by the sultan to establish a
form of political organization which would curb the
power of the local chiefs (Snouck Hurgronje, 1906:
I, 80 ff.). Presumably the mosque officials, the *imeum*,
were to be the rivals of the local chieftains. The sultan, however, was not very successful in this endeav-
or, for when the sultanate declined, the sultan was
under the control of some of the *uleebelang* of Atjeh
proper.

Although the sultan may have been without influence in the internal affairs of Atjeh, he was not completely without power to collect tolls and regulate
Atjehnese trade. In fact, the British in Penang considered the sultanate important enough to their in-

terests to support one of the claimants to the throne
in the middle of the nineteenth century. It was a dispute over the sultan's right to collect tolls, however,
which was one of the chief causes of the Atjehnese
War. The *uleebelang* dealt directly with traders who
refused to pay the sultan's tolls. In retribution for
these transgressions of Atjehnese law, the sultan
charged these traders with piracy, an act which led
to the Dutch decision to "pacify" Atjeh (Anderson,
1840; Tarling, 1963: 186 ff.).

In their rivalry with the *uleebelang*, the sultans
tried to make them into officers of the state. The term
*uleebelang* itself was probably derived from court
usage. It appears in the *Adat Atjeh* where it refers
to "great warriors," according to Braddell (1850:
729n.).[4]

The *sarakata*, the letters patent mentioned before,
give us an idea of the way in which the sultan conceived of the office of the *uleebelang*. These documents have a seal at the top with the name of the
sultan in the center. Around the center of the seal are
the names of eight other sultans. According to
Snouck, "the choice of these eight names rests with
the reigning Sultan; those of Eseukandar Muda [Is-
kandar Muda] . . . and of the immediate predecessors
of the reigning king are never omitted, but great freedom of choice is shown as regards the rest" (Snouck

---

[4] The version of the *Adat Atjeh* edited by Drewes and Voorhoeve dates from the nineteenth century, but the section referred
to here seems to be considerably older (Drewes and Voorhoeve,
1958: 19).

Hurgronje, 1906: I, 130). A *sarakata* that Snouck
translated begins with an invocation to Allah; it then
goes on to appoint a person to office and lists his
duties:

It is the bounden duty of all chiefs [subordinate to him]
to hear and follow his commands and prohibitions, insofar as they be in accordance with the law of our prophet
Mohammed (may Allah bless him and grant him peace!),
the law of the adat and the sacred institutions, even as
they held good in the days of the earlier sultans; on the
way of righteousness, so that no injustice may befall the
servants of Allah.

Let orders be given henceforth to duly perform the
Friday service and the five daily prayers, to build meuseu-
gits [mosques], deahs and meunasahs [buildings for religious purposes], also to contribute zakat and pitrah [the
religious payments] on all things that be subject thereto,
and where any is able to accomplish the journey to Mekka
to undertake the haj.[5]

The document continues, saying that the *uleebelang*
is the sultan's deputy in matters of divorce and marriage "in respect of all our subjects who are within
his jurisdiction," and adds that he may appoint an
*ulama* as his deputy in these matters. It ends by saying
"that should the uleebelang fail to act conformably
with the word of Allah, the law of Mohammed and
our institutions, then shall he forfeit his high office"
(Snouck Hurgronje, 1906: I, 191 ff.).

[5] This *sarakata* is for the Panglima Meusigit Raya, "the General of the Great Mosque." The title should not deceive, however;
the Panglima Meusigit Raya was an *uleebelang* like all the others
(Snouck Hurgronje, 1906: I, 129).

Snouck rightly points out that the *sarakata* give no indication of the actual behavior of the *uleebelang*. But the great desire of the *uleebelang* to have them, and the willingness of the sultan to issue them,[6] make them seem less than meaningless. As I have mentioned before, the *uleebelang* through their relationship with the sultan regularized their position within the *nanggrou* and defined their otherwise anomalous social status. The sultan on the other hand saw the letters patent as a way to assert his authority over chiefs who otherwise gave no sign of their subordination.

The value of the *sarakata* as a source of prestige for the *uleebelang* should not be underrated. Snouck noticed that "the Achehnese himself, when questioned as to the institutions of his country, will refer with some pride to these documents" (Snouck Hurgronje, 1906: I, 9). The *uleebelang*'s position may have rested on his control of local resources and on his command of his *rakan*, but it was only through the idiom of Islam that this position became meaningful to himself and acceptable to the residents of his *nanggrou*. "A Moslim prince," Snouck wrote, "augments his prestige vastly by . . . concessions to the law of his creed" (1906: I, 6).

The *uleebelang* appeared to Snouck only to make concessions to Islam and not to be centrally concerned with it. The *sarakata* were, in Snuock's eyes, "expensive luxuries" (1906: I, 141). In this Snouck

[6] To be sure, he was paid.

was right when he meant that the actions of the *uleebelang* never matched the picture the *sarakata* contained. But he greatly underestimated the role that Islam played in furnishing a framework of agreement between villagers and *uleebelang* and in providing an ideology for a class otherwise devoid of one.

The terms of this agreement should not be misunderstood, however. The *uleebelang* were wealthy men who used their wealth to achieve power. In turn they tried to make themselves part of the myth of Atjeh as an Islamic state. As a group they succeeded. Officially, *uleebelang* were officers of the state with the duty of administering Islamic law. In practice, they were never officers of the state but wealthy men with a personal force at their disposal. As there were always rivals who wished to usurp their position (Snouck Hurgronje, 1906: I, 151), *uleebelang* had to concentrate first on making sure they had sufficient resources to retain their *rakan*. They could not of course rely on the sultan for assistance.

This dependence of the *uleebelang* on their supporters to maintain their power conflicted with their duties set forth in the charters. The result is a dual image of the *uleebelang*. On the one hand, they are seen as officers of the state and thus are an accepted part of Atjehnese tradition. *Ulama* today still speak of Atjeh as "the land of the ulama and the uleebelang"[7] in the same way that, according to Snouck, "Atjeh-

[7] The quotation is from a speech by an Atjehnese *ulama* Daud Beureuèh in 1963.

nese referred . . . with some pride to the charters" (1906: I, 9). On the other hand, in person *uleebelang* were figures to be feared, not admired. Their distant presence was an accepted fact of Atjehnese tradition; their use of power conflicted with that tradition but was accepted because there was no alternative. The incongruity of power and cultural conception indicates the isolation of *uleebelang* from villagers. It is difficult to conceive that such a gap would have continued to exist if they had interfered in village affairs to any extent.

It was the tenuousness of the bonds between villagers and *uleebelang* that made the tie of the *uleebelang* to the sultan important. Yet the interests of the sultan and the *uleebelang* conflicted. Recognition of the sultan by the *uleebelang* meant, theoretically, that they must pay tolls to him. There was, I believe, an attempt to resolve this conflict by making the sultan into a magical figure and thus divest him of political significance.

Snouck reports that the sultan was "the object of a somewhat extraordinary reverence in the minds of Achehnese" (1906: I, 140).[8] As an example he cites

[8] Snouck maintains that this reverence dates back many centuries. That may well be so, but it is not any older than the conflict between the sultan and the *uleebelang*. He also says that this reverence was the result of the sultan's association with Atjeh's greatness; if this is so, it would date back to the sixteenth or seventeenth century, and not to the beginning of the sultanate itself.

Gullick notes the same contradiction between sultans and chiefs in the states of Western Malaya (1958: 48 ff.). He stresses the dependence of the chiefs upon the sultan for defense and trade, as well as for legitimacy, a dependence that contradicted their

the case of Teuku Ne' of Meura'sa, an *uleebelang*
whose father had submitted to Dutch authority. After
Teuku Ne' had succeeded his father, he went to visit
the sultan (who had not yet been captured by the
Dutch) to get a *sarakata*. "All who accompanied him
were implored by their friends and relations to bring
back with them some water wherein the pretender to
the Sultanate had washed his feet. We may add that
this young ne'er-do-well [Teuku Ne'] was for some
time regarded by a portion of his subjects as *kramat*,
i.e., one miraculously revealed as the chosen friend
of God" (Snouck Hurgronje, 1906: I, 141). Other
beliefs about the sultan were that the mouth of anyone who abused him would swell, and that a sick
child could get well if rubbed with the sultan's saliva.*
Such beliefs were not likely to have been part of the
conception of the sultanate during its greatness; they

---

freedom in their own districts. In Atjeh, however, one does not see
the sultan as in any way helpful against outside attack after the
early eighteenth century. Snouck, for instance, notes that resistance to the Dutch attack in the 1870s was spearheaded by "separate and independent bodies of troops, led by either adat-chiefs
or by some newly-arisen commanders of energetic personality, that
turned their arms against the invaders through their own impulse
or to advance their own interests" (1906: I, 147). Moreover,
from the *uleebelang*'s point of view, the sultan only hindered
trade. It is possible that the cooperation between *uleebelang* necessary to move goods from the interior to the coast was carried
out within the framework of the confederations of *uleebelang*.
There were two of these in Pidie and three in Atjeh proper.
Snouck thought these were defense pacts to protect *uleebelang*
from one another (1906: I, 91); no doubt they were, but they
could also have been useful in transporting goods. Thus, the only
real similarity in the relations between Malay chiefs and their
sultans and in those between Atjehnese chiefs and their sultans
was that of cultural position.

seem incompatible with the idea of the sultan as protector of the law. Also, the *Adat Atjeh*, which lists the qualities of a sultan, makes no mention of any supernatural powers.

There is an inconsistency in the relationship between the *uleebelang* and the sultan. On the one hand, there is the great honor the *uleebelang* paid him; on the other, there is the complete flouting of his authority. The honor can be explained by the lack of any source of legitimacy within the *nanggrou* and the *uleebelang*'s consequent search for a way to make sense of their status. The flouting of the sultan's authority can be attributed to simple self-interest. Yet this explanation of the inconsistency leaves us with the contradiction that although in theory the sultan had control over the *uleebelang*, in practice he was usually helpless before them. He was always culturally their superior, as the very issuing of the *sarakata* indicates. Furthermore, his cultural superiority was to the *uleebelang*'s interest, as was his powerlessness. Making the sultan into a magical figure resolved the contradiction in favor of the *uleebelang*. It sustained the cultural position of the sultan but said nothing of his rights. That Islam did not become synonymous with a magical sultanate, however, was due to the presence of another group in Atjehnese society, the *ulama*.

# 3 THE *ULAMA*, THE *PESANTREN*, AND THE VILLAGE: REFORM AND TWO TYPES OF THE *RANTAU*

The *uleebelang* and the sultan appear encapsulated in their own worlds rather than integrated into rural society. The same is true of the *ulama*, the religious teachers. In nineteenth-century Atjeh we see them in the religious schools, the *pesantren*, in the country. The *ulama*, however, are not a natural outgrowth of the rural scene. They appear first in the ports of the sultans. Their goals for Atjeh, we shall see, seem to differ little from the goals expressed by the sultans in the *sarakata*.

*Pesantren* are always separated from the villages themselves. They consist of an enclosure within which are the student dormitories, a building used for instruction called a *dajah*,[1] and, sometimes, a separate house for the *ulama*. Often the *pesantren* own lands which are either let out to neighboring villagers or worked by the students themselves. Such lands were often given to the *ulama* by wealthy men. Occasionally *uleebelang* would support them, although ordinarily the *ulama* were an embarrassment to the *uleebelang*. The *ulama* did not depend on either villagers or *uleebelang* for economic support. Culturally they

[1] Actually the traditional Atjehnese term for the entire *pesantren* is also *dajah*. *Pesantren* is used here, however, as that is the term currently used for the institution in the rest of Indonesia.

were at odds with both groups, as I shall show (Snouck Hurgronje, 1906: I, 165).

According to Snouck, Atjeh was frequently swept by *ulama*-led reform movements. Snouck saw the reformist *ulama* as political figures, and he speaks of them as "rivals of the traditional authorities" (1906: I, 151). Yet if they were rivals of the *uleebelang*, they were peculiar rivals: they wanted neither the office of the *uleebelang* nor their revenues. "The ulama," said Snouck, "say in effect, 'I do not want an inch of your territory, but I want from you submission to God' " (1957: 51). The goals of the reformist *ulama* seem innocuous enough. For example, one *ulama*, Sayyid Abdurrachman Zahir, known as the Habib, led a movement "against ram and cock fighting, gambling, opium smoking, paederasty and other illicit intercourse, while the people were strongly urged to the fulfillment of their principal religious duties, as for example the five daily seumayangs or series of prayers" (Snouck Hurgronje, 1957: 161). During the colonial war the greatest Atjehnese leader, Teungku diTiro, asked for very similar reforms. He said that in the areas restored to the *uleebelang* through the endeavors of the *ulama* "efforts should be directed to the restoration of fallen mosques, the orderly perception of religious duties, the renouncing of gambling and animal fights and especially the orderly collection of zakat [religious payment] and other contributions to the war chest" (Snouck Hurgronje, 1924: 65). These aims very closely parallel the duties of the *uleebelang* outlined in the *sarakata*.

Snouck thought the reform movement threatened the *uleebelang* because it exposed their maladministration of Islamic law and thus, according to him, put their chief source of revenue in jeopardy. "A reformation of the institutions of the country conducted in a religious spirit would rob the uleebelangs of everything. . . . The whole administration of justice now in the hands of these chiefs, and which forms the main source of their revenues, would pass entirely away from their control" (Snouck Hurgronje, 1906: I, 159 ff.). As I have indicated previously, Snouck greatly overestimated the conflict of *ulama* and *uleebelang*. In the first place, a reform of legal administration would not have weakened the *uleebelang* since, as I have tried to show, their revenues came chiefly from the collection of tolls. Moreover, some *uleebelang* actually took part in these reformist movements and enhanced their prestige by their participation. The *ulama*, for their part, showed no opposition to the office of *uleebelang* nor any desire to occupy it themselves. The conflict of *ulama* and *uleebelang* was much less fundamental and, I would speculate, focused more on the personal immoralities of particular *uleebelang* (such as "cock fighting, gambling, opium smoking, paederasty and other illicit intercourse") than on political differences (Snouck Hurgronje, 1906: I, 161, and II, 210 ff.).[2]

[2] Even today, after the revolution of 1945–1946 in which most *uleebelang* were slain, Daud Beureuèh, the most respected *ulama* in Atjeh and one who advocates nearly the same program that the Habib did, considers the *uleebelang* a legitimate part of the Atjehnese scene.

Perhaps the most peculiar feature of the reform movements was that although they had enormous appeal in the Atjehnese countryside, they never achieved their goals. The movements were a recurring feature of Atjehnese life, testifying both to their failure and to their popularity. The reason for their appeal and their failure lies in the nature of life in the village.

In the nineteenth century, most Atjehnese lived in terms of village and kinship. A man's associations and the course of his life depended on the ties given him at birth. The only exceptions to this pattern were offered by the reform movements and the *pesantren*. Men took advantage of these opportunities at the point in their life cycle when they were most deprived.

Atjehnese children are born in the house of their mother.[3] The idiomatic expression for wife is, in fact, "the one who owns the house" (*njang po rumoh*). Women acquire a house, or at least a portion of one, at the time of their marriage. The house is a gift from the woman's parents. From marriage until the birth of the first child, or sometimes for a period of three to four years depending on prior arrangements, a bride does not legally own the house. It still belongs to her parents, and during this period she is fully

[3] What follows is a mere outline of village social structure which will be amplified in Chapter 7. It is based on my field notes and differs in some details from Snouck's account (1906), mostly, I think, because Snouck collected his material in Atjeh proper, whereas my field work was done in Pidie. There are, of course, changes which have occurred in the seventy years since Snouck wrote. My statements hold, however, for both then and now unless I have noted otherwise.

supported by them. At the end of this period there is
a small feast (*chanduri*) at which it is announced
that the woman is now "separated" (*geumeuklèh*)
from her parents. She is given full possession of the
house and, if the parents can afford it, a rice field as
well. At the birth of every child thereafter the parents
try to give their daughter another rice plot.

Girls grow up in their mother's house and remain
there or nearby for the rest of their lives. Parents
build a new house for themselves and the rest of their
family when their first daughter marries. (This is
done on the condition that the parents can afford it,
but most can and could.) If possible, the new house
is built in the same yard as the old one; otherwise it
is placed close by. When the next daughter marries,
they move again, leaving the second house to her.
Often they end their lives in a shack surrounded by
the houses of their daughters.

A typical village consists of clusters of houses
owned by sisters and aunts (mother's sisters), with
the compounds often sharing a well and a fence. The
size of the clusters depends, of course, on the size
of the families and the availability of land. The largest
cluster in the village I studied had six houses, and
four houses in the village belonged to no such cluster.
In addition to houses, each village has at least one
*meunasah*, a building that the men use as a meeting
place to discuss village problems and to pray together
during the fasting month. At night unmarried adoles-
cent boys sleep there.

In the nineteenth century boys married when they were between the ages of fifteen and twenty. Marriages were arranged by the parents of the couple; the parents also bore the cost of the ceremony. After marriage, men had obligations both to their wives and to their wives' parents. During the first year of marriage, they were obliged to provide their wives with new clothes, and they were expected to give meat to their wives' parents before the last day of the fasting month and before the celebration of the month of the pilgrimage. When they stayed in their wives' houses, they were expected to reimburse their in-laws for their expenses if their wives had not yet been "separated." If their wives had been "separated," the men were expected to provide for themselves and to bring something extra for their children. Women, as we shall see, provided for themselves and their children from the yield of village agriculture during the time their husbands were away from home.

After the death of their parents, boys usually inherited the rice fields that had not already been given to their sisters. Girls were given their own rice fields as soon as they were separated from their parents, whereas men usually had no resources when they were married. Men could stay at home and work their wives' rice fields or those of the rich. But Atjehnese rice cultivation is not very labor-intensive, and only a handful of men are needed in each village to cultivate the fields. Also, women do half of the work, sowing, weeding, and husking the rice while the men

plough, harvest, and thresh it.[4] Thus, most men had
to leave the rice-growing areas for the pepper regions
in order to fulfill their duties as husbands.

The Atjehnese *rantau* pattern (*rantau* is an Indonesian word meaning "to leave one's home area")
should not be overly romanticized. It was not expected that a man go on the *rantau* in order to become
a man. He "went to the East" (*dja' utimo*), or on the
*rantau*, because he had no other means of earning a
livelihood. If a man could make a satisfactory income
in Pidie, he stayed at home.

At the time of their marriage, boys belonged
neither to their families' homes—we think of them
sleeping in the *meunasah*—nor to their wives' homes,
to which they came empty-handed. But even when
men lived up to their material obligations, they had
little place in their wives' homes. Women were independent of them, even if men could pay their own
way. "The woman is, so far as lodging and maintenance are concerned, practically independent of her
husband, since she continues to form an integral part
of the family wherein she was born. An Atjehnese
woman whose husband has gone as a pepper planter
to the East or West Coast and gives no sign of his
existence for years may indeed feel unhappy, but as
she lives in her own house either together with or in
the immediate neighborhood of her own family, she

[4] The participation of women in rice cultivation is denied by
Snouck, and this may have been the case in Atjeh proper. Today,
however, women do work in the fields in both Atjeh proper and
Pidie. (Personal communication from Chandra Jayawardena.)

is seldom constrained to demand a dissolution of marriage" (Snouck Hurgronje, 1906: II, 356).

As the preceding quotation indicates, although men tried to create a role as husbands and, especially, as fathers, women thought of them as essentially superfluous. They allowed men no part in raising children and tolerated them only so long as they paid their own way and contributed money for goods that a woman could not obtain through her own resources. It is naturally difficult to gather such information about the past, but a few additional passages from Snouck indicate that a man's role as a husband-father in the nineteenth century was small indeed: "The children of a fairly happy marriage receive the greater part of their up-bringing from their mother and her family . . . The father is indeed the recognized guardian and educator [under Islamic law] but he is not always at home; and though the members of his family show an interest in the lot of the young children whom he leaves behind, such an interest expresses itself in mere formalities" (1906: I, 407). In a footnote, Snouck remarked that men are like "guests in the houses of their wives" (1906: I, 339; also, I, 327), and that same remark was made to me to describe the way a man in the village felt ("*Lon na lageei djamei dirumoh ineonglon*"; "I am like a guest in my wife's house").

According to Snouck, the result of this lack of a role within the family for adult men was feelings of obligation toward the wife's family and dependency: "The man feels himself under a deep obligation, for

many reasons, to the family of his wife, his relations
with whom border on dependence" (1906: I, 361).
Undoubtedly these feelings were alleviated as men
contributed to the building of new houses and the
buying of rice fields for their daughters. One feels
that becoming a father-in-law had an importance in
the nineteenth century that, as we shall see, it lacks
today.

Islam did not furnish a basis of relationship and
self-esteem which replaced kinship and locality for
men on the *rantau* in the pepper areas. Kinship and
locality were still the terms of relationship there, as
we have seen. However, through the role of *ulama*, it
offered men release from their traditional obligations;
to those who did not become *ulama* it offered an oc-
casional alternative to village life.

One became an *ulama* through study in a *pesantren*. *Pesantren* graduates did not have an obligation
to provide for their families. Snouck notes that "well-
to-do people very often prefer to give their daughters
in marriage, with sufficient provision for their maintenance, to these *literati*" (1906: II, 25).

Release from the material obligations of village
life is only one sign of the profound change that took
place in those who studied in the *pesantren*. Through
their experience in the religious schools they were
removed from the world of the village and brought
into the world of Islam. *Pesantren* life can be seen as
a form of the *rantau*. The word meaning "to study in
a *pesantren*," *meudagang*, originally meant "to be a
stranger, to travel from place to place" (Snouck

Hurgronje, 1906: II, 26). One could not become an *ulama* by studying in the region in which one was born. "Achehnese assert . . . that no man ever becomes an *alem* [a person with some learning in Islam], to say nothing of an ulama, in his own gampong. To be esteemed as such in the place of his birth, he must have acquired his learning outside its limits" (Snouck Hurgronje, 1906: II, 25).[5]

The result of the *meudagang* is the transformation of ordinary villagers into *ulama*. Unlike the returned pepper grower, the *pesantren* student came back a different person. One indication of this is the attitude of *pesantren*-educated men toward the village. According to Snouck, they had "an ever-increasing contempt for the adat [custom] of their country (which conflicts with Islam in many respects) so that later on, as dwellers in the gampongs, they look[ed] down on their fellow countrymen with somewhat Pharisaical arrogance" (1906: II, 31).

The *meudagang* took the students out of one cultural world, the village, where men were linked as kinsmen, and left them in another, the school, where men acted as Muslims and not kinsmen. The experience of two radically different cultural worlds, which were not linked by the normal expectations of the life cycle, led the *ulama* to stress that man's nature could be the basis of unity between men even when sociological distinctions separated them. In the absence of

[5] Moreover, renowned *ulama* seldom taught in the area of their birth. The famous *ulama* in Pidie were from Atjeh proper and conversely (Snouck Hurgronje, 1906: II).

cultural bonds between men, the *ulama* formulated
ideas out of their own experience which could tie
men together. Islamic ideas provided an idiom by
which unity despite social distinction could be expressed.[6] These ideas were effective, however, only to
a certain extent.

*Pesantren* students studied Islamic law (*fikh*)
primarily. The reform movements stressed *ibadah*
(religious duties) and especially prayer which, according to Snouck and to Atjehnese today, villagers
almost totally neglected. Yet when an *alem* or *ulama*
returned to his village, he was honored not for his
superior knowledge of the law and for his understanding and practice of *ibadah*, but for the practical aid
he was thought to offer village life: "Those who have
devoted themselves to study and all who have for
some reason or other a claim to the title of teungku
[one learned in Islam] are regarded by the mass of
people not only as having a wider knowledge of religion than themselves, but also as having to some
extent control over the treasury of God's mercy. Their
prayers are believed to command a blessing or a
curse, and to have the power of causing sickness or
ensuring a recovery. They know the formulas appointed of Allah for sundry purposes" (Snouck Hurgronje, 1906: II, 32).

*Pesantren* students looked at the village religious
practitioners, the *leube*, "with contempt and sometimes even with hatred" (Snouck Hurgronje, 1906:

[6] The substance of these ideas is discussed in chapters 6 and 9.

II, 24) for their participation in practices that consistently bent Islamic belief into ritual useful for life in kinship units. Prayer, for instance, was neglected in favor of curing rites, saint worship, and feasts to celebrate birth and death. The reform movements were directed as much against these heretical practices of the village as they were against the immorality of the *uleebelang*.

The *ulama* did not express the overriding unity of villagers any more than the *uleebelang* did. We must see them as living in a world apart from the village and expressing beliefs very much in conflict with the practices of village life. For the most part villagers and *ulama* coexisted because their worlds did not interpenetrate. When the *ulama* attempted to bring these worlds together in the reform movements, however, they attracted much attention and respect. As usual, Snouck has cogently expressed both the separateness of the *pesantren* and the village, and the attraction of the reform movements: "The mass of the people believe in the absolute truth of the ulamas' teaching, yet transgress it from their youth up. The ulama are wont to conceal their aversion to such sins so long as forbidden acts and objects are not obtruded on their notice. [But when] an ulama goes beyond these everyday limits and travels about the country to enforce reform according to the spirit of the law, the respect he inspires increases to the highest degree. . . . Many Atjehnese sinners sympathize in the fullest sense with such a revival" (1906: I, 160 ff.).

The attraction of the reform movements for the villagers was, I think, due to an almost cosmic misunderstanding. The *ulama* preached reform in this world as a prelude to the next. They had in mind the abolition of the rituals that expressed particularistic ties in favor of the union of men through the law. Villagers, however, understood them to be offering an alternative to this life in the next world. The reform movements did not mean to them that life in this world should be different but, rather, that through ritual one could attain an alternative to this world in the next.

If we look at the program of the Habib, the most successful reformist *ulama* in nineteenth-century Atjeh, we see that it is identical to that of Daud Beureuèh, the most prominent *ulama* in contemporary Atjeh.[7] The Habib advocated the fulfillment of *ibadah* with special stress on prayer (Snouck Hurgronje, 1906: I, 161), and he also linked *ibadah* with public works projects: "The Habib . . . compelled the Achehnese to do what they were powerless to undertake at their own initiative, viz., to carry out useful objects by general cooperation. Not only did he get a new chief mosque erected by public subscription and cooperative labor, but bridges and roads were

[7] Daud Beureuèh was the leader of the POESA (All-Atjeh Union of Religious Scholars) before World War II. During the revolution of 1945–1946 he was Military Governor of Atjeh, and from 1953 to 1961 he led the Atjehnese rebellion against the central government. The public works projects discussed below were carried out by villagers in rural Pidie after Daud Beureuèh came to terms with the government.

also put in hand in the same manner" (Snouck Hurgronje, 1906: I, 163).

A century later, Daud Beureuèh was instrumental in having a mosque built, in having roads and bridges repaved, and in having a new irrigation channel constructed and old ones cleaned up. These projects exemplify the way in which *ulama* create among villagers a new, albeit temporary, sense of identity outside of kinship; they also illustrate the meaning of reform for *ulama* on the one hand and villagers on the other. If we look at one of these projects, the building of a new irrigation channel which took place in 1963, we can see how this is so.

In Pidie, about six kilometers inland from the Strait of Malacca, there is a large swamp in which grows a species of palm tree (*rumbia*) whose leaves are used to make thatch for roofs. The trees are a source of income for some of the people who live in that area, but the swamp had a more important use. The people to the south of it had dammed it up and were using it as a source of water to irrigate all of the rice fields between there and the sea (see Figure 1). As a result of the damming however, the swamp overflowed during the rainy season, killing many of the trees and, more importantly, flooding the rice fields to the north. This had been a long-standing problem, and no regency head (*bupati*) had been able to solve it. The *bupati* had all said that while it was unfortunate that trees were damaged and rice in the fields to the north was often lost, it was better to leave the situation as it was because the benefits of the irrigation provided by

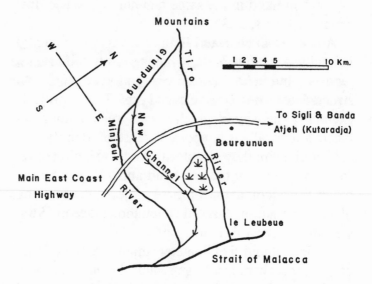

FIGURE 1. Sketch showing the location of the new irrigation channel constructed under the supervision of Daud
Beureuèh.

the swamp outweighed the destruction of the floods.

Sometime before I arrived in the area, the villagers
owning rice fields to the north of the swamp brought
the problem to Daud Beureuèh, threatening that if
something was not done, they would drain the swamp
by digging channels into the Tiro River. Daud Beureuèh asked them to be patient and then summoned
the people from both the north and south sides of the
swamp to a meeting. There he proposed that they not
only dig a new irrigation channel, which would furnish water from the mountains to both sides of the

swamp, but also drain the swamp to prevent flooding. The northerners agreed immediately, but the people from the south asked for a few days to think it over. They then sent him a letter, signed by the head (*tjamat*) of their district (*ketjamatan*) and the *imeum*, agreeing to undertake the project. Since Daud Beureuèh is a private citizen with no government position, I asked the villagers to the north why they went to him. Most said because the government had done nothing in the past and because they thought he could do it, particularly inasmuch as he had supervised the cleaning out of the four biggest channels the year before.

The completed channel is seventeen kilometers long, two-and-one-half meters wide, and one-and-one-half meters deep. Work on the project began on July 14 and continued until August 18 with a break of only two days to celebrate Muhammed's birthday. There were never less than 300 men working each day, and at times there were as many as 2,000. Although the new channel followed the path of an old one, it still required a great deal of adjoining rice land and destroyed valuable coconut and bamboo trees. No one was paid for these, Daud Beureuèh having convinced the owners to consider the property as *wakaf*, land given for religious purposes. The governor visited the men working on the channel and said that if the government had built it, the cost would have been over Rp.100,000,000 (at that time, about U.S. $100,000).

The core of laborers came from the north and south

of the channel, those areas which were going to benefit from it. But this group seldom amounted to more
than 200 men a day. The rest came because they
agreed that it was a good thing to do—there would
be a reward for them in the afterworld. It was arranged that the people from certain *mukim* would
come on certain days. The *imeum* announced the
days to their villagers, but participation was purely
voluntary, and no one was pressured to come. No
one, that is, except those who were going to benefit
from the channel. On about the third day of work,
very few of them showed up. Daud Beureuèh therefore sent the *imeum* to summon this group of workers,
and when they got there, he showed them the letter
in which they had promised to help. "Don't promise
to work," he said, "and then not show up. The only
one working is me, Teungku Daud. You're swindling
me."

Work usually began about 8:00 in the morning
and continued until 4:30 or 5:00, with only a short
break for lunch and prayers. Each man brought his
own lunch and his own tools, mostly long-handled
hoes and shovels. Daud Beureuèh set out bamboo
poles indicating the width of the channel, and then
while some dug others hauled the dirt onto the banks.
There was no special division of labor by village; each
man worked wherever he pleased, and no one gave
orders except Daud Beureuèh. Just before the men
went home each evening, Daud Beureuèh made a
short speech telling them how the channel would
benefit the community in terms of the increased

amount of rice that could be grown, or about the progress they were making, or how it was their duty as Muslims and Atjehnese to aid the community. During the last five days of the project, the men worked day and night, using pressure lanterns for illumination. Many, including Daud Beureuèh, did not return home at all, sleeping instead on the platforms in the rice fields that were ordinarily used as resting places for farmers.

In building the irrigation channel, everyone involved acted not as a resident of a certain village but as a Muslim. It was only because they acted as Muslims, willing to give up their interests as villagers, that the channel was built. Although it is true that Daud Beureuèh's solution to the problem of the flooding swamp did work to the advantage of nearly everyone, it was not the advancement of personal interests that permitted it to be built. The *bupati* had tried to resolve the problem on the basis of such interests and had failed. Even if they had been able to imagine Daud Beureuèh's solution, they would not have had the resources to carry it out—they would have had to pay for most of the labor and all of the land. It was only when the building of the irrigation channel was conceived of as an Islamic act that it could be done.

The religious character of the work is evident in its organization and in the fact that it was thought of as something apart from ordinary life. Large-scale cooperation itself is infrequent in Atjeh. Although women work in large groups when they sow and weed, men in the rice fields work separately except at harvest time when a couple of men may work together. There was often a sense of elation in the work on the irrigation channel which is never present in agricultural work.[8] This feeling was consciously fostered by Daud Beureuèh in his daily speeches and by such acts as calling in a photographer to "boost the spirit of things."

The men worked on the channel without thought of the distinctions between them that prevailed in everyday life: where another man came from or what his position might have been made no difference. With shirts off and stripped down to their shorts, all men in the trench looked and acted alike. As I mentioned previously, no one but Daud Beureuèh gave orders. He himself expressed the special nature of his authority in a speech he gave on the day the work was finished: "Now I am an important person [*ureung rajeuk*; in Indonesian, *orang besar*]. There is no one higher than me but God. But in a moment we will all go home. The channel is finished. Then I will be only an ordinary person [*ureung ubut*; in Indonesian, *orang ketjil*]. There will be no one lower than me but an ant."

Daud Beureuèh's authority rested on the consent of those who had asked him to solve the problem of the swamp and on the consent of the others who had agreed to help before the work began. Behind his

[8] One exception is threshing, which is done not by the men who work in the fields, but by the boys who sleep in the *meunasah*. They work as a group and have the same sense of elation that one saw among the workers building the channel.

willingness to undertake the assignment was his view of the project as part of religious duty, *ibadah*. To him, the project was only a part of the principle that governed all of social life. The improvement of the community was part of the law governing the relations between men. He made this clear in a speech which initiated the repair of a road: "Maybe you think this is not *ibadah*. Maybe you think it is enough just to pray and read the Koran. Maybe you think the relations between people are not the concern of religion." For him these projects were part of religion, as was everything social.

But the villagers saw the projects quite differently. Nearly all of them helped not because participating was something of the same nature as the rest of their life, but because it was essentially different. Most of them said they took part because they would be rewarded for doing so in the *achirat*, the hereafter. (The phrase was *"na fallah"*—"there is a reward.") For them, then, it was a departure from their ordinary social life, and their actions were not those of people from a particular place but those of people who had temporarily left that place behind. However, so long as kinship and locality were the bases of social organization, reform movements could not succeed in making Islamic law as the *ulama* conceived it the basis of social life in any permanent way. The appeal of these movements to villagers was not the reform of social life but the dissolution of traditional social bonds in favor of another, albeit temporary, kind of identity.

# 4 ATJEHNESE SOCIETY AND THE ATJEHNESE WAR

I have tried to present nineteenth-century Atjeh not as a hierarchical, vertically integrated society, but as one composed of four encapsulated groups existing side by side. These groups did not interpenetrate but met only at their boundaries. Each group had its own conception of Atjehnese Islamic tradition, bent to its own needs. No one depended on his relationship with someone in another group for a basic conception of social identity. Villagers were first of all husbands and fathers; the *nanggrou* they lived in was of little importance to them, as was their adherence to any reformist movement. *Pesantren* were located in particular *nanggrou*, but this did not influence the *ulama*'s conception of themselves. *Uleebelang* wanted *sarakata* from the sultan, but if they did not get them they were still *uleebelang*. *Uleebelang*, it is true, did make demands on the residents of their *nanggrou* when they were powerful enough to do so; but they existed as *uleebelang* just as well without doing so.

Nineteenth-century Atjeh may seem fragmented and almost unintegrated. But this is only if we think of it as tending toward, but never reaching, a hierarchical, feudalistic society. If we think of the society as one in which the roles of a member of one group did not feed into those of another, so that, for instance, there was no one similar to a serf who could only exist in relation to his lord, Atjeh appears as a whole. There was general agreement that Atjeh was an Islamic society that enabled the groups to live side by side, although each of them had different conceptions of the nature of both Atjeh and Islam. The only crosscutting of roles took place among the *uleebelang* and those to whom they extended credit in the peppergrowing *nanggrou*. This crosscutting, I have tried to show, only existed on a very small scale and only lasted so long as the *uleebelang* had a force of retainers. Nevertheless, there was a context of agreement between all of the groups, and this undoubtedly was based on the tradition of Atjeh as Islamic.[1]

These groups, then, existed side by side and lived their lives apart from one another but in mutual acceptance based on agreement and sometimes on misunderstanding expressed in a religious idiom. That there was sometimes friction when the groups met obscures the fact that there were few occasions when they had to meet. Moreover, most of their interconnections were not disruptive. If we give up the notion of hierarchy and feudalistic relations, we can see that the interconnections were actually often integrative: for example, the reform movements took pressure off the village; the sultan through the *sarakata* helped regularize the *uleebelang*.

The alternative view of Atjeh is Snouck's view of

---

[1] One must visualize, too, thousands of men leaving their homes annually to go to the frontiers of an area that was known as "Atjeh." Nationality may not have entered in any central way into the relationships they established there, but, nonetheless, there was a culturally defined geographical area.

it as a feudal society based on *adat* or custom. Atjehnese, Snouck pointed out, saw no conflict between
*adat* and Islam. From their standpoint, what was
Atjehnese was Islamic. It is no doubt true that *adat*
never existed as a distinct and independent standard
of action. *Adat* and Islam were generally viewed as
closely linked, the first dependent on the second. But
the meanings of "Atjehnese" and "Islam" were not
agreed upon by all groups within Atjeh. *Adat* as the
means of fulfilling Islam meant one thing to the
*ulama,* another to the *uleebelang,* a third to the sultan, and something else again to villagers.

Snouck saw Atjeh as basically united by ignorance.
In truth, Atjeh was governed by *adat,* but owing to a
lack of knowledge *adat* became identified with Islam,
while the basic rituals and the law of the latter were
ignored. From this point of view (Snouck's), Atjeh
was a feudal-like society. The *uleebelang* were not
political and commercial figures, but rulers. The maladministration of the *sjariat* was a form of *adat* which
linked *uleebelang* and villagers. The *ulama* who insisted on the fulfillment of *ibadah* were acknowledged
by Snouck as part of the Atjehnese scene, but he considered them as mostly foreigners and always as dis-
rupters of a society based on custom. He denied their
identity as religious figures. They were, in his words,
"rivals of the traditional authorities" (1906: I, 151),
who vied with the *uleebelang* for the allegiance of the
people.

To Snouck, then, Atjeh was a hierarchically integrated society disrupted by alien agitators. But while he thought of Atjeh as a feudal-like society, his own observations refuted this. For this reason it is difficult to say what Snouck really thought about the *uleebelang*. But his policy for ending the Atjehnese War and for maintaining peace was based on his idea of the *uleebelang* as *adat* rulers, despite all of his observations to the contrary that he reported in *The Achehnese*.

Snouck saw the Atjehnese War as the great opportunity for the *ulama* to wrest power from the *uleebelang*. Early in the war, many *uleebelang* surrendered to the Dutch. Some could not raise sufficient troops to resist; others who did resist could not cooperate with neighboring *uleebelang* for a common defense. Still other *uleebelang* surrendered in order to get additional territory. With the failure of the *uleebelang* leadership, the *ulama* took over the direction of the war.

Under the leadership of Teungku Tjhik diTiro, they constructed forts and manned and provisioned them. In the areas surrounding the forts, they collected "Holy War" contributions. They were able to liberate areas in Atjeh proper, which they returned to the *uleebelang*. Owing largely to the perseverance and leadership of the *ulama*, as well as to the policies of the Dutch before Snouck and General van Heutsz, they were able to prolong the war for over thirty-five years.

Snouck attributed the *ulama*'s success in winning

popular support solely to the confusion that the war
had created. In his opinion, they would lose this support if the hostilities were ended:

Their rise, their greatness is as closely as possible connected with the existing confusion. Even if we should
abandon Atjeh altogether they would lose more than win.
Their holiness alone is not sufficient to call up great
bands which not only do the company [the Dutch] much
damage but also fill the uleebelang with great fear of the
ulama. Were the war wholly decided in favor of Atjeh
the ulama could no longer collect sabil money; their great
weaponed gampong reserves and their fixed bands would
have no more reason for existing. Their great appearance
would thus fly away and in place of the greatest actual
power and government they go clothed in now, one would
[only] go to them for advice or to get an amulet; their
great reforming aims would meet the usual hinderances.
(1957: 72.)

His argument was that the confusion of war disrupted
the bonds by which the villagers were attached to
the *uleebelang*. To replace these bonds people turned
to Islam. The *ulama* took advantage of this to initiate
reforms they had always wanted and, in doing so, to
undermine further the authority of the *uleebelang*.
There is, however, no evidence that these bonds ever
existed. Had they been real, one would have expected
a different course of events in the Atjehnese War.
European experience, among others, has indicated
that such bonds are strengthened rather than weakened in periods of disorder as peasants turn to lords

for protection. One would have thought, then, that the disruption caused by the Dutch invasion would have resulted in closer ties between villagers and *uleebelang*.

Yet the fact remains that the *ulama* could successfully appeal to villagers whereas *uleebelang* could not, and if we reject Snouck's explanation for this, we must find another one. The reason lies in the nature of the *ulama*'s appeal and in their peculiar experience. Ties between *uleebelang* and villagers emphasized the distinction between lord and peasant, although, as I have tried to show, these bonds were not strong. The *uleebelang*'s view of their own position in Atjehnese society was contradicted by their actions, and they thus weakened the loyalty of their subjects. Rather than trying to strengthen the bonds between themselves and their subjects, *uleebelang* concentrated on gaining wealth through trade and, in effect, existed most harmoniously with the people of their *nanggrou* when they had the least to do with them.

There were not strong ties between *ulama* and peasants either; indeed, I have tried to indicate that there was a tension between *ulama* and villagers which paralleled that between lords and peasants in many respects. Furthermore, the appeal of the *ulama* was not to the obligations of men in society; they did not speak, for example, of the duties of villagers to *ulama*. Rather, they appealed to the peasants because they stressed the unity of all men despite the social identities which separated them. And associated with this appeal was an idea of personal transition that urged men to leave behind the ties of kinship in order to unite as Muslims.

The source of the *ulama*'s ideas was partly in their own experience. As we have seen, they alone of all Atjehnese experienced two radically different ways of life. They were born into the village and yet had to leave it and their ties of kinship behind and live as Muslims in the *pesantren* in order to become *ulama*. Consequently, they perceived the limits of society in terms of the common elements in man, which enabled them to be Muslims and disregard social position. They appealed to men to act not as villagers but as Muslims; to the *ulama*, this meant forgetting traditional social identities.

While the *ulama* envisioned a community of believers on earth, the effective symbol of their appeal in the Atjehnese War, and in the reform movements, was paradise. One can see how paradise entails transition, the leaving behind of the world, in the popular epic of the war, the *Hikajat Prang Sabi* (Story of the Holy War).[2]

The *Hikajat* tells of man's journey from the *donja* (world) to the *achirat* (afterworld). It begins with

---

[2] This work is popularly attributed to Teungku Muhammed Hadji Pantè Kulu, a follower of the greatest leader of the Atjehnese War, Teungku Tjhik diTiro (Muhammed Saman). There are several published versions varying greatly in content. The one I have cited here was edited by H. T. Damsté (1928). The quotations are, of course, out of context; they do not necessarily follow the order in which they occur in the *Hikajat*.

the conventional "In the name of God," announces that this is "the story of the command to fight the Holy War," and then cites the Koran:

> God has bought from the believers their selves
> and their possessions against the gift of Paradise;
> They fight in the way of God; they kill, and are
> killed; that is a promise binding upon God in the
> Torah,
> and the Gospel, and the Koran;
> and who fulfils his covenant truer than God?
> So rejoice in the bargain you have made with Him;
> that is the mighty triumph. (IX: 112.)[3]

The thesis of the *Hikajat* is thus evident: to those who fight the Holy War is given the reward of paradise. This is described as "the merciful place of the fulfillment of all desire":

> The blessings of God are unlimited for those who
> serve,
> Who fight the *prang sabi*.
> To those He gives Paradise full of light,
> Seventy heavenly princesses.
> More than can be counted He gives . . .
>
> You will get a new face, a young one . . .
> God will give you wealth and life . . .
>
> Each day you get food brought on rows of trays.
> The form is the same, but the taste different.
> Delicious indeed is the food that never ceases to
> come.

[3] All passages from the Koran are from the A. J. Arberry translation (1955).

Those who refuse the call are punished: "Remember the punishment of those who do not go to fight. Burning bodies, stinging insides." Moreover, death as a *sjahid* (a martyr in the Holy War) is pleasant and simple, whereas any other type of death means confronting the Angel of Death:

> To see the Angel of Death
> Is more terrible than being hacked by a sword.
> Your heart pounds then, more than if you were
>     hacked a thousand times.

But,

> . . . to die as a *sjahid* is nothing.
> It is like being tickled until we fall and roll over . . .
> Then comes a heavenly princess,
> Who cradles you in her lap and wipes away the
>     blood,
> Her heart all yours.
> And there are others who stand there, aligned as in
>     war.
> They do not go home, but await the fall of their
>     husbands—
> They see their husbands fall and rush off—
> And with a wave of spicy scent they become visible.
> If the heavenly princesses were visible, everyone
>     would go to fight the Dutch.

The price of heavenly bliss is thus the leaving behind of the world:

> . . . If your fathers, your sons, your brothers, your
>     wives,

your clan, your possessions that you have gained,
commerce you fear may slacken, dwellings you
love—
if these are dearer to you than God and His
Messenger,
and to struggle in His way, then wait till God
brings His command; God guides not the people
of the ungodly! (Koran, IX: 24.)

... Do not waste more time with possessions—those
who seek profit will lose.
Do not love your children and your wife. Push them
behind you. ...

Free yourself; and put your heart at rest.
If you can say you have no more desire
Then you can truly go to the war of the unbelievers.

In nineteenth-century Atjeh, with its weak links between institutions, the basis of effective ties between
people from different sectors of society was not common dependence and mutual need for each other as
villager, lord, sultan, and *uleebelang*, but common
identity as Muslims, which superseded all other distinctions. Only the *ulama,* drawing on their experience of crossing institutional boundaries, could appeal on this basis and thereby mobilize masses of
people, and yet they, too, failed. This was in part because the Dutch were superior in strength, but also
because, while the *ulama* wanted to build a new
society on earth, only the afterworld appealed to
villagers. It was not until the 1930s that men began
to realize a new life in this world was possible.

# PART II
## CONSCIOUSNESS AND SOCIETY IN THE 1930s

# 5 ATJEH UNDER THE DUTCH

Under the leadership of General van Heutsz and acting on the advice of Snouck, the Dutch finally brought the Atjehnese War to an end, approximately forty years after they had first tried to capture the palace of the sultan. Snouck had pointed out to the Dutch that their policy of controlling the capital and the ports and then trying to work out agreements with the *uleebelang* would not work because the war had become a religious one and because Atjeh was not a unified state. Accordingly, van Heutsz undertook a more aggressive military policy, attacking the forts of the *ulama* and imposing penalties on villagers who aided the *prang sabi*. Even with direct military action, it took nearly fifteen years for the Dutch to destroy the last bands, but gradually they were able to replace the militant *ulama* with those less inclined to pursue the *prang sabi*: "Habib Samalanga [one of the militant *ulama*] died a natural death. His spiritual successor now sits where he belongs, in a *gampong* in Boven–Samalanga, and busies himself with the study of sacred *kitabs* [books]. They say that if he hears anything about the *prang sabil*, a shiver goes through his body" (Snouck Hurgronje, 1924: 1).

Snouck's policy for establishing peace remained

Dutch policy for keeping that peace throughout the
colonial period. The *ulama* were to confine themselves
to "religion," that is, they were to stay out of political
matters, and their influence on village affairs was to
be restricted to domestic law. The "*adat* rulers," the
*uleebelang*, were to govern. Since Dutch policy was
intended primarily to keep the peace, and since the
basis of the peace was thought to be *adat*, they interfered little in the *uleebelang*'s affairs, at least initially.

This policy seemed to work. With the defeat of the
last bands of Atjehnese, resistance to colonial rule
was limited to what the Dutch called "Atjehnese
murder" (Atjeh-*moord*), the slaying of Europeans
by Atjehnese, which became a private form of the
*prang sabi*. Through the murder of a kaffir (an un-
believer), an Atjehnese man hoped to gain paradise.
According to former Resident Jongejans, "The murders are simply carried out. The perpetrator goes to a
place where he knows he will find a European—a
military encampment, a bivouac, a station. He waits.
When a European passes he runs at him and does him
in. He himself is usually captured or killed" (Jongejans, [1939]: 323). A Dutch psychiatrist, Dr. F. H.
van Loon, interviewed a person who made an unsuccessful attempt to commit Atjeh-moord: "Some
time ago he intended to go and murder a 'Kafir' and
especially a Dutch 'Kafir.' . . . He sold his property,
sharpened his *rentjong* [dagger] and left his village.
When it became known what his intentions were he

was arrested. He said he 'preferred to die rather than to live like this.' He wished to do in a Dutchman first as a good introduction to the hereafter" (1920: 15). This particular person did not seem to van Loon to be mentally ill, and Jongejans has noted that the perpetrators were "not people who were publicly opposed to Dutch authority, but those who seemed to be happy citizens, acquiescing in our rule" ([1939]: 321). For the most part, then, Atjeh-moord was not the manifestation of mental illness but a religious act.

There were at least 120 cases of Atjeh-moord between 1910 and 1937, but its frequency declined considerably in the later years. Between 1913 and 1918, there were 43 cases; twenty years later, between 1933 and 1938, there were only 19 (Jongejans, [1939]: 331). Jongejans and Piekaar (1949) attribute the decline to improved living conditions. I would suggest that the decline was owing instead to the promise that Islam, through the POESA (All-Atjeh Union of Religious Scholars), offered to men.

We have seen that throughout Atjehnese history *ulama* had repeatedly tried to reform Atjehnese culture and had never had lasting success. The conditions in which reformist efforts finally became effective were created by changes in the economy, in particular the end of pepper growing. As a result of these changes, the reforms of the *ulama* were seen for the first time as pertaining to this world. In the following sections, I intend to delineate these economic changes and their social consequences, as well as the

changes in popular religious outlook that accompanied them.

## THE DISTRIBUTIVE SYSTEM AND THE POSITION OF THE *Uleebelang*

In order to move troops more swiftly during the
Atjehnese War, the Dutch had built roads along the
entire length of both coasts, with secondary roads
into the interior branching off from the coastal roads.
By 1914 even Laut Tawar, situated in the deepest
(and highest) interior of Atjeh, was accessible by
road. By 1914, the Dutch had also completed a railroad that extended the entire length of the East coast,
and by 1919 this had been expanded so that one could
go from Medan to Kotaradja by train. As the new
transportation system came into being, the flow of
trade naturally altered to follow its routes. Traffic
concentrated in the large ports of each of the divisions
—Ulee Lheei (the port of Kotaradja), Sigli, Lho
Seumawè, Kuala Langsa, and Kuala Simpang; these,
along with those places situated along the railway
between them, became the major markets, serving as
the centers for both the distribution of imported
articles and the collection of Atjehnese goods, and
servicing a series of weekly markets in the surrounding areas (Encyclopaedisch Bureau, 1916: 211 ff.).

This, then, constituted a new distributive system,
the major traders of which were non-Atjehnese.
There was one major European import firm in Atjeh,
the N. V. Atjehsche Handel Mij., as well as several

others based outside of Atjeh but with branches in various Atjehnese cities. All but one of the European firms confined their activities to importing. A number of Chinese also had a part in this trade (Jongejans, [1939]: 222 ff.). In fact, Chinese merchants did most of the exporting of Atjehnese products, while other Chinese acted as intermediate traders. The latter established shops around the garrison markets located along the railroad; they then purchased goods directly from the Atjehnese and sold them through their shops to exporters (Encyclopaedisch Bureau, 1916: 211). In some cases, they also provided advances for certain crops. (For a while, the N. V. Atjehsche Handel Mij. provided loans to pepper growers, but it discontinued this practice when the advances were not repaid.) Some Atjehnese, most of them apparently from *uleebelang* families, did take part in exporting and intermediate trade, although the Chinese controlled the former and owned most of the shops. In the weekly markets, the traders were Arabs, Indians, Minangkabau, Batak, and Atjehnese (Jongejans, [1939]: 229).

With the development of the new distributive system, the *uleebelang* lost their position as the foci of trade in their *nanggrou*. Dutch policy limited the kinds of taxes that could be levied; goods were to be taxed only at the point of export from Atjeh. The major markets were brought under the control of the colonial administration. Some of the smaller markets were still considered the private property of the *ulee-*

*belang*, although the Dutch hoped to bring them eventually into the public domain (Jongejans, [1939]: 231).

The Dutch attempted to make the *uleebelang* into colonial administrators. They established supra-*nanggrou* treasuries into which all levies collected by the *uleebelang* were to be paid. In return the *uleebelang* and his staff drew salaries from this treasury, the surplus being used for improvements within the *nanggrou* concerned. The *uleebelang* had the duty of collecting taxes, including those on rice lands and other productive real estate. They were also supposed to hold court for the hearing of minor crimes, major offenses being heard by the *controleurs'* courts. (The controleur was a Dutch administrative officer.) Above all, they were supposed to keep order.

Because the Dutch were afraid of upsetting the peace they had won at such a great cost, and because they felt that the basis of peace was the maintenance of *adat*, they hesitated to interfere too much in the affairs of the *nanggrou*. Thus, while on the one hand the Dutch wanted the *uleebelang* to become colonial administrators, on the other hand their policy for peace-keeping encouraged the *uleebelang* to remain *adat* chiefs. In the short time the Dutch ruled Atjeh, they were never able to reconcile these two conflicting concepts of *uleebelang*. They did, however, favor the sons of *uleebelang* with Western-style education, but most of these young people had not yet succeeded their fathers by the time the Japanese took Atjeh. Moreover, those who had taken office, such as Teuku

Moehammed Hasan of Glumpang Pajong, found it very limiting to confine their activities to *nanggrou* affairs (Piekaar, 1949: 12).

The effect of Dutch policy was to make the *uleebelang* completely dependent on them. Having no real connection with the people of their *nanggrou*, and with the sultanate abolished and the *ulama* out of politics, *uleebelang* had nowhere else to turn. Their position, however, was more secure than ever. They no longer had to fear rivalry from other *uleebelang*, and their *rakan*, now turned into *upaih* (*upas* in Indonesian), salaried officers of the *nanggrou*, no longer had to be placated. Their power now stemmed from the guarantee of Dutch support.

The *uleebelang* made varied use of this new security. Some used it to enrich themselves: Teuku Keumangan Oemar, for example, came to own half the rice fields of Keumangan. Others took advantage of the situation to maintain their traditional monopolistic control over goods leaving their *nanggrou*. In theory people could complain about the conduct of the *uleebelang* to the controleur; in practice such appeals were futile at best and dangerous at worst.[1]

---

[1] Atjeher (1939), the writer of a column in *Penjedar*, a magazine published in Medan before World War II, described how the *uleebelang* were able to maintain their monopolies, in this case over rice:

The *uleebelang* get capital from the regional treasury with the help of the officer of the B/B [Binnenlands Bestuur], while the efforts of ordinary people get no attention from the government. But the [Dutch] officer is interested only in the amount of rice exported each month. He does not want to look into the hundreds of other problems in the area. He enters the amount exported [from the *nanggrou*] in his report and that's all he bothers with. Actually the people are crying out be-

The Dutch were not insensitive to this problem, but they felt themselves in a bind, being afraid to interfere in the affairs of the *uleebelang*. There were some *uleebelang* who used their new security to improve conditions within their *nanggrou*. Teuku Hadji Tjhik Moehamad Djohan Alam Sjah of Peusangan, for instance, saw a great opportunity to learn about Western techniques and culture. "Agriculture, irrigation, cattle breeding, education, hygiene and religion all had his interest" (Piekaar, 1949: 19), and his

---

cause the rice has become the monopoly of the chiefs and their relatives. Others have a very difficult time buying *padi* in their areas. In such a situation of course there is no competition and the price is whatever the *uleebelang* makes it. There has already been one incident where a European set up a rice mill and began buying *padi* from the villagers. When this happened, the brother of the *uleebelang* summoned the people together and told them that before they sold rice to the European they should come to him and he would give them whatever the European offered. With this the people no longer dared to sell to the European, even though they had promised to do so and even though he had raised his price. The European went to the administration and complained but with no result, so he sold out to an Atjehnese. Now this fellow is in trouble too.

And there are other ways of working things out. The chiefs can forbid the export of all rice from their areas except that which has already been milled. And any milled rice must be reported to them. Anyone who reports that he wants to export milled rice can only get a permit for one or two *guni* [sacks] at most. But there is also a rice mill owned by the *uleebelang* which buys the rice at f. 50 less than the price outside the area and exports as much as it wants.

In another *Penjedar* article (1940), Atjeher described how difficult it was for the villagers to report their grievances to the authorities and receive any satisfaction: "The government has no direct connection with the people and does not know how they feel about their chiefs. . . . The hundreds, nay thousands of letters that ask the government to look into the wrongdoings of the chiefs get no reply when they are sent via the Government Officer in Atjeh. Most of them disappear into thin air, in other words are suppressed."

daughter was the first Atjehnese woman to receive a Western-style education.

But both types of *uleebelang* found themselves isolated from the rest of Atjehnese society. As I have indicated, they were dependent on the Dutch, separated more than ever from the villagers, unable to turn to the sultan, and lacked a satisfactory relationship with the *ulama*. Teuku Tjhik Peusangan, for example, was interested in advancing education and so became the patron of the POESA. But when he detected nationalist sentiments among its younger members he quietly withdrew. He was then accused of being pro-Dutch and was exiled to Takengon by the Japanese. He was kept there for most of the remainder of his life, first by the Japanese and then by the post-war nationalist administration of Daud Beureuèh. Among the *uleebelang*, Teuku Keumangan Oemar was Daud Beureuèh's greatest enemy. He prevented Daud Beureuèh from establishing a school in his *nanggrou*. He was no favorite of the Dutch, however, and was deposed and exiled by them to Uleei Lheei before the war for disruptive activities. In spite of this he joined the *uleebelang* effort to aid the return of the Dutch after the war and was killed by nationalist forces in 1946.

By the end of the 1930s, then, the *uleebelang* had not become professional administrators with talents that would have been of value to the nationalists. Nor were they traditional *adat* figures with popular backing. And they were not even what they once had been —essential figures in the economy. With the new dis-

tributive system their old-style monopolies were largely eliminated. The one thing that they did have was
the support of the Dutch.

THE OCCUPATIONS OF ATJEHNESE MEN AND THE POESA

The figures the Dutch give for the value of exports
from the "native" sector of the economy (in Dutch,
*bevolkingsproducten*) show a continual rise from
1904 until the worldwide depression struck in the
early 1930s. The value of the native exports in 1904
was f3,575,000; in 1913 it was f5,542,000 (Encyclopaedisch Bureau, 1916: 132 ff.). By 1929 it reached
an apparent high of f8,382,000,[2] a figure which represents not only a rise in prices but also a rise in pro-
ductivity. In terms of volume, exports in 1904 were
16,004,000 kilograms; in 1913, 20,923,000 kg.; in
1929, 36,173,000 kg. (Encyclopaedisch Bureau,
1916: 132 ff.; and *Verslag over 1935*: 21). Although
there was a serious drop in the value of exports during
the depression, this trend was reversed in 1936.
Moreover, by 1939, for the first time since the
Dutch "pacification," Atjeh was producing more than
enough rice for its own needs.

By the late 1930s, then, the Atjehnese economy
would have appeared to have been quite healthy.
This cheerful picture, however, is misleading, for the
cultivation of pepper, the major occupation of Atjeh-

[2] I say "apparent" because no figures are available to me for the
period from 1921 to 1928. The figure quoted for 1929 is from
Economische Vereeniging "Atjeh" (De Handelsvereeniging te
Koeta–Radja), *Jaarverslag over 1934*, p. 21. Hereafter, these
reports will be cited as *Verslag(en) over*, followed by the date(s).

nese men, declined seriously after 1924. Thus, in spite of the export figures which indicated post-depression recovery and growth, most Atjehnese men were actually without income in the 1930s.

In 1904 the production of pepper (in terms of volume of exports) was 4,127,000 kg. (Encyclopaedisch Bureau, 1916: 149). This level of production was maintained, with dips and rises, until 1923. (The average annual export figure for the years 1914–1918 was 3,101,000 kg.; for 1918–1923, 3,936,000 kg. [Kreemer, 1922: II, 20; and *Verslag over 1935*].) In 1918, however, insects began attacking the gardens in Idi. Although many gardens were entirely ruined, new ones continued to be laid out, but by 1924 production began to fall sharply. From 1924 to 1929 the annual average export figure was only 1,806,000 kg. (*Verslagen over 1926–1929*). This decline in production is not a reflection of fewer people growing pepper; it is the toll of disease and pests. Interestingly enough, however, the value of the crop in 1929 was still greater than any previous year for which I could find a record, although it was only a third of the size of crops produced in the years before insects took a large toll. This was, of course, the result of rising prices. The price of pepper in 1924 ranged between f16 and f27 per kilogram (*Verslag over 1927*: 10); in 1925 it rose to f60 per kilogram; and by 1929 it reached f91 per kilogram. It is not surprising, then, that even though gardens were devastated by disease, new ones were being constantly laid out.

It is remarkable, however, that even after the price began to fall in 1930, new gardens continued to be planted. Each year from 1930 to 1936, with the exception of 1934, the price of pepper was lower than that of the preceding year. The highest price per kilo in 1930 was f55; in 1936 it was f8.25. But pepper production actually rose after 1929. The export figure in that year was 1,414,000 kg.; the average annual export figure from 1930 through 1934 was 1,492,000 kg. When production did finally fall in 1935, it was not because people were planting less pepper but because of disease. The *Verslag over 1932* states that, "In spite of the low price, there was a modest upswing in pepper cultivation in Peuereula and Edi [sic], while in Sigli and Meureudu the people went on laying new gardens" (p. 14). The report of 1936, the year during which prices were at their lowest and production itself was only two-thirds of the 1934 figure, says that, "Natives have made a remarkable number of gardens in the subdivisions of Sigli, Bireuen, and Idi. Unfortunately this is balanced by the loss of extensive areas of gardens in Meureudu which fell victim to fatal sickness" (p. 25).

At a time when the pepper gardens were being stricken with disease and pests and when pepper itself was worth little even when it survived, why did men continue to cultivate this commodity when others brought in more money? The reason is that there was no other outlet for their labors. If we look at the crops that replaced pepper as the most valuable exports, this becomes apparent. The leading export in 1936 was areca nut. This had increased greatly in value since 1934, but this did not mean that vast new areas were opened up for the growing of areca palms. Production in 1936 (27,000,000 kg.) was only slightly greater than it had been in 1923 (24,000,000 kg.) (*Verslag over 1936* and *Verslag over 1924*). The increase in value was owing to the Dutch stratagem of exporting the crop directly to Calcutta, bypassing the Chinese middlemen in Penang and Singapore (*Verslag over 1936*: 28). By contrast, pepper production in 1923 was greater than it was in 1936, and pepper prices were just beginning to rise. Areca-nut growing therefore did not expand sufficiently to absorb the labor of men who might have left their pepper gardens.

Copra was the second highest earner of foreign exchange in 1936. But it, too, did not offer employment opportunities for men who might have wanted to leave their pepper gardens. In the first place, the price of copra went up in 1934; this can be attributed to new, Dutch-instigated methods of drying the coconut meat which improved its quality and made it suitable for direct export to Europe (*Verslag over 1936*: 29). As a result of this, there was some increase in production as well, but this was found not among the Atjehnese growers, but among the foreign-owned estates. In 1913, 4,000,000 kg. of copra were exported (Encyclopaedisch Bureau, 1913: 146). In 1923, when there were 189 hectares in production on estates (Kreemer, 1922: I, 434), copra exports rose to 7,000,000 kg. (*Verslag over 1924*). By 1938, there were over 1,000 hectares in production on estates (Jongejans, [1939]: 166), and in 1936 exported production had already reached 9,000,000 kg. (*Verslag over 1936*).[3] The laborers were primarily Javanese, the Atjehnese having refused to work on foreign-owned estates. So copra, too, offered no substantial outlet for labor that might have moved out of pepper production.

Dutch policy was to encourage the use of Javanese labor on estates, while the Atjehnese and Javanese grew rice to feed them and eventually the estate workers of the East coast of Sumatra as well. This policy seemed to work, and rice production did rise extensively. Once a rice-deficit area, Atjeh became a rice exporter, with a surplus of 36,000 tons in 1941 and expected surplus of 45,000 tons in 1942 (the actual surplus figures are not available) (Piekaar, 1949: 24). But even this increase in rice production did not absorb Atjehnese laborers from the pepper gardens since it was the result either of more efficient methods of cultivation in those areas already in production, or, if in new areas, of the use of Javanese labor. Resident Jongejans stressed that there was sufficient rice land already available to Atjehnese growers. The aim, then, was not to increase the amount of land under cultivation but to increase the yield through the use of better seed and more efficient

[3] No copra production was reported for the European sector of the economy, even though copra was grown on European estates. Therefore, the assumption is that it was reported in the native sector. Furthermore, there is no evidence of the expansion of Atjehnese copra gardens in the period before World War II.

growing practices. Some new wet rice lands were created, but these were in areas where people were already growing rice with rain water (Piekaar, 1949:
169 ff.; and Jongejans, [1939]: 160). In fact, the
Dutch irrigated 40,000 hectares, but very little of
this was available to men who were unsuccessfully
planting pepper.[4]

The depressed position of Atjehnese men in the
economy was not visible to the Dutch, and with sufficient reason. Atjeh was peaceful, export figures
showed it to be reasonably prosperous with even better prospects, and it was producing its own food. If
one could have entered a village in the 1920s or
'30s, he would have seen little to indicate that anything was amiss. In Pidie at least, the villagers seemed
to be living nearly as well as they had been at any
time in the past. Yet one might have noticed a large
number of apparently idle men in the village. Men
today say that before World War II they spent their
time mostly sitting in the *meunasah* or by the side of
the road, chatting. Men did not go hungry, but this
was only because of the resources of their wives. The
discontent this produced among men and women did

[4] The figure is from Piekaar (1949: 25). Of the 40,000 hactares,
only 980 were in Pidie. The rest were nearly all in the East. Atjehnese rice production was never very labor intensive: "In place of
the intensive agriculture of the Javanese, the Atjehnese as a rule
has a more extensive method of cultivation. He plants more than
is necessary for a good yield per acre and also more than he can
successfully weed and care for. In this way a less than average
yield per acre still gives a satisfactory total yield" (Anonymous,
1923: 13). In spite of Dutch efforts to improve the means of cultivation, rice production never became labor intensive.

not appear in economic statistics, but it was visible
to Dr. van Loon (1920), although he attributed it
to the shock of losing the war: "Atjehnese women . . .
reproach their husbands for their weak nature. . . .
Their attitude towards Atjehnese men seems before
all to reveal contempt for their [husbands'] general
psychical decline which causes them to lose their
pride."

It was in this situation that the teachings of the
*ulama* were first popularly accepted as the *ulama*
had intended them. The *ulama* accomplished this
through the Persatoean Oelama Seloeroeh Atjeh
(All-Atjeh Union of Religious Scholars), which was
formed in the late 1930s. Founded as an educational
organization, the POESA soon had branches all over
Atjeh. In some villages in Pidie nearly every adult
joined. These local branches sponsored lectures on
every possible occasion. In addition a youth organization, the Pemoeda POESA, was established, as was
a scout group, the Kasjafatoel Islam.

The *ulama* founded the POESA with the intention
of standardizing the curricula of Western-style religious schools which had started to appear in Atjeh
in the late 1920s.[5] It soon developed into a mass or-

[5] The Atjehnese War had badly disrupted the *pesantren*
(Snouck Hurgronje, 1906: II, 28). As part of the reconstruction,
several new schools were founded. These schools had Western-
style classes, although initially the subjects were all religious. (By
the outbreak of World War II, half of the subjects were secular.)
The first of these schools was the Madrassah Nadatul Islam in
Idi, established in 1928. Daud Beureuèh founded the Djamiah
Dinijah school outside of Sigli in 1930, and there were several
others as well. The founders of these schools were *ulama* who had

ganization with the aim of reaching all Atjehnese, whether enrolled in schools or not. The goals of the POESA were the same as those of the reformist *ulama* of the nineteenth century. The situation in the 1930s differed from that of the nineteenth century not in the programs of the *ulama*, but in the willingness of villagers to understand them. In the next chapter I shall try to outline the ideas the POESA put forward.

---

been educated in Atjehnese *pesantren*. Looking back on the founding of these schools today, these men see nothing startling about them. Rather they see themselves as continuing, with a technique adapted to new conditions, a tradition which the Dutch had disrupted. There was some, but not much, resistance to these schools by a few *ulama*, but this did not focus on the schools themselves so much as it did on such issues as whether certain *chanduri* (ritual feasts) were objectionable.

# 6 RELIGIOUS IDEAS IN THE 1930s

With the economic changes that occurred in Atjeh before World War II, there was, as we have seen, a gradual dissolution of the traditional bonds of kinship and locality which had linked men to one another in all phases of life. Although statistics indicated that the Atjehnese economy was healthy in the 1930s, large numbers of Atjehnese men were unable to make a living, and their position vis à vis their wives was, if anything, more humiliating than it had been in the past. It was these men to whom the POESA appealed, primarily because it offered them the opportunity to create for themselves a new society. It is not possible, however, to understand the message of the POESA by looking solely at the dilemma of villagers; it is necessary to understand POESA ideology in its own terms, insofar as we are able to do so. To this end, I have drawn on conversations that I had with *ulama* and on material from the POESA journal, *Penjoeloeh*, published from 1940 to 1942.

## PRAYER AND THE IDEA OF HUMAN NATURE

The POESA view of society rested on a particular conception of human nature and the role of *ibadah* (religious duty), and especially prayer, in controlling this nature. The *ulama*'s ideas of human nature must therefore be discussed before we can turn to their ideas of society itself.

The Atjehnese versions of the Islamic myths of the

creation and destruction of the world describe man as a creature with two parts to his nature. I want first to talk about these myths and then to describe the expression of man's dual nature in prayer.

Before God created the world, He made the angels (*malèkat*) out of light (*nur*). The angels had various tasks; some worshipped God, others hauled water, some brought rain. No matter what their tasks, though, the angels were perfect in carrying them out because there was nothing in their nature that would make them disobedient to God. Since the angels were perfectly faithful to God, there was no indication of His omnipotence. If there was a hell at that time, it was empty. God therefore made the world as a testing place for a new kind of creature who could be either faithful or disobedient to God. In this way, both heaven and hell would be filled, and God's omnipotence would be demonstrated.

Before making man, God created the earth as a place for him to live. The earth and the natural world (*alam*) were made from nothingness (*wab*). After making the world in seven days, God created Adam out of earth (*tanoh*). Once man had been created, God made Hawa, the first woman, from Adam's rib.

God gave Adam (and hence Adam's descendants) *hawa nafsu*, the part of man's nature that he shares with the animals. It is everything that arises from within man, and hence hunger and sexual yearning, as well as love for the world, are manifestations of *hawa nafsu*.

When man responds to *hawa nafsu*, he is led away from God, for his response to himself diverts him from obedience to God's commands. If man had only *hawa nafsu*, he would not be able to obey God at all. But God also gave man a means to respond to Him—*akal*, or the ability to know. *Akal* is similar to our conception of rationality. Through the use of *akal*, man can know God's commands and control his (man's) instinctive nature, *hawa nafsu*.

It is the outcome of the struggle between the two parts of man's nature that determines his lot in the next world; some earn paradise, others earn hell. The outcome is evidence of God's omnipotence; both heaven and hell are filled.

God did not put Adam directly on earth. Adam and Hawa lived in paradise with the *malèkat* at first. The story of their expulsion explains the meaning of *hawa nafsu* and *akal*. After making Adam, God told the *malèkat* to honor him; he also told them that He was going to give the earth to man. The *malèkat* protested: " 'Why?' they asked. 'If man is put on earth there will be only bloodshed and destruction. Man has *hawa nafsu*; he will not be perfectly faithful [to God].' God, however, had taught Adam the names and uses of things. He called the *malèkat* together and asked them the names of the things of the earth. They did not know. Then Adam recited the names and uses of the things of the earth, and so demonstrated the superiority of man to the *malèkat*. The *malèkat* then understood why man and not the angels would be given the earth."[1]

---

[1] This and the following quotations are statements of Atjehnese informants.

Man is superior to the angels because he has *akal*. But man is also better suited to earth because he has *hawa nafsu*. "If the *malèkat* were put on earth, no use would be made of the world. They would only sit with their mouths agape, having no desire for anything. They would not use the world."

When God demonstrated the superiority of Adam to the *malèkat*, they all honored Adam except one, the *iblis*. The *iblis* refused because Adam was made of earth, while he and the other *malèkat* were made of light. The *iblis* therefore had to leave paradise, but before he left he asked God for someone to go with him. God answered that anyone who wanted to (*na meuhadjat, berhadjat*) could join him. The *iblis* therefore tempted Hawa with forbidden fruit.[2] Adam, as well as Hawa, ate, and God expelled them from paradise.

The story of creation thus delineates the two parts of man's nature. *Hawa nafsu*, or passion, desire, nature itself, leads man away from God. The very eating of the fruit was the satisfaction of *hawa nafsu* and so paradise was lost. *Akal*, however, makes man superior to the angels; it is the faculty which can lead man back to paradise. After Adam ate the fruit, he asked God to forgive him. God did and told him that if he and his descendants were faithful to His word, He would allow them to return to paradise. By using *akal* to know God's commands, man can regain paradise.

[2] In one version in the Koran, the *iblis* first tempts Adam; in two other versions it is unclear whether Hawa or Adam eats first.

Man's nature itself is neither good nor evil. It is only man's acts that are judged. Yet evil acts are the expression of one part of man's nature, *hawa nafsu*, unmediated by rationality, *akal*. Evil as a potential of man's nature which may be countered by the use of *akal* is emphasized by the role of the *iblis* in tempting Hawa and Adam to eat the forbidden fruit. Had Adam not lived in paradise first, the *malèkat* would not have known that Adam was their superior by virtue of possessing *akal*. The *iblis* was expelled from paradise not for having tempted Adam and Hawa, but for having refused to recognize that *akal* made men superior to the *malèkat*. He actually obeyed God in not honoring Adam so that the *malèkat* could see the significance of *akal*. In this light, the eating of the fruit by Adam and Hawa is more clearly their own responsibility than it is in Genesis, where the serpent is punished for tempting Eve. The lack of responsibility of the *iblis* for the expulsion of Adam and Hawa is indicated again when God says that "anyone who wants to" can leave with him. It is something within Adam and Hawa that makes them disobey God.

The nature of the temptation shows us something about *hawa nafsu*. In the Atjehnese myth, the fruit is only fruit. It is not the fruit of a special tree of knowledge of good and evil; man already has *akal*, the faculty of knowing. Nor does the fruit contain the promise of eternal life, as it does in the Koran. In the Atjehnese version, Adam and Hawa eat out of pure desire, demonstrating their animal nature, *hawa nafsu*, and the way in which *hawa nafsu* leads man away from God.

The extent to which sinful acts are thought of as the expression of *hawa nafsu* is illustrated in a story told by an *ulama*. He said first that if we ever felt a great desire for something and satisfied that desire, we would surely commit a sinful act. Then he told us about a learned man who liked to eat meat. "One day the man went to a feast. Meat was served, and he had a great desire to eat it. However, he recognized the strength of his desire and so contained himself. He arose, left the feast, and went to the market. There he asked the meat-seller when the steer had been slaughtered. Sure enough, the beast had not been slaughtered at all; it had died of disease." I asked the *ulama* if all desires led to sinful acts. What, for instance, if we had a great urge to read the Koran and did so? "That," he replied, "would be doing a good thing for the wrong reason. Surely we would be doing it only to impress the woman next door." (The Koran is always chanted aloud, and the sound carries easily through the walls of Atjehnese houses.)

*Hawa nafsu* is the cause of all evil acts, yet it is not synonymous to the curse of original sin. It existed as part of man's nature before he ate the forbidden fruit. It is in itself neither good nor bad. It has good consequences when man, motivated by *hawa nafsu*, uses the things of the earth in accordance with God's will as he perceives it through *akal*. It leads man to do evil acts when it is unmediated by rationality. In any event, *hawa nafsu* is an immutable part of man's nature, impossible to alter. He can only try to control it, to make it subservient to rationality.

Fortunately God has given man a means to control

himself. Through the performance of the five ritual prayers, he can achieve the dominance of rationality over *hawa nafsu*. This is how an *ulama* explained it:

"God has given us two characteristics [*tabiat*], *hawa nafsu* and *akal*. *Akal* guides us and restrains us from giving in to *hawa nafsu*. But *akal* alone is not sufficient. The sharper *akal* is, the more trouble it can lead us into if it is not guided by religion. Religion is a guide to *akal* and by means of *akal* we know religion. Without thinking of God and thus of religion, *akal* would mislead us. We would risk our place in the afterworld if it were not for prayer. Therefore God has ordered us to pray."

"Religion is a guide to *akal* and by means of *akal* we know religion" in that prayer not only puts the believer into a state of control over himself but is itself an exercise of this control. Moreover, this control of self continues after the prayer is completed so that rationality does not become the mere instrument of *hawa nafsu*.

Prayer is a part of the lives of most Atjehnese men; they seem actually to pray five times daily. Most of them claim that prayer does result in self-control, but statements about the relation of prayer to self-control are difficult to confirm from observations of daily life.[3] Consequently, I want to describe an instance which I observed where a man actually lost control of himself and then regained self-possession through prayer.

The man was Abdullah, a tobacco trader who worked in a town about five hours away by bus from

[3] Of course the Atjehnese know of many non-Atjehnese who do not pray. An *ulama* said, for instance, that in the Chinese one sees an example of *akal* existing only as the tool of *hawa nafsu*.

his own village. He was married to Sjarifah, one of a group of six sisters, cousins, and aunts who lived in adjacent houses. Sjarifah was twenty-six; Abdullah was thirty-five. They had two children, one a girl of nine, the other a boy about a year and a half. The boy fell sick, and for two months he ate very little. Finally he became so weak that he could no longer hold his head up. Sjarifah sent for the village healer several times and also took him to the male nurse in the market place, but the boy's health did not improve.

Both Abdullah and Sjarifah were especially attached to their son. Sjarifah's neighbors said that for a long while she and Abdullah had wanted a second child but that she had not been able to conceive. When the boy became seriously ill, Sjarifah sent a note to Abdullah asking for money for medicine. Learning that his son was sick, Abdullah came home.

About 9:30 one night, a week after Abdullah had returned to the village, there were cries from Sjarifah's house. The boy had just died, and his body was laid out on the bed. Sjarifah and all of her female relatives were wailing in the back room. Abdullah was by himself in another room. He had fainted and had just come to when I arrived. A few minutes later some teen-aged boys arrived and were directed by one of the female cousins to write notes announcing the death to relatives in neighboring villages.

By 10 P.M. the wailing had decreased somewhat. More relatives had arrived, including a sister of Sjarifah's mother who lived in another part of the village. Each time Sjarifah and her kin began to cry again,

Sjarifah's aunt would warn them that it was a sin to cry, that it was *sjétan* (the devil) who provoked them to do such things. Instead of crying, she said, they should "remember that the baby is going back to God. He is going before us. Be glad; the baby is free of sin and will be received by God." In spite of these words, the crying continued all night. Neither Sjarifah nor any of her female relatives who had cared for the baby during his lifetime could be comforted by such thoughts.

Abdullah, however, immediately regained control of himself. He told us how Sjarifah had noticed that the baby had stopped breathing. "The last four days the baby couldn't swallow. We took him to the male nurse but it didn't help. Then tonight Sjarifah looked at him and he was not breathing. Since then she hasn't stopped crying. That's not right. The baby is free of sin. He will be received by God."

The death was announced to the village the next morning. Learning about it, the village men came to the house to accompany the body to the graveyard. They gathered below the house and talked and smoked as usual. Abdullah was there as well. He was subdued but not much different than usual.

Upstairs, in the back of the house, the body was being washed before burial. Meanwhile Sjarifah and her relatives were still crying. The woman who teaches the girls to read the Koran repeatedly urged them to say "There is no God but God" (the first part of the confession of faith), but none of them listened to her and she herself occasionally dissolved into tears. When the body was wrapped, the men recited the special prayer said before burial. Then they brought the body to the graveyard for another service and buried it. The women stayed behind in the house.

For the next seven evenings men came to the house to recite the Koran in honor of the dead boy. There was also a feast so that, according to Sjarifah, she could recognize the boy on the Day of Judgment and they could go to paradise together.

Sjarifah did not stop grieving for her son for at least a month after that. Although she no longer cried continually, she secluded herself in the house. She was seldom alone, however, one of her female relatives usually being with her. Together they mourned, heedless of the warnings that mourning is sinful. Abdullah, however, refused to give in to his grief. Just thirty days after the boy died he said:

"Last week, the night before Lebaran [the day celebrating the end of the fast], I woke up and found Sjarifah crying. 'Don't do that,' I said, 'it is the work of the devil. When the child comes into your mind you should do away with the thought by reading the Koran or by praying. To carry on like that is sinful.' I told her the story of Ibrahim and Ismail. If God asked for the son of a prophet, how can we complain if He asked for our child? We should be happy he died so young and is free of sin. The next day [Lebaran], Ainsjah [his daughter] and I went to visit my mother. Sjarifah would not come [as she should have on Lebaran]. She stayed home and cried. If an *ulama* sees anyone mourning, he immediately becomes angry. It is sinful. I loved my son but I won't grieve. When I think of him, I pray or read the Koran instead."

Whenever Abdullah felt himself about to surrender to the grief that arose within him, he prayed or read the Koran. This is what the *ulama* meant by "religion as a guide to *akal*." The recitation of the prayers put Abdullah into a state of full possession of *akal*. That it did have this effect is shown by the fact that from the time he recovered from the first shock, he maintained a state of being that allowed him to act and be accepted as any other man. Sjarifah, however, was considered to be in an altogether different and unacceptable state. Her response to death, shared by her relatives, was not considered a normal reaction.[4] She was not supposed to grieve; she did so in spite of attempts to prevent her. That she herself found this socially unacceptable is demonstrated by her refusal to visit her mother-in-law on Lebaran and by her self-imposed seclusion. None of her actions was considered "customary" (part of *adat*); most of the women sympathized with her, but the men, including her husband, did not. The contrast between Sjarifah and Abdullah is the contrast between the expression of *hawa nafsu* on the one hand and that of *akal* on the other.

Abdullah's response to the death of his son illustrates "religion as a guide to *akal*." But to learn how "*akal* is a guide to religion," we must look at prayer itself. Prayer is not communication with God in the ordinary sense. God is completely transcendent, un-

---

[4] "Normal" in the sense of what is valued, not in terms of what happens statistically. Atjehnese women often grieve and are always warned and chastised for doing so.

approachable by man. God revealed himself and his teachings through Muhammed, who was the seal of prophecy. Man is left thus only with the teachings of Muhammed, and all that he can try to do is to retain the awareness of God that these teachings conveyed. Man accomplishes this through prayer. However, for prayer to be valid, there must be complete control of body and mind, that is, absolute control of self.

Prayer begins with ritual purification. Certain kinds of contamination, such as that received from touching a pig or a dog, can only be removed by a complete bath. Usually, however, it is sufficient to free oneself of all bodily excretions and to wash the face from forehead to beneath the chin and from ear to ear, the feet, and the arms up to the elbows, and to wet the hair. Before performing these ablutions, one must say to oneself, "Because of God I wash myself as is my duty." After washing, one is ready to pray.[5]

Several things can invalidate the state of ritual purity necessary for prayer. One cannot get dirty, for instance, or do anything that might leave one in less than full possession of *akal*. Falling asleep, touching the skin of a woman, or becoming dizzy makes one unfit to pray.

The spot on which a Muslim is about to pray should be clean. Atjehnese often use prayer mats, but this is not required. If an Atjehnese is to pray outdoors, for instance, he first cleans off a spot of ground. The

[5] There is the further requirement that the body be covered. The minimal regulation is that the body be covered from waist to knees. No one, however, prays without a shirt.

prayer must, of course, be recited while facing toward Mecca.

The times at which the five daily prayers must be recited are carefully specified. The first must be said during daybreak (*subuh*)—from the time the first rays of the sun are visible until the sun has risen; the second at noon (*zuhur*)—from the time the sun is at its zenith until the shadow of a stick stuck vertically into the ground is the same length as the stick itself; the third in the afternoon (*ashar*)—from the end of *zuhur* until sunset; the fourth at sunset (*mohgreb*)— from the time the sun sets until its rays are no longer visible; and the fifth at night (*isja*)—from the time of darkness until daybreak.

The prayers differ from each other not in content but only in the number of *raka'at* or "bowings" which compose them. The recitation of the prayer begins with a silent declaration of intent (*niat*), such as "It is my intention to perform the obligatory *zuhur* prayer with four *raka'at* because of God the sublime." This can be said in Atjehnese, but everything after this must be said in Arabic with the proper pronunciation. Most Atjehnese have no understanding of Arabic, but they are very concerned about pronouncing the words correctly. An incorrectly pronounced word invalidates the prayer. Atjehnese are taught the meaning of the prayers and are told to concentrate on it while pronouncing the Arabic.

The concern for exact pronunciation is duplicated by a concern for correct postures, since an incorrectly struck posture also invalidates the prayer. After the *niat*, which is said standing, the worshipper raises his hands, with his fingers open and his palms turned toward each other, to the height of his ears. In this position, still standing, the worshipper says, "God is most great" ("Allahu Akbar"). Then he brings his hands to the level of his waist and folds them, the right over the left, and chants the first *surah* of the Koran:

In the Name of God, the Merciful, the Compassionate

Praise belongs to God, the Lord of all Being,
the All-merciful, the All-compassionate,
   the Master of the Day of Doom.
Thee only we serve; to Thee alone we pray for
   succour.
   Guide us in the straight path,
the path of those whom Thou has blessed,
not of those against whom Thou art wrathful,
   nor of those who are astray. (I: 1.)[6]

After this *surah* is recited, the worshipper may follow it with any *surah* from the Koran. A common one is entitled "Sincere Religion":

In the Name of God, the Merciful, the Compassionate

Say: 'He is God, One,
God, the Everlasting Refuge,
who has not begotten, and has not been begotten,
and equal to Him is not any one.' (CXII: 1.)

[6] All passages from the Koran are from the A. J. Arberry translation (1955).

If this *surah* is recited during the first *raka'at*, it is best to recite a different one during the second. "The Afternoon" seems to be frequently used here:

In the name of God, the Merciful, the Compassionate

By the Afternoon!
Surely Man is in the way of loss,
save those who believe, and do righteous deeds,
and counsel each other unto the truth,
and counsel each other to be steadfast. (CIII.)

The worshipper then bows from the waist while saying "Allahu Akbar." When bowing, he raises his hands again as they were when he said "Allahu Akbar" at the beginning of the prayer. With the trunk of his body parallel to the ground, he places his hands on his knees and faces toward the ground. Then he says, "God is the most pure and the most great. Praise be to God."[7] After this he stands erect again, but while rising, he repeats, "Hear God, those who praise You." When fully erect, with his arms hanging straight down, he continues, "Praise belongs to God. Our praise fills the heavens and the earth and anything else You wish." After this he makes a full bow by lowering himself first to his knees, then putting his hands on the ground palm downward and lowering his nose and forehead to the ground. In this position he says, "God, the highest, is the purest. All praise belongs to God." This phrase is recommended but not obligatory; it may be repeated from three to eleven times. The bow is then repeated.

[7] This phrase is recommended (*sunat*) but is not obligatory.

During the first *raka'at* the worshipper sits between bows with his legs tucked under his body. In the sitting position, the thighs must be parallel to each other and the feet crossed, the left foot under the right, and the right sole perpendicular to the ground. The back must be straight, and the hands should be placed over the knees. While sitting, he says "Allahu Akbar" and then says:

> Forgive me God, be merciful to me.
> Correct my weaknesses and raise my sight.
> Give me livelihood and guide me.
> Give me health and pardon my errors.

This concludes the first *raka'at*, which is then repeated with only slight variations up to the number prescribed for each prayer. The prayer ends with the confession of faith and the pronouncement of the greeting, "*Assalaimu aleichum warachmatullah.*"

Prayer is not a ritual means of making a request of God. One prays because it is, literally, one's sacred duty, complete in itself. The worshipper performs that duty with precision, not because he is afraid that some end outside of prayer will be denied to him if the ritual is improperly performed (except, of course, one will be punished for not praying), but because precision is part of his duty. To be sure, there is a request made ("Correct my weaknesses and raise my sight . . ."), but it is a very general one and cannot be considered the reason for prayer itself.[8] Rather,

---

[8] It is true that a line can be added for the welfare of one's parents at the end of prayer. But this is in Arabic and, like the

the words of this request, like those of the rest of the prayer, are to the mind what the motions are to the body—a form to which one accommodates oneself. Atjehnese are taught to fill their minds with the meaning of the Arabic words and so to exclude any other thoughts that might arise within their minds. In this way they obliterate anything that comes from within them, physically as well as mentally, and so give themselves over, "surrender" (the meaning of "Islam") themselves to God.[9]

In one sense, the lack of initiative allowed the believer in prayer seems a denial of *akal*. He must recite what is given him to recite and is allowed only to add *surah* at certain points. But it is this very arbitrary character of prayer that expresses the self-control of the believer. Prayer is not an outpouring of inner feeling but the believer's conformation of himself to God's commands. By making his words and actions, literally his whole mind and body, fit God's prescriptions, he enacts in a sacred context what is required of him in secular life afterward. In this way, prayer becomes an intense, sacred microcosm of the larger world that precedes and follows it. It at once demonstrates not only the believer's freedom by his conscious control of his actions, permitting him to tri-

---

rest of the prayer, the emphasis is on precision. One can ask God for things, but this is *doa* (which Poerwadarminta [1960] defines as request—*permohonan*), not prayer (*sembajang*).

[9] The effectiveness of this can be seen when Atjehnese pray in public places such as the market. They seem to remove themselves completely from their surroundings, giving no indication that they are aware of what is going on around them.

umph over that part of his self that urges him to do otherwise, but also his submission to God in the performance of the acts themselves. The intensity, the sacred character, and especially the symbolism of "giving-over" of self in prayer explain perhaps how Abdullah could so effectively reenter the secular world in full possession of *akal*.[10]

Through prayer men make themselves into rational beings in control of their own actions. They thus distinguish themselves from animals, as well as from children (*aneuk*). The latter do not yet possess a fully developed rational faculty; therefore they do not pray and have not yet become people (*ureung*).

Prayer is, then, a framework within which men struggle with themselves in order to realize one part of their nature, rationality. It is this quality, rationality, that is requisite to the performance of all social roles. Man's dual nature remains with him, but it is periodically controlled or, better, realigned through prayer so that *hawa nafsu* is subservient to *akal*. The promised result—the creation of relations between men on earth, undisrupted by the passions that set men against each other—was expressed by one Atjehnese writer in this metaphor: "Men want to bind themselves together with the rope of God, the rope which neither rots in the rain nor cracks in the sun."

THE PROMISE OF *ibadah*

Among the *Penjoeloeh* articles on Atjehnese so-

[10] The reading of the Koran requires the same precision as prayer.

ciety is one by Teungku Oestman al Muhammady
entitled "What Is the Reason for the Backwardness
of the Islamic Community? What Went Wrong?—
How Can the Situation Be Improved?—Is Islam a
Religion of Backwardness, a Religion of Chanduri
and Selamatan [Ritual Feasts]?" Because Teungku
Oestman so well displays the idea of society as a
manifestation of *ibadah*,[11] I would like to quote extensively from his article:

The best medicine for the backwardness of the Islamic
community today is the understanding of the meaning
of Islam and knowledge of its first principles. This will
bring mankind to a state of refinement and material well-
being [*keadaban dan kebendaan*] and will raise its spirit
to the place of perfection prepared for it.

*Men must be assured that the word* ibadah *does not
merely mean the act of prayer* [ruku dan sudju]. *It is intended as the means to regulate person, family, society,
and mankind generally, as well as the creatures of God.*
. . . *Ibadah* is the strongest basis for the material and
spiritual well-being of the household and of society . . . .

The Dutch writer Dr. E. Rijpma, in his book *De
Ontwikkelingsgang der Historie,* has described the progress of Islam in its golden age. He wrote about science, art,
letters, education and industry, agriculture and trade, and
so on. All of this was achieved not through formal psy-
chology [*psychologisch formeel*] but by the true teaching
of Islam. It was the result of *ibadah*; *ibadah* based on the

[11] *Ibadah* literally means religious duty, which includes the five
pillars of Islam, the indispensible duties of all Muslims: the confession of faith, the five daily prayers, the fasting month, the
religious payments and, for those who can afford it, the pilgrimage. It also includes ritual purity and, sometimes, the Holy
War. See "Ibadat" in Gibb and Kramers (1953).

principles of learning and philosophy, true *ibadah*, not the sort we find today.

What is true *ibadah*? It means, in short, that everything is done legitimately, according to law. The meaning of each duty is thought about, and the intention is understood in the light of general science. . . .

I will analyze one part of *ibadah*, prayer, in this way. . . . If we take the time to think about it, we will see that logically prayer is an injection into society so that society will achieve material and spiritual well-being. . . . Prayer has a very intimate connection with all the problems of life. . . . In matters of health, industry, economics, agriculture and education, and so on, prayer has a very special role.

Prayer does not mean merely the act of prayer itself. It includes the forms of work and social intercourse in daily life. As you know, one of the requisites of prayer is that nakedness be covered. Because of this, the person who prays must also pay attention to such things as the cloth industry, cotton mills, thread, machines, and so on, so that he can cover his nakedness.

Here we see the wisdom of prayer in material things. The requisite of covering oneself in prayer means that prayer regulates daily life. In this one problem alone, we meet with concerns about industry, agriculture, chemistry, and economy . . . and this is just a beginning. We have not space enough to go into all the things connected with prayer.

But we can see that *the meaning of prayer is not just the actual prayer itself; it includes all the forms of social intercourse in daily life as well. In this way prayer leads to unity and harmony of nation and fatherland.*

This is the true intention of prayer. . . .

We are surprised that we have become a backward community, one commanding no respect and without value.

But we should not be. Not at all! It is all our fault.
Our great error was in violating the command of God
and His prophet. . . .

This [backwardness] is the result of our way of being
Islamic, of not honoring the essence of Islamic history.
We have not heightened and purified Islam; we have
degraded and soiled it. . . .

We have the duty to pray in our homes, in our mosques
and to act accordingly in society.

God forgive us.

Show us the way of Your straight path! Amin!!![12]

Teungku Oestman claims that all of social life is
based on *ibadah*. We might well wonder how considerations of "health, industry, economics, agriculture
and education" are included in five ritual prescriptions. If we take Teungku Oestman to mean that because we must cover our nakedness in order to pray
we must necessarily have a cloth industry, we would
not be fair to him. He does not mean that religious
duties *require* certain kinds of economy and society.
Rather he means that if *ibadah* is rightly understood,
a certain kind of society comes about naturally.
*Ibadah*, then, "is intended as the means to regulate
person, family, society, and mankind generally, as
well as the creatures of God." The implication of his
statements is not that we must build a cloth industry
in order to pray, but that prayer and the four other
duties of *ibadah*, if rightly understood, will encom-
pass the cloth industry as well as the rest of life.

For the writers of *Penjoeloeh*, society is based on

[12] *Penjoeloeh* (August 1941: 121–122); emphasis supplied.

the restraint of man's nature. Once man responds not to his own nature (*hawa nafsu*) but to God's commands, harmonious social relations are possible. The only way for man to resist inner promptings is through fear of God. *Ibadah* is the most perfect way for man to become aware of God and thus to fear Him. When *ibadah* is rightly performed, rationality (*akal*), and not passion (*hawa nafsu*), will permeate all of society. It will naturally follow that in economic life, for instance, factories will be built. The result of a true understanding of *ibadah* is the control of self brought about by prayer and extended to all of life. The connection between *ibadah* and cloth industries is not merely that *ibadah* requires cloth factories in the specific sense, but that rationality, once found through the fear of God, will then guide the rest of life.

*Ibadah* does not give a specific *form* to social life; it does not provide an *image* of a perfect society. Instead it imparts a special *quality* to all of human life —the control of self, or the expression of rationality. This quality dominates life nearly automatically after it has been brought into being through the fear of God. In the reconstruction of society, therefore, it is not necessary to talk of the form society should have; it is only necessary to bring about the proper control of inner life and a good society will automatically develop. It is for this reason that Teungku Oestman ends his article not with an injunction to build factories, but with an admonition to pray.

In accord with this view of society, the Atjehnese see their past as periods of either rationality or irrationality. They think of history as cyclical; not, however, as the repetition of certain events, but as the emergence and recession of *akal*. The writers of *Penjoeloeh* considered the time in which they were living as the beginning of a new era, a time of "awareness" or "consciousness" (*insjaf, keinsjafan*). One writer, Oesman Raliby (1941: 178) began an article entitled "The New Atjehnese Society" by saying: " 'Atjeh is greatly different today than it was ten years ago.' This was said to me during the fasting month. It is true indeed.

We cannot yet say that Atjeh is entirely conscious, but our experience has shown us that it really has begun to be conscious."

The editor of *Penjoeloeh*, Ismail Jakoeb, began a letter with the same thoughts and the same image:

"This is the era of progress, this is the Twentieth Century." This is what we hear everywhere from all the descendants of Adam. Without exception, all elements of society, old and young, here and abroad, are active. They are comparing thoughts, and they talk of the spirit of the century. . . .

The Muslim world or the world of the East was asleep in the last century. Now they are awake and full of the spirit of life. . . .[13]

"Sleep" as the opposite of "consciousness" in history is developed more fully in a *Penjoeloeh* article by Ismail Taib (1941: 40) called "Youth and Unity in Atjeh":

[13] Quoted from the typescript of a letter Ismail Jakoeb sent to the committee formed to establish the POESA. No date [1939].

According to history, there was one era which we cannot forget—the era of Al Raniri and Fansoeri [two famous *ulama* who lived in Atjeh at the time of its greatness], the time of the flying of the flag of Islam in the land of Atjeh. The flag of Islam flew in Spain for eight centuries while Cordova was the center of learning; the Abbasid Caliphate shone for five and one-half centuries while the power of Islam was at its peak and Bagdad was the center of knowledge. In the same way in a corner of Indonesia, in Atjeh, the star of Islam glittered for many eras, lighting up the heart of the community until faith truly was in the hearts [of the inhabitants], unshakeable in the strongest wind.

Famous *ulama* arose, men of letters, philosophers of the deepest contemplation. Everywhere there were schools, from the most elementary to the highest.

. . . Youth were educated in all branches of learning until they genuinely understood all matters of religion and their duties to God. . . . In the body of every youth flowed the blood of heroism that comes only from faith in God. . . .

But except for God, nothing is eternal. After night comes day, after life, death, as though a turning wheel; once on top, then to the bottom. So too with the kingdom of Atjeh. After a period of brilliance, a time of unity, after the time of its pride in its *ulama* and its poets of the greatest titles, came the time of turning. The turning of the wheel to the bottom. The star became dim, the rope of unity slackened. There were disagreements. The longer time went on, the dimmer it got. Then the light went out altogether. Atjeh was dark. Quarrels arose. The people of one region became the enemies of those of the next.

The youth of that era were scarcely educated. Into their veins flowed the spirit of vengeance. They took sides, divided into groups; they became provincial. Finally the names of regions became famous—Pasè, Gajo, Peusangan, Pidie, and so on. Enmity between regions did not end in one era; it descended to the next.

With the end of unity came the end of a good society, the end of the progress of religion.

Atjeh has slept long. . . .

Sleep is the state in which nature overcomes consciousness. It is used as a metaphor for the overcoming of man by his own nature, by *hawa nafsu*. During the period of sleep, "Quarrels arose. The people of one region became the enemies of those of the next." One thinks of the prediction of the angels when they learned that man had *hawa nafsu*: "If man is put on earth there will be only bloodshed and destruction." So long as this state of sleep persists, inner compulsion is reflected in outer disorder: "Enmity . . . did not end in one era; it descended to the next."

Light, the opposite of darkness, is a force from without which awakens, which brings consciousness. It is "the star of Islam, . . . lighting up the heart of the community." The changed state of being is then reflected in social life. Atjeh is great, and there is "a time of unity." Darkness, however, is not the direct opposite of light: it is not an outer force but merely the absence of light. (The light became dimmer until it "went out altogether. Atjeh was dark.") In darkness, *hawa nafsu* dominates man; there is sleep. Devoid of the restraint produced by the light of Islam, passion causes disorder. (Into the veins of the youth "flowed the spirit of vengeance.")

The decline of Atjeh, then, was not caused by historical events as we know them but by "darkness," "sleep," which appears both inexorable and inexplicable. "After night comes day, after life, death, as though a turning wheel. . . . After a period of brilliance, a time of unity . . . came the time of the turning. . . . The star became dim, the rope of unity slackened."

This imagery is found in many articles in *Penjoeloeh*. Perhaps the most notable is by A. So'dy (1941: 190–191). The article is called "The Dawn of Consciousness Breaks on the Eastern Horizon of the Land of the Rentjong."

There is nothing eternal in nature. Everything changes. There is a time to sleep and a time to wake.

In the time of Iskandar Muda, Atjeh progressed, bathed in the gleam of sunlight. Everywhere Atjeh made itself felt, not merely because of the bravery of its people on the battlefield, but because they struggled to call out to others. They called to them to leave behind sin and to spread the rays of Islam.

Who is not astounded to hear that Atjeh colonized Djohor, Riau, Djambi, and so on. Atjehnese arose [*bangun*] and crossed the seas not to add luster to their name but to obey the utterance of God, to spread Islam.

Whose hair does not stand on end to hear Atjeh called "the doorway to Mecca" [*serambi* Mecca]? People greatly respected this name, as they should have.

In short, Atjeh was at its peak. Islam was truly alive; its rays prodded [*mendjolok*] the atmosphere. Religion was truly felt in the souls [*djiwa*] of the inhabitants. The Land of the Rentjong bathed in the rays of victorious Islam.

But the rays gradually dimmed. The Land of the Rentjong darkened beneath a blanket of gloom. Atjeh fell into retreat, its advances suffocated by the era. Atjeh slept in a cradle of illusion [*ajoenan maja pada*]. It was time to sleep.

But now the dawn of consciousness has broken. Its
rays are transforming the horizon of the Land of the
Rentjong. Slowly the light appears, purifying. In a moment
the sun itself will appear, showing its sweet face. Its rays,
carrying the stuff of life [*bahan bahan hidoep*], will shine
in all the corners of Atjeh. They will awaken the people
from their cradle of ignorance.

Clearly the people of Atjeh have begun to awaken. . . .

*Ulama* and youth everywhere in Atjeh are conscious of
unity; the construction of a new generation has begun . . .
step by step, from theory to practice. Everywhere the
people are aware [*insaf*]; they have begun to improve
themselves. The advisors have begun to teach and have
planted seeds which will grow in the new generation.
Writers have begun to take up their pens and to write of
the soul which has been hidden for so long. Everywhere
a great desire for unity is developing in the soul of the
people.

Atjehnese used to fear learning. Now they are thirsty
for knowledge of religion. And this has carried over to
secular knowledge as well. . . .

Atjeh has been through bitter experience which has
been its first teacher. Now there is a spirit of unity. Men
want to bind themselves together with the rope of God, the
rope which neither rots in the rain nor cracks in the sun.
True unity can be neither asked for nor sought after but
can only come of itself with the awakening of consciousness. Wherever mankind has fully developed *akal*,[14] has
great will, no longer bothers with trivia, wherever people
do not hold back in carrying out their responsibilities,
there the spirit of unity in its pure state will arise by
itself. . . .

Here again religion is conceived of as an outer

[14] The word used is actually *tjerdas*, which is defined in Poerwadarminta (1960) as "*sempruna perkembangan akal budi*,"
"the perfect development of *akal*."

force producing a new state of being, which in turn produces a new state of society. Again "light" is a metaphor for "Islamic religion." It is "light," or religion, whose "rays prodded the atmosphere [*mendjolok ketjakrawala*]" and thus entered "the souls of the inhabitants [*djiwa penduduknja*]." As a result, the Atjehnese "arose" (*bangun*, meaning both "to wake up" and "to get up" [Echols and Shadily, 1961]) and "crossed the seas" to colonize "Djohor, Riau, Djambi, and so on."

A. So'dy stresses that Atjeh's greatness was the result of the desire of the Atjehnese to advance religion. "Everywhere Atjeh made itself felt,[15] not merely because of the bravery of its people on the battlefield, but because they struggled to call out to others. They called to them to leave behind sin and to spread the rays of Islam." A. So'dy clearly indicates in an earlier sentence that this greatness was the result of the changed state of the Atjehnese: "In the time of Iskandar Muda, Atjeh progressed, bathed in . . . sunlight." And he stresses the religious motives of the Atjehnese again when he says they colonized "not to add luster to their name but to obey the utterance of God." He continues by pointing out that the basis of Atjeh's reputation is not its political power (which merely "astounds"), but its religious significance as "the doorway to Mecca." In any case, Atjeh's political position was owing to the religious motivation of its subjects.

---

[15] Literally, *"Seloeroeh tempat mentjioem baoe Atjeh"*—"Everywhere the odor of Atjeh was smelled."

An awakened society is a unified society. Unity is a product of consciousness. (A. So'dy even implies that consciousness means the consciousness of unity itself. ["*Ulama* and youth everywhere in Atjeh are conscious of unity."] Unity comes from a changed state of being: "Everywhere a great desire for unity is developing in the soul of the people." It cannot come from any other source: "True unity can be neither asked for nor sought after but can only come of itself with the awakening of consciousness."

A. So'dy gives us our best understanding of what this changed state of being is: "Wherever mankind his fully developed *akal*, has great will, no longer bothers with trivia, wherever people do not hold back in carrying out their responsibilities, there the spirit of unity in its pure state will arise by itself." The first phrase of this sentence, "Wherever mankind has fully developed *akal*," refers directly to the change in state of being. The rest of the sentence describes the results of this change, which add up to "the spirit of unity." Here, fully developed *akal* is the state of being which contrasts with the state of sleep, or the dominance of *hawa nafsu*.

Alternating eras of rationality and irrationality do not conform to specific images of good and less good societies. Atjeh in the time of its greatness, for instance, is not thought of as a model of the relations between people. It is only an example of a society permeated by *akal* and, hence, of the unity of men.

The POESA writers offered no suggestions about the shape of a unified society. There is in their writings nothing like the Western conception of a just society, for instance. Nor are any specific social reforms suggested. The only concrete proposals the POESA made were to establish more religious schools and a printing press. On the major political issue of the 1930s, the restoration of the sultanate, the leaders of the POESA were divided.[16]

The absence of specific conceptions of society is to be expected if society is a reflection of the inner states of its members. There is no need to think of what society should be; it is enough to concentrate on changing man's state of being. A good society is not a just one in our sense. It is one in which men have control of their selves. No single political or social form best suits this condition. The development of *akal* takes the form appropriate to the moment in history. Cloth factories, for example, may be appropriate now, whereas they were not in the time of Muhammed. One looks to history not for an image of social organization but for an expression of a state of being. It is not the form but the state of being which brings the form into existence that defines human worth. "Unity" means harmony among men; the shape harmony takes is of only temporal significance. "Nothing worldly is eternal," the writers of *Penjoeloeh* often said, and the societies of

---

[16] Some of the POESA youth-group members wanted the sultanate restored because they hoped it would diminish the power of the *uleebelang*. But Daud Beureuèh, for instance, was against this because he disapproved of the character of the pretendant sultan.

the past were at best only expressions of *akal* appropriate to the time.

There is, however, one way in which the past is used as a model of what the present ought to be. This can be seen in a *Penjoeloeh* article by Asmara Aini (1940: 138–139) entitled "Strengthening the Power of the Young: Important Materials for Giving Life to the Spirit [Semangat] of the Youth in Their Work." The "materials" referred to in the title are examples from the past. He begins by telling us why the youth are so important: "It is indeed the youth who will risk the energy of their maturity to bring about a very special state in the time to come. Our nation has the greatest hope of them. With the power of ordered ranks, youth, still strong in their struggle with the world, able to withstand heat and cold, exhaustion and weakness, will surmount the peak and take on the duties of nation and religion." Asmara Aini sees the struggle with the world, the withstanding of heat and cold, and the overcoming of exhaustion and weakness, as the overcoming of *hawa nafsu*, and the result is the fulfillment of religious and national duties.

Some experts have showed us that there are many ways of giving life to the spirit of the youth [*menghidoepkan semangat pemoeda*]. For example, one can narrate the life of prominent people in the community who have given of themselves for the best interests of society and religion. We are indeed pleased that the leaders of this journal have begun doing this by publishing the biographies of *ulama* (and especially Atjehnese *ulama*) whose lives have until now been hidden from the people.

Another important factor in these efforts is the study of the history of our fatherland. The strengths and weaknesses of our ancestors in the spread of religion in past centuries can be assessed now. What level has our civilization reached? How far have we progressed?

Calling to mind national days [*hari kebangsaan*] is another very important means to strengthen the spirit of awareness. Actually, the study of the past is not for the purpose of the past itself; it is [to find] a guide and a compass for the time ahead.

One uses the past as a guide to the future not to emulate the structure of previous societies but to reawaken the spirit that motivated the deeds of men. It is not even the deeds themselves that are important but the spirit behind those deeds. Here is the next paragraph: "All the national victories which the course of time has obscured, all the efforts of the leaders of the past must be retold and brought back to us so that the spirit of the youth will be moved and come alive and they will want to follow in the footsteps of the *ulama* in the inner sense [*timboellah rasa hendak mengikoeti djedjak-djedjak oelama itoe dalam sanoebarinja*]." Here the past is seen as "a guide and a compass for the time ahead," but Asmara Aini is really interested in the "inner sense" of past events. It is not sufficient for youth merely to "follow in the footsteps of the *ulama*"; they must also emulate the spirit or "the inner sense" (the true meaning) of the *ulama*'s deeds. Thus it is the state of being which brought about the events, rather than the events themselves, which is important.

## SOCIETY, UNITY, AND CONSCIOUSNESS

*Akal* and *hawa nafsu* conceptualize interior experience, but they also refer to the nature of society. *Ulama* in the 1930s, speaking of Atjeh's past and future, did not distinguish between society as perceived in terms of *akal* and *hawa nafsu* and society as *akal* and *hawa nafsu*. Nor, I believe, would such a distinction have made sense to them. The reason for this lies in their experience. Their own transition from village to *pesantren* was itself conceived in terms of *akal* and *hawa nafsu*, as we shall see in the next chapter. In a society with as little cultural unity as nineteenth-century Atjeh, passage between institutions was most easily thought of in terms of common human nature rather than in terms of the natural succession of roles that men played. *Akal* and *hawa nafsu* conceptualized the experience of passage from institution to institution, and thus the limits of society. Awareness of society in nineteenth-century Atjeh was expressed not by the features of the institutions as such, but by the characteristics of men which enabled them to have grossly disparate types of social experience in a lifetime.

Indeed, the idea of a new society was conceived of in terms of transition. The pairs of images by which it was expressed all indicate movement from one state to the next: from darkness to light, from disorder to unity, from backwardness to modernity, from sleep to awareness. It is as though the idea of a new society made sense only in terms of what it would come from. No doubt the great appeal of reformist Islam in the 1930s can be attributed to this notion of transition which the *ulama* expressed in their teachings. On the one hand, it delivered men from their families (the topic of Part III), and, on the other, it promised a new society to replace the bonds between men which, with the decline of pepper cultivation, had lost meaning.

The *ulama* expected a new society and a new consciousness to appear together. It was soon apparent, however, that consciousness and society were distinct from each other. A few men began to speak of the difference between themselves and the world, and stressed not the reformation of the world but their own purity. For example, one *Penjoeloeh* writer, who signed himself T.T. (1942: 279), said: "We believe in appearances and our eyes deceive us. . . . Where can we put our trust?" He then went on to answer his own question: "My advice is to use the method of the French, the *method of scepticism* [*methode ragu*]. . . . Use *akal*, pure thoughts, and Afala Ta'Qiloen." Another *ulama*, Nadhroen Adamy Medan (1941: 167), said, "If we really think how falseness blossoms and spreads, upsetting everything in its path, we want to flee this earth and run to escape the fumes of hell that fill this world with poison." As we can see, his solution also emphasized the distinction between awareness and the world. His article, which appeared in *Penjoeloeh*, was entitled "Education in the Truth," which meant, of course, education in *ibadah*. "The fence that holds a person back from doing evil things is clear thought and a true feeling of not liking evil."

If men began to doubt that awareness would manifest itself in a new society, they did not doubt that, at least at certain moments, it could appear in the unity of men. In the meetings of the POESA, the new consciousness seemed visibly expressed, at least in retrospect. In 1940, the POESA held a congress in Sigli, which was attended by members from all over Atjeh. Here is a description of that meeting by the editor of *Penjoeloeh*, Ismail Jakoeb (1940):

At first glance this was just a group of *ulama*. . . . We did not expect the congress to turn out this way. Sigli seemed as usual. But then it was filled, crowded with every kind of people from every part of society. They wanted a change in their fate, they wanted to bring in a new era, one of triumph. Atjeh at one time was famous. Then it quickly declined until it was left behind to sleep.

But apparently it will advance as quickly as it declined. Ten years ago it was still asleep. Then it awoke and began on the road of expansion. It is no longer morning now; it is already afternoon. . . .

The congress began Friday night, the 19th of April with a reception. The city was filled with not less than 6,000 members of the community of Islam, men and women both. Five minutes before the reception opened, the sound of an exploding bomb shook the inhabitants of Sigli, pounding on the eardrums of the members of the congress. The congress was about to begin. Two minutes later a second bomb followed, heightening the spirit of things, knocking at the doors of consciousness. At pre-

cisely eight, a third bomb was heard, adding even more
to the spirit of things.

. . . Saturday afternoon the atmosphere in Sigli was like
the great holidays. The crowds flooded the city, thronging
the road to Kota Asan [the meeting place]. By seven
o'clock the city was packed, filled and overflowing. Most
had to wait outside the meeting hall. There were about
10,000 people at that meeting.

After more meetings, at which *ulama* as well as
*uleebelang* and students spoke, and a special radio
message from an *ulama* in Singapore, the congress
closed with "the exclamation that the age of awareness had at last dawned" (Ismail Jakoeb, 1940).

A feeling of unity was achieved most vividly in
meetings such as these, but the teachings of the
POESA also affected the way in which men viewed
themselves and the course of their own lives. In the
next chapters, we shall look at the influence of these
teachings.

# PART III

## CONSCIOUSNESS AND SOCIETY IN THE 1960s

# 7 MEN AND BOYS IN ATJEHNESE FAMILIES

By the 1960s Atjehnese men had gained a place in the market. Today most men are traders in the distributive system created by the Dutch, although some are growers of cash crops in the mountains of central Atjeh and a few have stayed in the village to grow rice. The assumption of roles in the market has not meant (to the Atjehnese) that a new society has come into being. Atjehnese do not see the market or the family as the manifestation of *akal* in the world. On the other hand, they do view themselves in terms of *akal* and *hawa nafsu*. In this chapter and the next, I want to show that there has been a divorce of consciousness from society, with men's ideas about themselves no longer being defined by their social roles.[1]

More specifically, in this chapter I want to show how *akal* and *hawa nafsu* now define passage from childhood to manhood but fail to delineate a role of husband–father. The result is that the structure of the family today is very similar to that of the family in nineteenth-century Atjeh, whereas men's ideas of their place in it have changed considerably. We can see how this is so if we look at the reasons why men

[1] I am not concerned in this study with the political changes that took place in Atjeh (and Indonesia) before and after World War II. These form a separate topic not relevant here and are the subject of another paper now in preparation.

today are unable to make decisions in their families,
even though they feel entitled to do so.

## KINSHIP, INHERITANCE, AND CONTROL OF LAND

The powerlessness of men is not a feature of the
Atjehnese kinship system. Atjehnese trace descent
through both males and females. Their kinship terminology is Hawaiian; that is, all cross-cousins and
parallel-cousins are referred to by the same term as
that used for sisters. While Hawaiian terminology
does not distinguish between relatives traced through
the mother and those traced through the father, Atjehnese do have terms for the two groups. Relatives on
the father's side are termed *wali* and those on the
mother's side, *karung*. Since residence is uxorilocal
and since approximately half of the men marry into
villages other than the one into which they were born,
the two groups are distinct. Children grow up in the
house of their mother and in the company of the
children of their mother's sisters. Men, however, feel
obligations to both sides, and this leads to conflicts
with their wives, as I shall illustrate. Nonetheless,
there is nothing in the kinship system as such that
prevents men from having authority in the families
created by their marriages as there would be if the
Atjehnese system were matrilineal.

Nor is there anything about inheritance which can
account for the powerlessness of husbands. Inheritance follows Islamic law, with two shares going to
male heirs for each one share going to females. This
is modified by the practice of giving women houses

at the time of their marriage. As we have seen, these become the full and legal property of the women from one to three years later. Those parents who can afford it also give rice land to their daughters, either at the time they are *geumeuklèh* (separated) or at the birth of their children. If parents with a son and a daughter should die before building a house for their daughter, their own house would go to the daughter and the rest of the estate would be divided according to Islamic law. If they had two daughters, their house would go to the elder daughter and a second house would be built or bought for the younger daughter before the estate was divided. Judges of the Islamic courts say that this procedure is not in conflict with Islamic law. If, however, the son sued to have the estate divided before the house was built, the judges assured me that they would have to decide in his favor. The astonishing fact, however, is that no such case has ever been brought before the Islamic courts in Pidie or in Atjeh Utara insofar as the judges there can remember. The principle of inheritance, according to the old men of the village who act as overseers of the division of estates, is that women are provided with house and house land, and after that the estate is divided according to Islamic law.

Islamic law dictates that the property men and women bring to marriage is kept separate until their deaths. That which they earn together after marriage is divided, after the death of the husband, in half, with one half going to the wife and the other half divided between wife and children. However, if a man goes away on the *rantau* and leaves his wife behind, his earnings are considered his property and not joint property to be divided between his wife and children. Villagers gave me this information, but I never witnessed the division of a merchant's estate and so cannot confirm it. I have no reason to doubt it, however. The important point is that there is no barrier to a man leaving his estate to the family created by his marriage.

When a man with young children dies, his estate is not usually divided immediately. Instead, control of it is given to his wife to provide for their children; legal responsibility for the estate rests with the husband's brother. As the husband's brother is likely to live in another village and in any case probably spends most of his time trading in the East, he usually has little control over the way in which the estate is handled. Disputes before the Islamic courts (which settle matters of marriage, divorce, and inheritance) sometimes concern conflicts between widows and husbands' brothers over the handling of these funds. Disputes arise, for instance, if the woman remarries, for the husband's brother is likely to fear that the estate may be used by the new husband. The husband's brother can claim the children if he thinks the estate is not being properly handled. Supposedly many widows with children do not remarry for fear of losing their children, although I know of no case where a widow in fact had to give up her children.

In case of divorce, men are supposed to provide for their children. In the cases I know of and according to the judges of the Islamic courts, they do not do so. The only recourse for women is to leave the children with their fathers, but as the women usually can provide for them without the fathers' help, they do not do this. No children that I know of went with their fathers at the time of divorce, even in those cases where the mother was mentally defective.

To see how these customs work in practice, we will look at a single village in Pidie. The villages of Pidie are set in the midst of rice fields and have from 500 to 800 inhabitants living in clusters of houses owned by related women, as they were in Snouck's time. Each village has from one to three *meunasah*, men's houses, as it did in the nineteenth century, and each house in the village is said to be affiliated with a *meunasah*.

In the area of one *meunasah* I surveyed, there were 65 houses with 83 nuclear families. Sixty-four of these families had living male heads. Of these 64 men, only 12 remained in the village to work in the rice fields. The others were away for extended periods; most of them were traders in the East, although some were traders in the local markets and came home weekly. The majority of those who traded in the East were only in the village a few times a year, usually on the occasion of an Islamic festival, such as the end of the fasting month. A few of the men absent from the village were in the mountains of central Atjeh growing coffee, and they, too, came home only infrequently.

Every married woman owned her own house and

the land on which it stood, provided she had been
*geumeuklèh* from her parents.[2] Of the 83 families,
there were 25 who held no rice land.[3] However, 9 of
these 25 families were not yet *geumeuklèh* and so
were not classified as landless in the distribution of
the religious payment to the poor.[4] Of the remaining
16 families, 5 are unknown to me, and at least 3 of
the remaining 11 were very old couples who had

[2] No men owned houses. If parents had no daughters, their
house was sold, following the death of the second parent, and
their sons divided the proceeds.

[3] Figures on land ownership are only approximate. Land is not
registered, and people are reluctant to say how much land they
own and where it is situated because, in theory, they should pay
taxes on it. In practice, the taxes are not collected, but they were
under the Dutch and in 1963 the government had plans to collect taxes again.

The figures given here are from two sources. One is a survey
made by Moh. Amin Aziz, an Atjehnese student at the Agricultural Faculty in Bogor, and by myself. This survey was made in
the rice fields while men were ploughing. It covered all of the
men ploughing three-quarters of the rice fields (25 hectares) surrounding the village. Since about one-third to one-half of the villagers own rice lands near other villages, the survey could not
yield complete information about ownership of land by people
from the village we studied. The second source of information
was the *imeum* of the *mukim* in which the village is located. This
man was formerly village headman. He knew of all of the people
born in the village and still living there who had inherited land.
He did not know about villagers who had bought land in other
villages, nor did he know about the holdings of men who had
married into the village but who had been born outside it. (Of
the 64 men in the *meunasah*, 37 were born in the village and 27
were born in other villages.)

[4] The division of the *zakat* (religious payment) provided information on landlessness; people without rice land received the
largest share of the *zakat*, and so one could at least learn who was
landless.

once owned land but had given it to their daughters. No one family owned very much of the total land surrounding the village: one person owned 1 hectare (3 percent of the total land), the greatest amount owned by a single individual. Seven percent of the land surveyed was *baitalmal*, land set aside for religious purposes, and 3 percent was owned by the *meunasah* of the village.

Women owned 31 percent of surveyed land in their own name,[5] but this figure obscures the fact that most women owned some land. In fact, 54 percent of the owners of rice land were women.[6] Of 40 couples in their first marriage, 27 of the women were known to have received rice land either at the time they were *geumeuklèh* or at the births of their children. Of the remaining 13 women, 2 were childless and the other 11 had some chance of inheriting rice land when their parents died.

In the absence of their husbands, the management of nearly all land is in the hands of women. Women whose absent husbands own rice land arrange for

[5] Rice land women receive when they are *geumeuklèh* is given to them in the name of their children, if possible, in order to exempt it from the provision of Islamic law which says that what a couple earns after marriage is their joint property. In any case, if the couple is divorced, the woman retains ownership of this land.

[6] Men own more rice land than women, but more women own land than men. This is owing to the fact that women get land at an earlier age than men, but they do not get much. Parents keep some rice land for their younger daughters, giving only small parcels to their older daughters when they are *geumeuklèh*. Also, some men buy land with trade proceeds, although they prefer to reinvest most of their money in trade.

other men to plow and harvest it and to watch the water level in the plots. This is usually done by leasing the land out in return for half the yield (two-thirds of the land was worked under this arrangement), but it can also be done by paying someone a fixed amount to plough the land.[7] A few men return home at harvest time to see that they receive their fair share of the crop, but most do not want to leave their business in the East. The income from this land is controlled by women. In addition to the return women get from their own and their husbands' land, they also receive about half the return to labor: they do the weeding and planting for which they are paid.

In 1963, 31 households planted secondary crops. Tobacco and ground nuts were the most extensively planted and the most profitable crops, but onions, cucumbers, and other vegetables were also grown. Women raised nearly all the secondary crops; only 6 men took part. A few families grew only what they needed themselves, but most found an important source of income in the sale of these crops. An average yield of 50 kg. of tobacco brought Rp.75,000. Secondary crops were particularly important to those who did not own rice land. The crops could be grown on a relative's or fellow villager's land at no expense or for a token payment.

[7] Crops can be cultivated by just a few men as they do only the ploughing and harvesting; women do the sowing and weeding. Men are able to handle the ploughing easily, but for the harvesting they receive help from other men who come from neighboring areas where the crops are at other stages of development. Threshing is done by the boys of the village and the resident farmers.

The women and children in the village lived off the yield of the rice harvest supplemented by the proceeds from the sale of the secondary crops. With these proceeds the women bought such items as fish and spices, but the men on the *rantau* had to provide the cash for items the women could not afford. One such item, an essential, was cloth, which the men usually brought or sent home at the end of the fasting month.

The result of Atjehnese inheritance customs, then, is to give the bulk of village resources to men. Women are certain to get a house and house land, and possibly some rice land. Most resources, however, are owned by men. In spite of this, women feel that men should contribute not rice but money to buy imported goods. We shall return to this later, but the point here is that regardless of ownership of land, control of it is given to women, and this underlies their expectation that men properly should provide not rice, which the women can obtain themselves, but money.

The other significant feature of Atjehnese inheritance is the fact that women get houses and sometimes rice land at marriage, or shortly thereafter, whereas men are usually without resources in the village until their parents die or they earn enough through trade to buy rice land (which they are unlikely to do until they are well-established traders). It is not, however, only young or poor men who are powerless in their families. Even wealthy men have little ability to make decisions involving their wives. There is, however, nothing inherent in Atjehnese kinship or inheritance customs which prevents men from establishing a place in the families created by their marriages. Nonetheless, men are powerless. To find the reason for this, we will turn to the way in which men and women conceive of their roles and the part modernist ideas play in these conceptions.

CHILDREN IN THE FAMILY

Men are infrequently in the village, but boys are always there. I want to describe the steps by which boys leave the family to show how this process is thought of in terms of *akal* and *hawa nafsu* and then compare it briefly with the absorption of girls into the family and the expectations they come to have of their husbands.

Nearly all Atjehnese families, like most peasant families, have children present in their house compounds. Of the 83 families surveyed, only 9 were childless. One of these families consists of a divorced woman living alone, 2 are families whose children have recently died, and 5 are couples married less than two years. The only couple who has long been without children of its own has been raising a child of the wife's sister. (Borrowing children is a common practice among Atjehnese families and is likely to be done both by childless couples and by those with only one child.)[8] Older couples whose children are now adults usually live in the same yard as their sisters,

---

[8] There were 191 living children born to the 83 families, an average of 2.3 per nuclear family. Another 42 children had died, most of them during infancy. Sixteen families had lost at least 1 child.

daughters, or nieces, almost always with young children present.

Mothers give their youngest children whatever they want. No matter what the mother is doing, if the child cries or asks for something, the mother attends to him. This indulgence stops only with the birth of a younger child. If there is no younger child or a child of a neighboring sister, there is literally no end to the mother's indulgence of her child, at least before he or she is married. When a younger child is born, the older siblings are denied in favor of the youngest. In our house we often saw the mother take something away from her six-year-old son in order to give it to his three-year-old sister. The younger child had only to ask.

Deprivation of the older siblings is only a matter of scarcity of resources. The younger child has the first choice, but as soon as possible the older child will be placated as well. Often it is the mother's sister or the grandmother who does this. Where there was a new, younger child in the house, the older sibling made more and more demands for attention. While he always got what he wanted eventually, it never seemed sufficient and the child often kept on crying, even after he received what he had asked for.

The crying of the child in these cases did not seem to upset anyone. They just let him cry, often for hours. At most there would be only mild chastisement. When a boy would not stop crying, the grandmother would taunt him, saying that he was a girl. I never saw anyone bribe a child to stop his crying, saying, for

instance, "If you stop crying, I will give you a ba-
nana." They did not make gratification conditional
on the behavior of the child. Eventually, some one
would pick the child up and soothe him. If the child
did not stop crying, they would put him down again
and let him cry. The attitude was that if it was at all
possible to give the child what he wanted, he should
have it. This was quite independent of the child's behavior.

By the time they are about six, boys already know
that there are certain activities that are properly performed by women. They learn this through the females themselves. Often, however, it seems as though
the women's desire to please the children, to give them
whatever they want, conflicts with their feelings that
some activities are not proper for little boys. For instance, one night the women in our household were
making rice cakes for a feast the next day. The oldest
child, a boy about eight, was already asleep, as was
the youngest, a little girl. But the middle child, a boy
about six, was still up although very sleepy. My wife,
according to her notes, was mixing batter when the
boy came over to her and started to help. No one
commented. After a while, though, the grandmother
came in and noticed the boy. She was amused and
said, "Don't play in the kitchen. Don't you know
you're a boy? That's for girls." The boy moved away,
but not far. His grandmother told him to go to sleep,
but he answered that he wanted to stay up and eat
ten pieces of cake. This won everyone over and he
stayed. After a while his mother got irritated and

told him to go to sleep, but he stayed until the cakes were baked. These prohibitions against participating in girls' activities are not very strong. This same boy, for instance, was making mud cakes with his little sister in the yard all of one afternoon.

Mothers indulge their younger children at the expense of the older ones not just because infants objectively need more attention, although of course they do. Their reason is related to their conception of *akal*. *Akal* is a capacity; it is not something that anyone can teach. The most one can do is create an atmosphere in which it can develop. One woman in the village explained it thus: "When a baby is born, he is a great emptiness, but as he grows up, he gradually becomes filled. As he grows, *akal* increases. In caring for the child, we can at most slightly hasten the growth of *akal*. But even if we did not care for the child, *akal* would grow anyway." Younger children have less *akal*. They are therefore more entitled to indulgence, not having the ability to know that gratification of desires is a bad thing. This does not mean, however, that older children should not be indulged. They, too, are still children; they, too, are still not fully capable of self-control. Therefore, if they ask for something, they are indulged. The asking itself is a sign that *akal* is lacking. Since one cannot teach a person to have *akal*, since it is innate, mothers can only give them what they want in the knowledge that they are less than adult.

The corollary to this first belief is that indulgence is never used as a reward for good behavior. A boy does not receive things from his mother or grand-mother because he has behaved properly. Rather, he is loved as a result of what is infantile in him, what is less than mature, his lack of *akal*, and thus his lack of self-control.

What a boy learns in the house is what it is not to be male. He learns at most that the love of his mother, aunts, and grandmother is given not as a reward for being a man, but for being a child. It is only outside the house that he learns that the self-denial of the instincts is what makes a boy an Atjehnese, a Muslim, and thus a man.

The boy learns about manhood through his progressive removal from the household, each step of which is associated with Islam. The removal begins at about the age of six when a boy starts to learn to read the Koran. This is the first activity which he does not share with girls. The boys go out of the house to a special building used only for the teaching of the Koran. There they are taught by the chairman of the *meunasah*, or by someone designated by him. They go every morning at about 6 A.M. (and, at least initially, with great eagerness) and chant together with the teacher. The teacher reads a passage, and the children repeat it after him. They learn to make the proper sounds associated with each of the Arabic characters and to chant the Koran in the proper way. They do not, however, learn the meaning of the words.

There is no division into classes in the village religious school. Nor is there any specific length of time the children study. Some continue on until they are about twelve or fifteen; others go only a few years. The level of learning can be seen in the competence of the men in the village—only a few can read the entire Koran. These few have had special training outside the village, either in a *pesantren*, a religious school, or through study in a mosque while away from the village.

Every man in the village, however, can chant at least the first two *surah* of the Koran, and they can also recite and know the meaning of the sixty-second *surah*. This is the *surah* about the nature of God which, according to Arberry's translation, reads as follows:

In the Name of God, the Merciful, the Compassionate

Say: 'He is God, One,
God, the Everlasting Refuge,
who has not begotten, and has not been begotten,
and equal to Him is not any one.'

When boys begin to attend religious school, they play less with girls than they did before. The girls usually stay inside the house yard, while the boys begin to go out to play with other boys.

At about the age of eight, a boy is circumcised.[9] This is not marked by any great ceremony, and there is no feast. At most, the mother cooks glutinous rice cakes and distributes them among the neighbors.

[9] There is no special person who circumcises the boys. Any man who knows how, and who also knows the proper ritual, can do it.

While living in the village for over a year, I was never aware of the occurrence of a circumcision (although I learned later that several had taken place). Yet, while the community as a whole takes little notice of the rite, it is important in the transformation of the boy into a man. After circumcision, the boy always wears pants (before this he often ran about naked), and he only rarely plays with girls.

The next step in the removal of the boy from the household comes at puberty. A man has the obligation to perform the five daily prayers from the time that he reaches physical maturity. Men say that when they dream they have an ejaculation they know that they are mature. This is also the sign that they should move out of the house into the *meunasah*. They say that they are ashamed to stay in the house after they reach puberty. If they do not move out of the house, the other boys tease them, saying that "they are still sucking at their mother's breast."

At this age, boys are no longer seen with women. No Atjehnese man is ever seen with a woman who is not his wife for more than a minute or so. Men say that if they are seen with a woman, people will accuse them of having an affair. Atjehnese often said that this custom was "specific Atjeh," something peculiar to the Atjehnese. Even with old women, as well as with their own mothers and sisters, the boys limit themselves to the briefest possible exchanges and rush away.

By puberty, boys are in the house only when they have something important to do there, such as eat or change their clothes, or when there is some particular function for which they are needed. Like the men, they never spend extended time in the house. Before puberty, boys do not have any chores around the house. When they reach puberty, however, their mothers may ask them to do part of the ploughing or some other labor that men generally perform. They are often reluctant to do this. One sister said this about her younger brother, then about sixteen years old: "Abdulrachman [the brother] is very lazy. He won't work because he knows that his mother can afford to give him anything he wants." She went on to compare him with a neighbor's boy the same age: "Djamin knows that he won't have anything but rice if he does not work, because his mother is poor. So he ploughs his mother's field."

Abdulrachman did indeed get whatever he wanted from his mother. This caused his other older sister to say that he lacked *akal*. "If he wants something," she said, "that's it [*kakeu*]—he just asks for it, he doesn't think first." Boys such as Abdulrachman who go to high school stay in the village until they graduate. The others go off to the East in their middle teens.

Boys learn, then, that the indulgence they receive from their mothers is not a reward for proper behavior but a recognition of their lack of *akal* and thus of their status as children. They are not refused this indulgence even after they have reached their teens, providing that their mothers can afford to give it. As we have seen, after boys reach the age of six, they begin a series of steps which remove them from the household; each of these steps is associated with Islam. Their first activity outside the gates of the house yard is to learn to read the Koran. Then they are circumcised and no longer run around naked or play with girls. When they reach sexual maturity, they begin to pray and move to the *meunasah*. Finally they leave the village altogether. Each step away from home is a step toward becoming a man, a person, and is associated with the development of *akal* and the refusal of *hawa nafsu*, a quality men associate with women. Childhood, or unmanliness, is the state of indulgence, of *hawa nafsu*; manhood, or adulthood, is the attainment of *akal*.

The transition of females from girls to women is not characterized by the same or similar stages. Girls also learn to read the Koran and, at the same time, are taught the proper rituals to use later when they menstruate and after sexual intercourse, yet their training is much more casual. It begins when the girls are older, about eight or so. They do not have their religious training in a special building but in the house of one of several women who are able to teach them. Their training, instead of coming early in the morning, comes at night when everything else has been done and the girls are free.

The girls, too, are circumcised, although not at the same age as the boys. They are usually about twelve. Circumcision does not mark any important change in their social activities. Neither, for that matter, does marriage. A girl does not obtain her full rights as a woman, the ownership of a house, until she has a child. Her activities and her attitudes after marriage differ little from what they were before.

Girls confine themselves to the house. Their play often is an emulation of the women's activities. They make mud pies and play house. As they grow up, they help take care of their younger siblings or the children of their older sisters. They also help in the kitchen by peeling vegetables, building the fire, or grinding the spices. Yet women always complained that girls did not really work hard enough. A woman with five children expected her thirteen-year-old sister to help in the house, but she said that the girl was never there. Her younger sister, she said, "just takes no interest in these things. She acts like a little princess. She doesn't really work." Another time this woman said that her younger sister always had to be told what to do: "She does not pay attention in the kitchen." Before, she said, when her younger sister did not work she would pick up anything in sight, "a glass, a pot, whatever there was," and hit her with it. "Then she would work."

It would not be right to say that the girls do not work hard. They seemed to do a lot. Yet what is important is their attitude toward what they were doing. They think of their chores as something imposed and burdensome. For instance, a seventeen-year-old girl, married about two years, when asked if she wanted her husband to come home from the East, said: "No, because when he is away I can play. I can go here and there. When he comes back to the village, I have to go home and cook for him." Actually, this attitude is not so different from what older women said about their husbands. Almost invariably they said that they liked to have their husband come home because he brought money, but it also meant a lot of extra work for them. Yet women do not regret the things they do for their children, but to unmarried girls and married girls who are not yet mothers any type of housework seems to be a burden.

There is a startling change in women's attitudes after they have given birth to their first child. While I do not understand the dynamics of the transformation that occurs in the mother at birth, I can describe the ritual itself or, rather, the series of rituals which precede and follow birth. The rituals after birth are unique among Atjehnese ceremonies in that, rather than a feast or at least the giving away of rice cakes, which marks all other significant events in Atjehnese life, these consist of a series of prohibitions and hardships imposed upon the woman.

The first pregnancy is marked by a ceremony during the fifth month in which the husband and wife are "cooled off" (*peusidjuek*). This is a brief ritual performed by a woman called the *teungku ineong*, a woman who is learned in Islamic and customary lore. The mother of the bride—Atjehnese women are referred to as brides until they have their first child—makes glutinous rice cakes and brings them to the mother of the groom. This is the announcement that the daughter-in-law is pregnant. The mother of the bride also gives some money to the groom or, if he is away, to his mother. This is usually about Rp.2,000 ($1.00).

In the sixth month of pregnancy, the mother of the groom returns the call of the mother of the bride and brings rice; a few days later, she brings rice cakes to the bride. The bride is supposed to eat them all, but this is impossible for her physically as well as socially because no one would think of keeping food from other members of the family.

In the seventh month, the mother of the groom comes again to the house of the bride, this time bringing with her the *teungku ineong* of her own village, who gives the bride a bath. The mother of the groom also brings about thirty packages of rice and spices, as well as a new sarong, some soap, and dusting powder.

In the seventh month the most important ceremony before birth takes place. A salad of raw, unripened fruit, *rudjak*, is made under the supervision of the *teungku ineong*. The women of the neighboring houses come to help. During the preparation of the salad, each piece of fruit is brought by the woman peeling it to the *teungku ineong* for her inspection. Just what she looks for she would not say. Also during this ceremony the *teugnku ineong* lights incense. She says this is an invitation to the souls of those of the family who have died and to the spirits who play a part in Atjehnese curing rites to come and eat. She does not name any of the spirits individually except for one called Nek, who, as we will see, plays a part in the birth itself. After the feast is prepared, the women present eat part of it and give the rest to whatever men might be in the neighborhood and to the boys who sleep in the *meunasah*. This is the last ceremony before birth. During the second, fourth, and sixth pregnancies the ceremonies before birth are abbreviated except for the making of the fruit salad. The ceremonies during the odd-numbered pregnancies are as outlined above.

Up to this point the midwife has played no role, the important ceremonial leadership being furnished by the *teungku ineong*. During, as well as after, birth, however, the midwife plays an important part. There are no male midwives in Pidie since men and childless women are not allowed into the room in which a woman is giving birth.[10] The midwife is someone who has been visited by the spirit known as Nek or Nek Rabi. Nek Rabi is the spirit of a woman who lived in Kotaradja, the capital of Atjeh. One night as she was returning home from reading the Koran, someone mistook her for a thief and cut off her head. The murderer brought her head to a place in Atjeh proper called Indrapuri and buried it. Her body was buried in Kotaradja.[11] Because Nek Rabi died before her appointed time, she goes about asking for things

[10] There is at least one male midwife in the East. This man has no supernatural powers, however. He was trained in school to be a midwife and works in the towns.

[11] Another version of the story is that Nek was having an affair and was killed when it was discovered.

from women while they are giving birth. She only appears, however, if something improper has been done in the ceremonies before birth, especially during the *chanduri* of the seventh month. She possesses the midwife, who then speaks with the spirit's voice and who cannot continue to deliver the baby.

Nek Rabi came while Aniah, one of the village women, was giving birth to her sixth child. One of the other women there seized the midwife and asked the spirit what she wanted. The spirit said that *nangka*, a certain kind of fruit, had not been put into the fruit salad during the feast of the seventh month and so she had come. Then one of the neighbors said she would give Nek Rabi a feast if she would go away. She went.

Nek Rabi on that occasion visited the midwife at a crucial time during the birth. The umbilical cord had not come all of the way out. To the Atjehnese, this is dangerous, because they believe that if it does not come out it can crawl back into the woman and kill her. Nek Rabi apparently comes often when there is trouble during birth, and if there is not trouble before she comes, there is when she gets there. She adds greatly to the dangers of birth, which is already considered a very dangerous time for a woman.

After a woman has given birth, she must not leave her house for forty-four days. During much of this time she must lie on a platform over hot bricks with her legs straight out and her ankles together. She must not lift her arms above her head. Her mother watches her to see that she keeps the proper posture and that she changes position in relation to the bricks so that she is roasted evenly on all sides.

During the first week the midwife comes and massages her with coconut oil. The new mother bathes as little as possible, for the idea of the roasting is to expel the aftereffects of childbirth and for the mother to become as dry as possible. The more the woman sweats, the better the treatment.

Roasting is begun the day after the woman gives birth and continues for at least twenty and for as long as forty-four days. The first week the woman can eat and drink as she pleases. But after the seventh day, when she is given a potion made from certain kinds of leaves, she is supposed to eat and drink as little as possible. From this time, certain foods, among them some of the most common items of the Atjehnese diet, may not be eaten for as long as five months or more. A few of these foods are glutinous rice, bananas, water-buffalo meat, which is the most common kind of meat, duck and duck eggs, and all fruit.

The seclusion of the woman ends on the forty-fourth day with a brief ceremony called *putron aneuk* (in Indonesian, *turunkan anak*), or "bringing down the child" (from the house, which is set on stilts). A respected person of the same sex as the child carries the baby down the steps of the house. If the baby is a girl, the woman may walk around the yard with the baby in her arms, sweeping the ground and doing other women's chores to the great amusement of the spectators. Occasionally the descent of a male baby is greeted with the firing of a gun. The *putron aneuk* ceremony is usually brief, but occasionally there is a *chanduri* to which neighbors are invited. The *chanduri* usually represents the fulfillment of a vow made by the mother at the grave of a holy man. She may, for instance, have vowed that if she had a child she would give a *chanduri* and bring an offering to the holy grave.

I do not understand most of the symbolism of the ceremonies surrounding birth. Villagers say that they do not know what any of the ritual means, and nothing we did could elicit any kind of explication. It is clear, however, that the ceremonies taken together have the structure of a rite of passage. The first three ceremonies before birth recognize the new state of the pregnant woman and begin her removal from ordinary life. The birth itself and the roasting and seclusion are the liminal period, whereas the *putron aneuk* ceremony marks the woman's return to society.

Women say that the result of roasting and following the dietary prohibitions is a healthy, trim body (*ramping*) and the ability to take care of the child. They claim that women who eat when they are hungry and drink when they are parched after giving birth will be without the strength to care for their children. Their bodies will be flabby, and they will have constant headaches.

It is difficult to describe the way in which a woman changes after having her first child. The difference in her attitude toward chores is only one sign of a fundamental change of identity. More importantly, when *birth signifies adult & lets her join world of mothers & aunts as more of an equal*

a woman becomes a mother, she also becomes an adult. She gets legal possession of her house. The whole focus of her life changes. One could almost say that women seem to exist only in relation to the young children in the household. Without children they feel themselves to be girls; with them they are genuine people whose activities focus on providing and caring for their children. My wife had a conversation with Aniah in which she expressed the importance of children to women:

Aniah commented that she had had five children and was now pregnant again. She said that if we looked around the village, we would see that she was actually the only woman with a large family. Most of the others had only two or three. "But that is all right," she said. "If I have a lot now, I won't have so many later."

"Why is that?" I asked. "You will just have more and more until you are old and can't have any more."

"No," she said, "I have seen that there is no woman who had more than twenty and that woman is in Bireuen [a city about a day's journey by bus from the village], and even there it is unusual. I already have six, there are not many more to go. Usually, if you have a lot, you have ten. Still, that is a whole regiment."

She paused and then continued: "I was talking to Mariah [her neighbor]. She came over and I told her to sit down and have something to drink. But I was busy with the children and so I couldn't even sit down with her. I told her, 'I haven't even combed my hair yet.' But she [the neighbor] said, 'Never mind, you are lucky to have so many children. Ahmad [the neighbor's only child, a son] has just come home from the university. He has a cold and I am so worried I can't eat.' " Aniah commented that her neighbor was worried because she thinks, "What will happen if my son dies?" Aniah continued: "Zubeida [another neighbor with only one child] is the same way. Whenever her daughter is sick, they all get very worried and think what will happen if she dies. When Mariah's son was in high school [in a town close by], she would sit home and worry about him. She worried about who was taking care of him, and if he was getting enough to eat. Sometimes she would cook some fish or some meat or even a chicken and bring it to him. Sometimes she would bring him food twice in a week. Now her son is away at the university, and she sits alone in the house and has nothing to think about and she remembers him until she is sick. At least," Aniah said, laughing, "when I sit and think a little, I am immediately bothered by Kasim and Fozziah [her two youngest children]. I complain, but look at Mariah, she wishes she had someone to bother her. She thinks and thinks about her son, and she is sick. There is nothing to keep her from remembering. That is why she wants to marry her son to the daughter of Ismail [a man from a neighboring village]. But maybe her husband doesn't even know about it yet, and neither does Ismail. . . . I don't know." Aniah then went on: "I look and I see how unhappy women who only have one child are. Like Sjarifah—her son died and now there is only her daughter. She is already like a childless woman."

Women with more than one child are not worried about their sons leaving them. Aniah, for instance, said she knew that her sons would leave her and that their wives would not like it if they saw much of her. Their wives would be afraid, she said, that their husbands' money would be spent on their mother rather than on them. "But," she told my wife, "by that time I will be a grandmother."

Mothers benefit very little from the achievements of their sons in the world because of the jealousy of their wives, as Aniah noted. Yet this does not worry women so long as there are other children in the compound to whom they can transfer their attention; in this case, they are willing to give up their sons. In addition, men find it very uncomfortable to accept the only thing their mothers can give them—namely, the indulgence they give to small children. It was for this reason that Mariah's son spent as little time with his mother as he could.

Women, then, are willing to give up their sons if they know they still have a place as mothers, aunts, or grandmothers in the compound. Mariah was not willing to give up her son, for he was an only child; moreover, she lived by herself without her mother, sisters, or aunts (and their children) nearby. Aniah's observation that women with only one child worry that the child will die carries the implication that mothers with many children do not share this worry. To a great extent they do not, for a woman with a single child is concerned not only for the child but for herself in that the child allows her to be a complete woman, a mother. However, if a woman with many children loses one, she still has others and is thus still a mother and no less a woman.[12]

## HUSBANDS AND WIVES

Having looked at the Atjehnese conceptions of

[12] This is a bit harsh. When Aniah lost her third child at birth, she grieved for months.

human development, we can now look at the specific factors that prevent men from exerting power in their families. Formal arrangements for marriages are made by the parents of the prospective couple. The couple has some initiative in the matter, however. Often a man will ask his parents to arrange a marriage with a particular girl. Girls have a veto: if they do not like the man, they may refuse to go through with the marriage. Ordinarily the couple is not well acquainted before marriage because there are few opportunities for them to meet. Nonetheless, both partners have ideas about the kind of person they want for a spouse. Women look for one quality in particular; they want a husband who will not be *kriet*, or stingy, meaning that they hope he will be willing to spend the money he earns on the *rantau* on his family. Women occasionally have other preferences as well, such as that their husband's skin not be too dark, but all agree that generosity is the crucial factor in making a man a good husband.

Men are less stereotyped in their desires and are usually reluctant to talk about women. One apprentice cloth trader on the *rantau* did, however, tell me what he expected in a wife. He said he badly wanted to get married, but at age twenty-five he still had not found a girl.

"For a while I thought of the daughter of Tgk. M. Hasan, but I did not press it. She is solidly built and would be healthy and have healthy children. But she has several defects. First, she is insubordinate. If her mother tells her to do something, she always argues. Actually, a woman should be supple [*lemah*]. She must be obedient and obliging. If not, it's not good. . . . Also, she wants too much. She wants someone with a motorscooter or at least a Honda [motorbike]. You can tell by the way she acts. This is not right. If she gets someone like that, thanks be to God, but if not, she must be content."

This conflict in expectations, women wanting their husbands to be generous to them and men being afraid their wives will demand too much, presages conflicts in marriage. Given unlimited resources, men would not mind giving their wives all they ask for. They feel, however, that they would like to spend some of their money in other ways. They ridicule the Minangkabau (a people of West Sumatra) for sending money back to their villages when they could use it for trade. "The Minangkabau," said one trader, "are out-model [old-fashioned]. They send money home instead of keeping it for business." Also, men feel obligations to their families of orientation, yet when they give money to their mothers, brothers, or sisters, their wives resent it.

Underlying the wives' expectations about money is an assumption about the obligations of men to their families. It is expected that men will provide their families with goods that the women cannot afford to buy with the money earned from the village economy. Rice-growing alone is not sufficiently profitable to buy imported goods, such as cloth, which women consider necessary. Men who do not go on the *rantau* are noticeably poorer and often have trouble with their wives. Kasem is an example. He was born of poor parents in the same village in which he married. He married Po Ti, all of whose relatives had died leaving her with four *gantjang* (one-third acre) of rice land. Kasem had no rice land inasmuch as all of his parents' estate had been used to build a house for his sister. Kasem had twice tried to trade on a small scale in the East, but both times he had lost his capital and had returned home to work the fields.

One evening there was a terrible racket in the village. People began running to Po Ti's house with buckets of water thinking there was a fire. Actually it was Kasem and Po Ti fighting. Their quarrel illustrates the situation of men who do not go on the *rantau* and who therefore cannot provide their wives with everything they expect. Kasem and Po Ti had just returned, separately, from working in the fields. Although accounts of the quarrel vary, it was initiated by a small incident. According to one account, Kasem had entered the house and had seen that the baby was unattended. Po Ti had gone down to the well in the yard for water to clean the baby who had just soiled himself. Kasem, having seen that the baby had been left alone, began to abuse Po Ti when she returned. Another account attributes Kasem's anger to the fact that there was no water in the house with which to clean the baby, but whatever the cause, the quarrel began and soon pots and pans were flying. Po Ti kicked Kasem and Kasem hit her. She tried to stab him and, when that failed, slashed at him with a cleaver. By that time they were in the yard, and neighbors intervened, restraining them. Po Ti told Kasem to go and never return. He went to his sister's house next door, being too ashamed to go to the *meunasah*.

The villagers' explanation of the intensity of a quarrel over such a trivial matter was that Po Ti had long been dissatisfied because Kasem would not go to the East like other men. Indeed, she had said as much to him during their spat. According to neighbors, she had told him, "What do I need you for?" which they took to mean that Kasem had nothing and would not even try to leave the village to get anything. He could not give her cloth or buy meat for her, while she had to cook for him.

Everyone expected that the quarrel would end in divorce because Kasem had been put into such a shameful position. In fact, there was a reconciliation. Partly this was because Po Ti had to furnish refreshments to the boys who were threshing rice on the land Kasem had rented. She was afraid that if she did not, no one would thresh and they would lose the income. But things are still not back to normal. Po Ti put a mattress in the gallery of the house and Kasem must sleep there. She told him to go sleep in the *meunasah* (where one of the farmers who is separated but not divorced from his wife sleeps), but he was too ashamed. Po Ti cooks for him but she will not serve him; he must go to the kitchen and get the rice himself. They still fight. People say that when Po Ti remembers Kasem hit her, she slaps him and rips his shirt. He stands there quietly and takes it. He once told her that he would take all of her abuse, but one day she grabbed a knife. At that point he threatened to divorce her if she did it again. Neighbors say that the only reason he does not divorce her is that he is fond of their son. Villagers may have exaggerated the details of the story, but nevertheless the quarrel demonstrates the kind of situation that drives men to the East or at least the situation villagers imagine a man confronts if he does not provide what his wife wants.

As I have pointed out previously, men own most of the resources of the village, but because they are expected to provide not rice but goods sold in the market, women are dissatisfied with men who try to provide for them through agriculture. It is therefore not only landless men who feel compelled to leave the village; older men who have earned money on the *rantau* and who may have bought rice land or who may have inherited it are also not to be found in the village. Of the 83 families in the *meunasah*, there was only one in which the grandfather was not away on the *rantau*. (This man was the chairman of the *meunasah*.) Thus we see that ownership and even control of rice land are not sufficient for men to fulfill their obligations toward their families.

When men do earn money on the *rantau* and bring some of it back to their families, they feel that they are creating a place for themselves which serves as a substitute for their standing in their original families. They see themselves as taking care of their families, providing for them in a way that equals their wives' expectations of them. One man, for instance, said that he had equal obligations (under the law) to his original family and to the family into which he married. But, he said, "Because I seldom go back to my own village, I am more likely to take care of the people here [in his wife's village]. . . . The obligations [*kewadjiban*] are the same, but the opportunities are greater here." Men feel that they contribute a good deal to their families and are responsible for their welfare. For example, Maun, a well-to-do trader married to Aniah, said that he took care of Aniah's widowed mother, her younger unmarried sister, her unmarried brother, and, until she was married, her other sister. He used the phrase "*tanggung djawab*," an Indonesian expression meaning "to bear responsibility," to describe his relationship with his wife and her family. He had even planned the future of Abdulrachman, his unmarried brother-in-law of sixteen, who was attending junior high school.

"I carry the expense for Abdulrachman and will keep on [providing] until he can take care of himself. Aniah's *adek* [younger siblings] are like my own *adek*."

"Do most men feel this way?" I asked.

"Yes," he said, "it is what Islam teaches. I want Abdulrachman to go to Medan to live with a friend of mine. He is lazy; a change of scene [that is, leaving the village] would do him good, make the laziness disappear. It's very important because if I die, Abdulrachman will be the one to take care of Aniah and the children."

"What will happen when Abdulrachman marries and lives in another village?" I asked.

"He'll always come back to his parents' house. He will [therefore] be more reliable than Amir [one of Maun's younger brothers] or my older brothers, although they have the duty [to care for my children] in law, and it would be a great sin if they did not."

Maun felt that he provided for his wife's family, bore responsibility for them, and could shape their future. He said he was an integral part of the family —"Aniah's *adek* are like my own *adek*." On another occasion he said, "Aniah's mother replaced my own" (who had died). These statements, however, were closer to wishes than facts; certainly his wife did not agree with them. Aniah felt that Maun wasted money on his own family, that he should give more to her, and that in business matters people were always taking advantage of him. When there were decisions to make, she made them, even in the face of strong opposition from Maun. In the case of Abdulrachman, for example, she opposed sending him to Medan and he stayed in the village. Other decisions also illustrate how she always managed to outwit her husband. The following episode was recorded by my wife.

A man came on a bicycle and said he was the man from whom Maun had bought a coconut plot during the fasting month. Maun paid him Rp.17,000 of Rp.50,000 and said he would pay the rest after the rice harvest. Now the rice was half cut in Gampong Pinong, where the plot is, and the man had come for the rest of the money. Aniah told the man she did not have the money and he said, "Just let me have some rice from your plot."

Aniah refused. The man said he wanted to be paid, and Aniah said, "Never mind, sell the land to someone else and give me back the Rp.17,000." Ma [Aniah's mother] was upset because when Bapak Usman [Maun] came home or found out that Aniah had cancelled the purchase, he would be angry with her. Aniah told Ma, "Let him be angry." Aniah told me later that when Maun paid the Rp.17,000, she asked him, "Why are you buying land

that's worth nothing? If you invest money, at least buy
rice land." But he wanted to buy that land so that it could
be used by Nuraini [the daughter of his older sister] when
she gets married. [Maun's sister wanted to build a house
on the site for her daughter because the plot was near her
own house.] Now Nuraini was about to get married. Aniah
went on: "I told him, 'You know you will never get the
land back.' 'Never mind,' he said. He wanted to help his
sister. He knows the land is as good as lost to us—you
can't take back land when people are living on it. He
shouldn't have bought the land to begin with. And besides,
I just got a letter from him yesterday. I wrote and told
him we needed money because Ma was trying to pay for
the house she bought for Zubaidah [Aniah's unmarried
sister]. He wrote back, 'sell rice land,' and that's all. He
didn't have to tell me that. I know I can sell *sawah* [rice
land]. And that's why I told the man to return the
Rp.17,000. If he [Maun] doesn't have money for Ma, how
can he have money to pay for the plot for Nuraini?"

Aniah continually felt that Maun did too much for
his own family and not enough for hers. Wherever
possible she limited what Maun gave to others. She
particularly felt that Maun's younger brothers, Zulkifli and Amir, made unreasonable demands on her
and got more than they deserved. As she explained
to my wife, relations between her and Zulkifli were
especially strained:

"Zulkifli lived with us before he was married. He would
come home from a trip, and, having just gotten off the
bus, would say, 'Tjut Po ["Older Sister," the usual term of
address for women], I feel sick. Buy some bones and make
soup.' He would order me to make soup, and the next day
I would buy bones and make soup. If he wanted meat,

I would cook meat for him. There was nothing he asked me to do that I didn't do. When he came to the house, whether alone or with friends, I would serve him tea. Then when he got married, he told me, 'I want you to buy my wife a pound ringet' [a U.S. $20 gold piece]. Well, I laughed, only because what else could I do? Talk about nerve [in Indonesian, *berani betul dia djuga*]. Later I told Bapak Usman, 'You have a brother like a child.' There was nothing I wouldn't do for him. He came to our house as if it were his own. And then he had the nerve to order me to buy a pound ringet. . . .

"Bapak Usman, when he found out, said, 'We'll buy him one.' 'Oh no we won't,' I said."

In fact, they did not give Zulkifli the gold piece, which is why relations between Zulkifli and Aniah are strained.

There was little Maun could do concerning money that Aniah did not find out about. Maun went into partnership with some Chinese in Medan without telling her, but she heard about it, and when he returned home during the fasting month she was furious. The terms of the partnership guaranteed him Rp.25,000 a month, a percentage of the profits at the end of the year, as well as the use of a house and car in Medan. He wanted her to move to Medan with the children. She thought he had been swindled.

"I told him, 'How can we live on Rp.25,000 a month in Medan?' It's enough in the village, but what's the good of a house in Medan if we have an income of Rp.25,000? At the end of the year they figure the profits and we get a percentage—but first of all it's not certain there will be profits, and anyway the Chinese always fool around with the books. And then after he went into the partnership he spent three months sitting around [the village][13] before he went back to Medan [to earn more money]. What's the good of a house in Medan without enough money to live there? And besides, who wants to live in a house that someone else owns? And the same with the car. Besides, I don't believe there is a house and a car. . . ."

Naturally, it is difficult to get details of marital conflicts from many families. We heard of many other couples with experiences similar to those of Maun and Aniah, but we were seldom able to obtain the full particulars. Atjehnese attribute most divorces to such conflicts over money, and the divorce rate itself is one sign that these conflicts are widespread. In Pidie as a whole, 50 percent of the marriages end in divorce (the figure is from the Pidie Office of Religious Affairs), although in the *meunasah* I surveyed the rate is somewhat lower, or about 39 percent. In the 22 cases of divorce that I learned about, 14 were attributed to conflicts over money, with the women always accusing their husbands of being *kriet*, stingy.[14] Most divorces are actually obtained by men because

[13] He stayed in the village for only two months, but this was longer than most men stay. One reason he remained so long was that I was anxious to talk with him and did everything possible to keep him there.

[14] Of the other 8 cases, 2 involved women who were mentally retarded; 3 took place because the couple was childless; 2 were granted to women whose husbands never returned from the East; and of those willing to talk about the last one, no one could remember the reason for it, and I could learn only that there had been quarrels. The seemingly lower rate of divorce in the village as compared to the district as a whole can probably be attributed to the difficulty I had in getting information about older people.

it is a much simpler procedure for them to divorce their wives than for women to get a judge to grant a divorce. But in all of the 14 cases just cited, the action that led to the divorce was in fact instigated by the women. In most cases the women felt that their husbands were not contributing sufficiently to the household and decided to throw them out of the house, ordering them not to return or putting their belongings at the bottom of the steps. The men were too ashamed to do anything but divorce their wives. In a few of the 14 cases, the husband had taken a second wife, and his first wife had then ordered him never to return. In each case she felt that the second, younger, and more attractive wife would get most of the money earned on the *rantau*, and the first, therefore, no longer wanted to cook for him.

Most conflicts in marriage do, then, concern money. If one asks whether men in fact live up to the financial obligations of marriage and so are entitled to make decisions, one can only answer that men think they do and women think they do not. Maun felt he provided well for his family, whereas Aniah thought he provided inadequately. In their case it is clear that Maun did give Aniah a great deal, even if she thought it insufficient. Aniah's father was a farmer who owned a little rice land, some of which he gave to her, but his resources were not nearly as great as those of Maun. Maun became wealthy during the 1950s (after his marriage) by smuggling coffee, tobacco, and rubber to Penang. He used part of his profits to buy more rice land for Aniah and their children and another part for extensive improvements on

the house Aniah received from her parents. (He replaced the woven walls with wood planks, put on a
new roof, and built three additional rooms around a
patio below the house.) And, as he said, he did give
to her mother and her brother and sisters. Aniah's
objections were not that he did not provide, but that
he spent too much money on his own family and that
he made poor business deals which jeopardized her
family.

Yet, even if men spent all of their trade profits on
their families, it is unlikely that they would satisfy
their wives. For one thing, as the example of Maun's
partnership with the Chinese shows, women would
still feel that men were not making enough. But more
importantly, women do not believe that the contributions men make to their families entitle them to
any special consideration. They feel that the husband
has a place in the family only for as long as the money
he brings home from the East lasts. When it is gone,
they no longer want their husbands around. Their
understanding of the marriage contract is that men
have a place in the home only if they pay for it each
day. Even the larger contributions of men, such as
buying a house for their daughters, do not entitle
them to a permanent role in family affairs. One village woman, when asked by my wife if she wanted
her husband to come home, replied, "Yes and no. If
he comes, there is a lot of work cooking for him. But
without him there is no money. No husband, no
money." Other women used nearly the same words
to describe their attitudes toward their husbands.

They feel that their husbands' contributions entitle them to be fed and deferred to while they pay for it; but when the money is gone, they should go too. They do not feel that men are entitled to share in the larger decisions of the family.

From the women's point of view, the family consists of the people who occupy the house compound —themselves, their sisters, mothers, and children. Their husbands have no place, and hence no right to make decisions. Women, for instance, envision paradise as the place where they are reunited with their children and their mothers; husbands and fathers are absent, and yet there is an abundance all the same. Quarrels over money reflect the women's idea that men are basically adjuncts who exist only to give their families whatever they can earn. Maun contributed substantially to Aniah's family, yet Aniah did not think that this entitled him to make decisions. Nor did she quarrel with him because she was in need; the family was very well off. It was, rather, that Aniah did not recognize any legitimate use for Maun's earnings other than to provide for her own family. So long as husbands do provide for their families, women are willing to give them deference, but nothing else.

Men recognize their obligations to their families, but what they cannot understand is why, when they do provide, they do not really achieve what they want—inclusion in the family itself and the right to make decisions. Maun felt that his wife's younger siblings were like his own and that her mother had replaced his own. Yet this was wishful thinking, as

Maun's relations with the family show. Regardless of how well he provided, he could never exercise what he felt was his right to participate in making decisions.

One reason for the powerlessness of men could be their prolonged absence. It is true that women must make many decisions when men are gone, but even when men are home, they have no power. Another reason could be the resources and tactics of women, but, as I have tried to show, men have greater resources, and tactics, too, are not the answer. Aniah, for example, explained how she would make Maun accept the fact that she had reneged on the buying of the coconut plot: "When he finds out," she told my wife, "he will get angry. He will say, 'Why have you done this?' And if I am quiet, he'll get angrier. But if I answer back, 'Why did you buy a garden and not pay for it?' he'll be silent, and I'll be the one to get angry. He's like that. If he's aggressive [beuhe; in Indonesian, berani] and you answer, he's silent. If you are silent, he gets angry. . . ." She laughed. Whether this is what happened I do not know, but she did force him to forgo his purchase of the garden. Another time when my wife was telling her about an argument, Aniah advised her, "Ah, we women can win if we're tough enough." Although it may seem otherwise from her relations with her husband, Aniah is a sweet and gentle woman who made demands upon her husband not for herself, but only for her family. Moreover, she resorted to such tactics only when she felt that Maun's behavior endangered her family's rights. In any case, she did not win because of her anger; one could just as well ask why she did not concede when Maun got angry.

The reason men are powerless before their wives and so are without place in their own families lies in a contradiction in what success means to them. On the one hand, men feel that, on the basis of their financial contributions, they deserve deference and indulgence from their wives, as well as the right to make decisions. On the other hand, they feel demeaned when they receive the deference and indulgence they seek. As a result, they are easy prey for their wives. Women, fulfilling their obligations as wives, are very deferential when their husbands first return home from the East. They acquiesce when their husbands order them to cook a special dish or to take care of the children.[15] They wait on their husbands, bringing them tea and seeing that they are comfortable. In fact, women treat their husbands just as they would a guest. But, like a guest, husbands can outstay their welcome and usually do. When their money is gone, wives urge them to return to the East.

For their part, men welcome the chance to relax. They feel that they deserve everything they get, and they take it quite for granted. They expect to be catered to when they return home. They do not think that they are guests, but rather that they are receiving their just reward for their efforts on the *rantau*. They

[15] Or at least they do so to their husbands' faces. When my wife was helping Aniah cook one day, Maun came in. He tasted the curry and told my wife to add some pepper. She was about to do so when, as Maun turned to leave, Aniah took her hand and restrained her. Later Aniah told her that it was not necessary.

think of the village as a place to rest and to be comfortable (*seunang*; in Indonesian, *senang*). Soon, however, their wives cease indulging them and the quarrels begin. Here is the way that Kasem described the process. He was naturally biased, having himself failed on the *rantau*, but his description is quite accurate.

"If you stay home all the time, there is trouble. If you spend one month a year here, it's all right. Women defer to you, just like a guest. But if you are home every day, it is not good. What's more, if you stay in the village too long you don't know what to do with yourself. Men come home, they stay for a month or less, and they dress in good clothes—nice shirts and pants [instead of the sarong usually worn in the village]. But all they do is sit around and talk to their friends. They are lazy. They don't look for work. They act like kings. They bring home Rp.10,000, and when that's gone they get scared and run back to the East."

Aniah's estimation of men in the village matches Kasem's. She, too, pointed out that they have nothing to do there and found it disgraceful:

"When Maun is home, he has nothing to do. He walks back and forth along the road looking for something to pass the time. He meets a friend, they talk a bit, and again he has nothing to do.

"He is like a child. He walks around the house looking for something to do. Then he goes back to the road and sits on the bench with the other men. The longer they sit the stupider they get [*maken treb, maken bodoh*; in Indonesian, *makin lama, makin bodoh*].

"What's more, he comes home with Rp.30,000, and by the time he leaves he has spent Rp.60,000. I don't know what he spends it on; it isn't for us. He doesn't waste much money on us."

Men cannot withstand their wives' complaints and go back to the East, usually sooner than they had anticipated, because they share their wives' estimation of themselves. Women treat their husbands like guests, being solicitous of their comfort (but not allowing them any share in decisions). Men accept the treatment, thinking initially that they have earned it. They come back to the village expecting to be indulged and in fact are. But the more they accept the indulgence their wives offer them, the more their wives think of them not as men but as children. Aniah explicitly compared her husband's behavior in the village with that of a child. In Atjehnese conceptions of development, indulgence is *hawa nafsu*, the very feature that defines childhood. Men, trained to think that indulgence is contrary to the kind of religious practice that makes a person a man, cannot help but share their wives' conception of themselves, especially when the money they have earned, and which they are sure entitles them to relax, is gone. To treat a man as a guest is to treat him like a child. Both guests and children are indulged, and neither is allowed authority. Guests differ from children only in the deference shown them. When women feel that their husbands are no longer living up to the contract between them, they defer no longer. Without deference, men are no longer guests, only children. At this point, they return to the East.

The question that remains is why men are prepared to accept indulgence if it is *hawa nafsu*. The reason is that indulgence comes to them under the guise of deference to which they feel entitled because of their possession of *akal*. Men's success in the market is to them an indication of their ability to act in terms of *akal*, as I shall try to show in the next chapter. In their thinking about the family, it is also clear that they consider women the source of *hawa nafsu*. When men return from the market, it is not surprising then that they feel entitled to authority, because of their possession of *akal*, and accept what women give them as a sign of that authority. They clearly are morally superior, and hence the deference they receive is their due. To women, however, the only recognizable sign of men's superiority is their money, and when that is gone, deference is exposed as indulgence. Men's relations to their wives then change in their own eyes, and in the struggle to make decisions they lose their effectiveness.

## THE FASTING MONTH AND THE CONCEPTUALIZATION OF EXPERIENCE IN THE FAMILY

The obligations of men to their families today are no different from what they were in the nineteenth century. Then, as now, men had to furnish their wives with cloth and money at certain times of the year and had to build houses for their daughters. Wives thought of their husbands as providers, but little more, and demanded of them everything they could give.[16] The difference between then and now is that in the nineteenth century, men, it appears, did establish themselves in the household by the time that they became fathers-in-law—Snouck, for instance, makes much of the obligations of sons-in-law to their fathers-in-law —whereas today being a father-in-law has little significance. The reason that men could find a place for themselves in the household in the nineteenth century is that they did not find the fulfillment of their social obligations undermined as the source of their authority. *Akal* and *hawa nafsu* did not conceptualize experience for men then as they do now, and the fulfillment of obligations was sufficient to establish men as members of their families both in their own eyes and in those of others.[17]

However much the interpretation of experience in terms of religious ideas works to the disadvantage of men, continued belief in the validity of these ideas rests partly on the fact that memories of the past are

[16] For instance, according to Snouck, Leube Isa, an *ulama* and the author of the *Hikajat Ranto* [The Story of the *Rantau*], said: "Many women embitter the lives of their husbands by demanding more than they can bestow in the matter of clothing and personal adornments. Thus they have themselves to blame if their spouses, weary of domestic strife, go forth to seek happiness in the rantos" (Snouck Hurgronje, 1906: II, 121).

[17] The family in the nineteenth century must have been much like the family in Negri Sembilan today. Swift has said of Negri Sembilan that the family there is "a joint enterprise which persists for so long as it is mutually profitable" (1965: 105). The point is that the Atjehnese family as a joint enterprise seemed in the nineteenth century to be one in which the partners eventually became equal, unlike the situation today.

reworked in a way whereby the future promises to be better. The celebration of the end of the fasting month illustrates this process. During the fasting month, *puasa*, men return home and go through the experiences with their wives which I have described. At the end of the month, however, men reinterpret these experiences. They ignore the actual relations between themselves and their wives and concentrate instead on the transition within themselves from one state to another that has taken place during their stay in the village. The effect is to change men's judgments about their place in the family.

If a man returns home at any time during the year, it is likely to be either during *puasa* or at the time of the other great Islamic festival, the celebration of the pilgrimage. Not all men return home from the East. Apprentices in the market usually stay to guard the stores, and some traders do not feel they can afford the expense. Business in the towns usually continues for the first week or two of the month, but by the middle of the month most men have returned home and there is very little commerce.

Both women in the villages and men in the towns begin to talk about *puasa* two or three months before it comes. Although the fast requires that they eat no food and drink no water from sunrise to sunset, neither women nor men are particularly concerned about the difficulty of doing this. Rather, women talk about the special delicacies that they will prepare for their families for the evening meal during the fast, and some tend to pass over the fast itself and talk about the first day of the month after the fast. At that time, there is a great celebration when, among other things, neighbors and kin exchange cakes. Because the men are home and the women have to cook for them, the fast means much extra work for women, but their attitude about this is the same as it is on any other occasion when their husbands come home. They are happy because the men bring extra money, but they regret having to go to extra trouble.

Before the fast, men also do not stress the hardship of going through the hot days with no food or water; they say that they get used to it after a few days. They talk instead about the forthcoming release from work and the fact that they will be going home. They are conscious of moving from one sphere of activities to another. When they talk about *puasa*, they nearly always reflect that the market towns will be deserted and that they can relax at home. In general, there is much pleasure and little discernible apprehension in their tone of voice.

The day before the fasting month begins is known as *urou ma'mugang*. On this day, meat is sold in the market; for the first few days of the fasting month, the fishermen do not put out to sea, and so the meat is a substitute for the fish the villagers usually eat. Husbands are expected to buy meat for their families at this time. They are also expected to give their wives money to buy material so that they can make new clothes for their children and themselves in time for the celebration at the end of the month. Some men return home for *ma'mugang*, but most do not leave the market for another week or two. In this case, they merely send money home.[18]

The routine of the household changes greatly during *puasa*. Women must get up much earlier than usual, about 3:30 A.M., to prepare a special breakfast, *soh*, for their families. This usually consists of left-overs from the previous evening's meal, and it must, of course, be eaten before sunrise. Unlike their husbands, wives cannot go back to sleep after breakfast because the children soon rise and must be looked after. Women are busier than usual since they must cook special delicacies for their husbands to break the fast in the evening. There is rice with ghee to make, as well as sweets.

At the beginning of the month, men rise shortly after their wives in order to eat before sunrise. As the month draws on, however, many of them sleep later, getting up only just in time for the sunrise prayer and then going back to bed. They rise again for the mid-morning prayer, stay awake usually until after the midday prayer, and then return to bed for a long afternoon nap.

In the evening, men break their fast at home with a snack and then go to the *meunasah* where they eat rice porridge cooked by someone selected by the chairman of the *meunasah* and paid for by the men of the *meunasah* as a whole. After their porridge, men pray the

[18] If the couple is still supported by the wife's parents, the husband sends the money for meat to his mother-in-law. He should also send home at the same time some cloth and various household supplies such as soap.

sunset prayer together and then return home to eat a substantial meal and rest. Occasionally during the month a family will cook for all the men of the *meunasah*, bringing the food there where it is eaten after the sunset prayer. No one is obliged to do this, but it is considered a good deed. There were five such meals provided during *puasa* of 1964 in our *meunasah*.

After they have rested at home and digested their evening meal, men return to the *meunasah* where they pray *teraweh*. *Teraweh* is the ordinary evening prayer with extra *raka'at*; it is recommended in Islamic law but is not obligatory. When they have finished, they read the Koran. On most occasions when the Koran is read in the village, only the first two *surah* are recited. During *puasa*, however, men try to read the whole book during the course of the month. Very few men can do this—only three in the *meunasah* in which we lived—but others sit and listen. The Koran recitation continues until 1:00 A.M. or later, but not all of the men stay to listen to the end: many return home to sleep.

Men characterize their activities during *puasa* as "*lalè puasa*"—the negligence, indifference, and absence of focus of *puasa*. Sleep is not only their main activity; it is also the best example of *lalè puasa*, although it would perhaps be better to say that men doze, rather than sleep, since even sleep seems too purposive. In waking moments when they are not praying or eating, men wander about looking for something to do, but their pace is always slow and drowsy. They correct their children, tell their wives

what to cook, amble over to the *meunasah,* or wander
out to the side of the road. They sit by the side of the
road in groups but chat, it seems, only when something happens to arouse their attention. A bus goes by
and someone comments that it is the second bus for
Lho Seumawè; someone passes and they say "*Assala-
mu aleikum,*" raising their right hands in greeting. No
topic is pursued for very long.

Men's behavior in the village during *puasa* is actually no different in character from their behavior in
the village during the rest of the year. *Lalè puasa*
matches Kasem's description of men in the village
quite accurately. It also illustrates what the POESA
leaders called sleep and which they equated with
being in the grip of *hawa nafsu.* Yet the end of the
fast is not a time of shame and defeat for men. It is,
rather, a moment of pride and triumph, and, especially, a time when men feel renewed and in full possession of themselves. It is not the experience of *hawa
nafsu* itself that produces these feelings. What men
commemorate is their response to *hawa nafsu.* They
acknowledge the attack, as it were, but claim victory
because they did not yield. In spite of their lack of
focus, they did not forget their daily prayers and they
did not eat or drink.

Both this feeling of renewal and the way in which
men interpret what they have experienced during
*puasa* are evident when they celebrate the holiday
of the first day of the new month, *urou raja puasa*
(Idulfitri, the first day of Sjawwal). The holiday begins when the new moon appears on the night of the

last day of the fasting month. This marks the beginning of the month of Sjawwal and thus the end of the fast. That night the boys of the village light firecrackers made from gasoline and bamboo, but there is no other special celebration. The next morning, however, there is a great deal of activity. Some of the boys, although so far as I could tell less than half, get up and recite the sunrise prayer at the graveyard in honor of their dead parents. People put on their new clothes and go to ask forgiveness from their neighbors. The men and women go separately, the women often taking cakes. This marks the beginning of the ceremonial visiting in which the young are expected to visit the old, after which the old will return the visits. Men visit neighbors first, then relatives, especially those in other villages, and, in the village itself, the *teungku tjihk* (in our village this was the man who taught the children to read the Koran) and usually, but not necessarily, the village headman and the chairman of the *meunasah*.[19]

These visits are carried out over two days. Visiting someone outside the village always means drinking tea and eating cakes. But visits to neighbors and other villagers, except for the *teungku ineong* and the *teungku tjihk*, are usually limited to the asking of pardon. (The first says, "*maaf lahe baten*" [forgive me in all ways], and the second responds, "*lahe baten*" [in all ways].)

[19] Sometimes the chairman of the *meunasah* is the person who teaches the children to read the Koran. "*Tjihk*" means "old." The title is given to the oldest man in the village with a reputation for learning.

Since the end of the Atjehnese rebellion in 1961, Daud Beureuèh has been leading prayer meetings on *urou raja puasa*. In 1964, this meeting was held in the morning at the site of the mosque Daud Beureuèh was building. People from three districts came, as well as various officials and dignitaries from the regency, including the head of the regency and the head of the regency military unit. Similar meetings are held in each district of Atjeh under the leadership of the local *ulama*.

Most people walked to Daud Beureuèh's meeting with groups of their fellow villagers, but many preferred to go alone.[20] Each group had one person who led a chant known as a *ratèb*, which is simply the repeated chanting of any of a number of religious formulas.[21] This particular *ratèb* consisted of the first half of the confession of faith—"There is no God but God"—repeated three times, followed by "God is the Greatest" ("Allahu Akbar"), also repeated three times. Leading the *ratèb* is a minor honor. In our village, the first person to lead it was a student who had just graduated from a university in Java and who was now on the faculty of the provincial university. Later the *teungku tjihk* led the *ratèb*.

Arriving at the mosque, men and women sepa-

[20] Women as well as men went to the mosque, but there were far fewer women. In fact, only about 10 percent of the women from our village attended the meeting. The majority of women came from the two villages where Daud Beureuèh has wives. (Daud Beureuèh has three wives, but one of them lives outside of the area within which people went to the meeting.)

[21] See Snouck Hurgronje (1906: II, 216).

rated. Each person lined himself up with his neighbors to form rows about a block long. Most had brought woven straw prayer mats and sat on these while waiting for the others to arrive. Many sat with groups of fellow villagers, with whom they had come, but others were separated from their neighbors when they performed the ritual washing in a nearby irrigation channel. There was no special seating order, and neither the regency head nor any other dignitaries had designated places. So far as I could estimate, there were about 7,000 people present.

While people were still arriving, the *ratèb* continued, this time with everyone in the meeting ground participating. The leaders varied, each village in turn sending a representative to the microphone set up on the foundation of the uncompleted mosque. Beginning about 9:00 A. M., Daud Beureuèh acted as imam, or leader of the morning prayer. He then gave a speech, which lasted about an hour. This is worth quoting rather extensively, since it expresses the meaning of the fast as confirmed by other men.

We are all God's slaves. We must all be joyful today. Why? Because we have been commanded to stay away from everything man desires—food, drink, slander, adultery, and so on. This leaves us with a feeling of power, of command over ourselves. We are able to control our desires. But at the same time we must remember our dependence on God, because everything we have comes from Him.

By fasting, we make *hawa nafsu* an instrument. It is for this reason that God gave us *hawa nafsu*. *Akal* is the head, the chief. *Hawa nafsu* is the instrument. *Hawa nafsu* is channeled thus into the simple path, the right way. This way we are not used by other men or other creatures.

People who want to live only for pleasure are stupid. Everything that is right comes only with difficulty. Nothing good is possible without struggle. Through struggle we learn, and thus we become masters of our passions. This is the meaning of the fast. It is a trial and an exercise so that man will know the true way.

Now, though, we must be happy, because we have fulfilled God's commandments. We must be thankful to God. We express our thanks by not doing what is forbidden, by not doing things that ruin our chance for paradise.

The fast is over, but God remains. So do not tell lies, do not disobey God's word. In this way, we profit from the fast. Our deeds will appear again when we confront God. Those who do not so profit will go to Hell. If we do evil acts, acts forbidden by God, all of the good of the fast disappears.

God is the Greatest, God is the Greatest, God is the Greatest [Allahu Akbar]. We have prayed today so that all the world will know that we are the community of Islam who obey God's commands.

Allahu Akbar, Allahu Akbar, Allahu Akbar.

We must be devoted and loyal to our parents if they are still living. We show this today with food and clothing. If they are dead, we go to the graveyard to pray. Thus both parents and children gain merit. We pray to open paradise for our parents.

Allahu Akbar, Allahu Akbar, Allahu Akbar.

Be truly terrified of God and carry out *ibadat*. Then you will go to the village of Adam, to paradise. If you are afraid of God, you will do no bad deeds, you will only follow *ibadat*. In this way you will fly to God. Those who do good deeds, who follow *ibadat,* will get good things later. You others, beware.

Those of you who go off on the *rantau* and squander your money on prostitutes, beware. Those of you who go off and forget your parents, your family, and your neighbors, beware. Tomorrow is the day of judgment. You will have no chance then.

Allahu Akbar, Allahu Akbar, Allahu Akbar.

Remember, you are Atjehnese, the nation of *uleebelang*, of Teungku Tjihk diTiro. Do not deceive your nation, but be charitable to it.

This was the end of the speech. It was followed by an invocation asking for the well-being of Muhammed, of parents, and of the Islamic community. Afterwards most people asked Daud Beureuèh's pardon, and he was there until after midday.

Daud Beureuèh's speech repeats the argument of the POESA that interior states are formed through *ibadah* and expressed in behavior. The opening of the speech concerns the tension between desire and action: "We must all be joyful today. Why? Because we have been commanded to stay away from everything that man desires—food, drink . . ." The speech continues by describing the effect of *ibadah* on *hawa nafsu*: "By fasting, we make *hawa nafsu* an instrument. . . . *Hawa nafsu* is channeled thus into the simple path, the right way."

Most of the speech focuses on the three consequences of acting properly after the fast, consequences which come from subordinating *hawa nafsu*. First is the ultimate reward of paradise: "Our deeds will appear again when we confront God. . . . Carry out *ibadat*. Then you will go to the village of Adam, to paradise." The second is the expression of the community itself: "We have prayed today so that all the world will know that we are the community of Islam who obey God's commands." The third, and perhaps the most interesting, is the social concomitants of acting properly.

Daud Beureuèh mentions parents and children ("We must be devoted and loyal to our parents . . ."). He also mentions husbands and their obligations to their families, warning those who go off on the *rantau* in particular not to "squander [their] money on prostitutes" and not to forget their families.[22] The injunction about the prostitutes is not realistic. There are, in fact, few prostitutes in Atjeh, and those are mostly frequented by non-Atjehnese soldiers. The other admonition is more meaningful and is directed to those men who have squandered their money through following their impulses rather than sending it home. Providing for one's family is seen thus as one of the results of following *ibadah*. If one is in a state where *akal* predominates, one gives to one's family and earns a place in it.

The most interesting aspect of the speech is the assumption that one attains the proper internal balance in order to fulfill social obligations. The effect of such thinking is that men feel they earn a place in the family not through actually fulfilling social obligations, but by achieving the right interior state which enables

[22] One might note that his remarks are addressed solely to men. Only men go to the graveyard to pray for their parents and only men go off on the *rantau*.

them to be good husbands and fathers. Remembering one's family comes from being in control of oneself. The result of making this connection between interior experience and social obligations is to reduce judgment of the second to the first and so to focus attention on interior states; social forms will take care of themselves.

Idulfitri, the first day after the fasting month, is a time when men have "a feeling of power, of command" over themselves, because they have combatted their desires. *Puasa*, the fasting month itself, is the period in which *hawa nafsu* was experienced. The month is portrayed in Daud Beureuèh's speech in purely subjective terms. Attention is focused not on the events of the month but on the interior states of the men who experienced them. Most men who came to the meeting had been in the village for two or three weeks. They had enacted all of the metaphors of sleep used by the POESA writers, and many had also had the kind of conflicts with their wives that I have described earlier. What Daud Beureuèh drew their attention to, however, was not their marital conflicts, but their feelings about themselves, their interior states.

The result of this new focus is that men's memories of their powerlessness are shifted away from their dealings with their wives and onto themselves. This, of course, is the cause of their lack of influence in the family, but it is also a way to dress their wounds. Viewing their problems from the perspective gained on Idulfitri, from their state of regained *akal*, men

attribute them to *hawa nafsu*. In their eyes, the celebration of the end of the fast rebalances *akal* and *hawa nafsu* and promises an improved future. However,
the position of men in the family remains unchanged.
They return home expecting to be full members of
the household, but because they cannot convince
their wives that this is their right, they again become powerless. Nonetheless, men continue to think
in terms of the promise of *ibadah*; the feeling of having experienced *hawa nafsu* is transformed into a
sense of renewal; and the cycle continues unbroken.

## *Akal, Hawa Nafsu,* AND THE *Rantau*

The lack of fit between social obligations on
the one hand and the interpretation of experience in
terms of the categories of reformist Islam on the
other reflects the genesis of *akal* and *hawa nafsu* in
nineteenth-century Atjehnese society. *Akal* and *hawa
nafsu*, as we have seen, conceptualize the ability of
men to leave family identifications behind and to
unite as Muslims. The idea of the unity of men outside of the family was partly an extension of the experience of the *ulama* who, in the nineteenth century,
did leave their families and unite as Muslims in
the *pesantren*. Given the discontinuous nature of
nineteenth-century institutions, an explanation of this
process necessarily stressed the qualities common to
all men despite their social identifications. *Akal* and
*hawa nafsu*, representing the faculties within men that
enabled them to transcend family identifications,

necessarily were incongruent with the obligations of membership in the family.

*Akal* and *hawa nafsu* accurately expressed the experience of the *ulama* in the nineteenth century because the *ulama* were released from the obligations of husbands. *Akal* did not have to explain the situation of men as husbands. Today, however, *akal* and *hawa nafsu* are the terms of the interpretation of experience within the family, as well as outside of it. There would be no lack of fit, of course, if social forms had changed with consciousness, as men had expected they would in the 1930s. But this has not been the case, and the expectation of social change itself has been abandoned. Nothing Daud Beureuèh said about the obligations of parents, children, and husbands would have been out of place in the nineteenth century. Old forms persist, but men view them differently.

The way in which conceptualization changes while society remains as it was, is evident on Idulfitri when men visit their relatives and their friends, asking pardon. Asking pardon is not asking for a release from transgressions committed against each other; only God can forgive. The fast itself is not atonement; one can in no way erase one's past. Rather, asking pardon signifies the awakened state of the person, making him fit for social intercourse. It says, in effect, that regardless of what happened in the past, the person is now capable of social intercourse as demonstrated by his keeping the fast. In the affirmation of ties between men, despite actions that might have pulled them apart in the past, one sees the unity hoped for and sought by the *ulama*. The expression of *akal* makes the past irrelevant, and a better future is anticipated. In effect, consciousness has been divorced from society.

# 8 ATJEHNESE FIRMS, THE DISTRIBUTIVE NETWORK, AND ISLAM

In the family, the traditional role of husband and father is incongruent with the terms of interpretation of interior experience. Men achieve a kind of resolution by interpreting memories of social relationship in terms of interior experience alone. In the market, the terms of interior experience and those of social relationships are not incongruent. There is therefore no need to try to resolve contradictions by reducing one to the other. In this chapter, I shall try to show how men think of their own experience in the market in one set of terms and their social relationships in another. I shall do so by first discussing the market itself, particularly the structure of business firms, and will then go on to indicate how the structure of firms and consequently the shape of the distributive system are limited by the ideas men have of themselves.

Specifically, I will try to show how Atjehnese business firms lack some features of corporateness. "Corporateness" is one of those terms which seem to mean different things to different people. What I will deal with here in terms of corporateness are two features of firms. First, Atjehnese business corporations have minimally developed structures of authority. There is little obligation to obey the commands of someone because he is your superior within the firm. Furthermore, firm owners do not feel it is their right to command their employees to the same extent that we find in Western business enterprises. Second, corporate personality is weakly developed. Relations in the market are not conceived of as relations between firms but between individuals, even where those individuals supposedly represent their firms.

I have not tried to describe the entire market. To illustrate the nature of Atjehnese firms, I have selected the cloth stores and bus companies since I have more complete information about them. I could have supplemented this material with information about other enterprises in the market, but it would have been redundant to do so. Coffee and tobacco are the chief export commodities in the area I studied. I chose them to illustrate the wider distributive system rather than outlining cloth distribution more fully, since the latter is implicit in the section on the structure of firms and would, therefore, make the section on the distributive system less clear.[1]

The study of the market was made in Bireuen, a town at the junction of the East Coast Road and the road to Takengon. Bireuen is the mid-point between the tobacco- and coffee-growing area and the export ports, and thus offered a particularly good vantage

[1] The social characteristics of Indonesian markets were first studied intensively by Alice Dewey (1962) and Clifford Geertz (1963: 28 ff.) in Java. This being so, it is interesting to note some of the differences between Java and Atjeh. Geertz distinguishes the atomistic pattern of the *pasar* (bazaar) traders, who work individually, from that of the corporate firms. He sees the latter as concomitant with the development of modernist Islam. I shall try to show how modernist Islam does foster firm-type organizations in Atjeh in the sense that Geertz intended. However, my chief argument in this chapter is that it also sets severe limitations on the development of these firms as institutions.

point from which to view the activities of Atjehnese commerce. It is the largest Atjehnese town which still has a weekly market, known in Atjeh as *peukan*. *Peukan* refers not only to the weekly market itself, but also to the place in which it is held. In Bireuen there is a covered area which is owned by the government and rented out to traders each Saturday; this is known as the *peukan*. The *peukan* spreads out from this area into the nearby streets. Traders who frequent the *peukan* in Bireuen on Saturday spend the rest of the week trading in neighboring *peukan*, traveling from one to another by bus, train, or bicycle. They buy most of their goods from any of the several stores in Bireuen.

In addition to shops and the *peukan* in Bireuen, there are rows of covered wooden boxes which serve as storage areas and selling space for small traders in rice, cloth, and other goods. These boxes and the place they are situated are known as the *los*, from the Dutch word meaning "shed."

Bireuen has a police post and barracks, an Islamic high school, and a grade school. There is also a residential section. No population figures were available to me, but a government official in Bireuen estimated the population of the town itself at about 5,000 inhabitants. Most of the population is Atjehnese, but some Chinese run coffee shops, bicycle repair shops, and produce firms.

ATJEHNESE FIRMS: THE CLOTH STORES
AND THE BUS COMPANIES

The cloth stores furnish the material for all Atjehnese clothing, since ready-made clothes are not easily available. None of this cloth is made in Atjeh itself and very little of it in Indonesia. Most of it is imported from Japan and India via Medan, although there is still some cloth brought in via Kutaradja (now called Banda Atjeh). Before Indonesia's policy of "confrontation" (*konfrontasi*) against Malaysia,[2] some cloth was brought from Penang into the smaller Atjehnese ports, especially Lho Seumawè. This stopped with confrontation, but even prior to the break in ties between Indonesia and Malaysia, the biggest importers and thus the cheapest prices were found in Medan.

It is convenient to divide the cloth stores in Bireuen into those which buy their cloth directly from the importers in Medan and those which buy from the larger distributors in Bireuen and Lho Seumawè. Although both types of stores sell directly to consumers, the former sell mostly to other traders on credit, whereas the latter sell only for cash and only to consumers. There are 12 of the first type of store and 19 of the latter. In addition, there are 12 cloth sellers in the *los* and, on market day, about 60 in the *peukan*.

Let us begin with the smaller stores first. An example is Toko Makmur. The owner of the store is Abbas, who was born in Samalanga. He went to public school there from 1922 until 1931. After graduating, he went to the modernist Islamic school Daud Beureuèh had established outside Sigli. He stayed there until the

[2] This is the Indonesian term for their policy of opposition to Malaysia, which resulted in the breaking of diplomatic relations between the two countries.

Japanese came; at that time he returned to Samalanga and became an apprentice in his older brother's cloth shop. By the time the war ended, Abbas thought he knew enough to go into business by himself, and so, with some capital borrowed from his brother, he moved to Lho Seumawè to trade in the *peukan*. By 1948 he had earned enough money to open his own shop there. He moved to Bireuen in 1950 thinking he could do more business, and later he brought his wife and children here as well, finding a small house for them. He has five children. The oldest boy is now in technical high school in Java; the girls are in senior and junior high school in Bireuen; and his younger sons are in grade school here. He hopes to send the younger boys to Java when they are old enough. He does not expect any of his sons to take over his store. He is not disappointed about this; he thinks they will be better off working as educated adults in government service.

Toko Makmur consists of a glass show case, a desk, a chair, and a lot of cloth hanging from the ceiling. There is a concrete floor, and, like all the other shops, the front of the store consists of removable panels put into place only when the store is closed. In addition to Abbas, there are three people associated with the store: Usman, Hanafi, and Abdullah. Usman, who is not related to Abbas but who is from the same *meunasah* in Samalanga, minds the shop with him and is always there if Abbas has to go out. Usman is about twenty years old and has been with Abbas three years. Before that he sold lamp oil in the market in Samal-

anga. Hanafi is also from Samalanga and is the grandson of Abbas' sister. He is twenty-five years old and
has been with Abbas about five years. He takes part
of the stock to the weekly markets around Bireuen.
Abdullah, the third person, is the tailor. He is from
Asan Kambang and is not a relative of Abbas. Abbas
owns all the equipment Abdullah uses—the sewing
machine, the iron, the ironing board, and the sewing table—and buys all the supplies necessary for the
tailoring, such as thread and the charcoal for the iron.
In return, Abdullah shares with Abbas the proceeds
from the tailoring, giving one-third to Abbas and
keeping two-thirds for himself. He also lets the apprentices, Usman and Hanafi watch so that they can
learn enough about tailoring to be able to sell cloth.
A person buying cloth from Abbas' shop need not
have the cloth made up there, but he usually will.
All of the tailors in Bireuen charge the same price,
and no one thinks that any of the tailors now working
are more skilled than others.

Abbas buys his cloth from one of the larger stores
in Bireuen and from a place in Lho Seumawè. He
buys on credit, which is extended for a month; at the
end of the month he repays the whole sum. He says
that he pays an extra 2 to 5 percent for this credit.
He sells the cloth at a markup of about 20 percent.
Once a year he takes inventory and figures what he
has made. He subtracts 25 percent of the profits as
the return on capital and divides the rest with his apprentices. At the moment, he takes 60 percent of the
remainder for himself and gives 30 percent to Hanafi

and 10 percent to Usman. The share he gives to his apprentices depends on his estimate of what they are worth. He has never paid more than 30 percent to any of his apprentices. No one gets a salary. If they need money, they take it from the till and leave a note. This is then deducted from their share of the profits at the end of the year. Abbas said that in places with more capital, half of the yearly profits are figured as return on capital. In his store, a larger portion goes to labor.

Abbas provides food for his apprentices, but he does not pay any of their other expenses. The boys sleep in the shop at night on mats on the floor. They thus get their lodging and also guard the shop. Unlike the larger stores, Toko Makmur has no back room which can be used as a kitchen. Abbas and his two apprentices eat at Abbas' house, with his wife doing the cooking. Abbas attributes half of the cost of the food his wife buys to the overhead of the store, a figure which includes his own meals, as well as those of his apprentices. The other half he pays out of his own pocket.

Since he began his store in 1948 in Lho Seumawè, Abbas has had two other apprentices. One was Rasjid Tjut, the son of an older brother of Abbas (not the same older brother from whom Abbas learned the trade). Rasjid Tjut had already worked for five years in a store that sold dishes, pots and pans, and other household goods. Since he had had this previous experience, he did not stay long with Abbas: he came to Abbas in 1950 and left in 1953. He started by working inside the store as Usman does now and then graduated to working by himself with Abbas' stock in the *peukan* around Bireuen. When he felt that he knew all there was to know about trading, he went into business for himself, moving back to Samalanga. Since he had used most of his share of Abbas' profits for living expenses, he had no capital of his own with which to begin trading, and Abbas furnished his original capital. Now Rasjid Tjut has his own shop in Samalanga, with his own apprentices. He has earned enough since opening his shop to acquire his own capital so that Abbas at present owns only 25 percent of Rasjid Tjut's total enterprise. Rasjid Tjut does not divide his profits in the same way that Abbas does; he gives one-third, instead of one-quarter, of the profits to capital and two-thirds to labor. This perhaps explains why Abbas has not asked for his money back. Although Abbas is a partner of Rasjid Tjut, he has nothing to say in the running of their business. Rasjid Tjut buys his cloth from different wholesalers than Abbas does, and they do not consult about any matters of business. Abbas' only right is an annual return on his money.

Abbas' other apprentice was Hasan, an older brother of Hanafi. He worked with Abbas from 1948 until 1955. He spent the first five years working in the shop. When Rasjid Tjut left, Hasan began trading in the *peukan*. Two years later he, too, left Abbas, and Abbas furnished him capital on the same terms that he had extended to Rasjid Tjut. Hasan is now trading in a small town about two hours by bus from Bireuen.

In Toko Makmur there are no employees. Apprentices work with the expectation of becoming independent, and when they leave the store, they work with capital provided by Abbas. Abbas does not have a voice in running their businesses. This atomistic character is typical of the larger firms as well, although in a more elaborate way. Let us now look at a larger store, Toko Saudara.

Toko Saudara is a partnership consisting of three brothers. Although all three brothers contributed capital to open the store, only two of them, the youngest and the oldest, have anything to do with its operation. However, the middle brother, who retired because of illness, shares in the profits as a return on his capital.

Before the World War II, all of the brothers were cloth traders in Uleè Glè, which is situated halfway between Bireuen and Sigli. Like most other traders, their father was a farmer. When the Japanese came, the brothers were no longer able to buy cloth and so returned to their village near Sigli until the war was over. They then took their capital and bought the store they now own in Bireuen. Beginning on a small scale, they now have one of the larger stores in Bireuen.

Toko Saudara not only does a larger volume of business than Toko Makmur; it is physically much bigger. The store has an upstairs that consists of three rooms in which everyone actively concerned with the store sleeps. On the ground floor there is a back room which is used both as a kitchen and as a place to bathe; the shop itself is the front of the ground floor. The store is actually run by the youngest brother, Umar, who is assisted by one apprentice. There are two tailors who operate on the same basis as the tailor at Toko Makmur; in addition, there is an apprentice tailor who also does the cooking. The oldest brother, Abdul Muis, trades in the *peukan* surrounding Bireuen during the day but sleeps in the store at night. In addition to these people, two others sleep in the store; both are tobacco traders from the same village as the owners of the store. They are known as *penumpang*, or (free) riders, and have nothing to do with the operation of the business. *Penumpang* are a feature of every store that has space for sleeping.

Umar's apprentice in Toko Saudara is Zulkifli. Zulkifli was the son of a cousin of the wife of one of the partners. His parents, grandparents, and aunts all died, however, so he was raised by the partner, who sent him through high school. Since graduating (five years before I met him), he has worked in the store. During the past two years Zulkifli has bought all of the cloth for the store in Medan.

Zulkifli goes to Medan about once a month. He takes two to two and one-half million rupiah each trip. He said that if he took less and went more often it would be cheaper to buy the cloth locally since his expenses in going to Medan are so great. By buying cloth at least once a month the partners gain first-hand information about prices, although this same information is readily available from travelers who arrive from Medan daily. Until the early 1960s, the partners used to receive credit from the importers.

Inflation, however, has eliminated this, and they now pay cash, although Umar said that if he went himself he could get a month's credit.

Since the brothers do not receive credit from anyone, they buy from whichever importers give them the best prices. Zulkifli says he goes to about a dozen importers in Medan before he buys. He said that he does not get special prices at any single importer. Most of the importers are Chinese firms which, owing to the Indonesian policy of discouraging Chinese traders, have Indonesian fronts. There are two major Atjehnese firms, however. Zulkifli said that he buys from whoever gives him the lowest price, without giving or receiving any special consideration from the Atjehnese importers.

The monthly business done by Toko Saudara is about the same as the amount the partners spend on their monthly buying trips—two to two and one-half million rupiah a month as of June 1964.[3] The inventory they maintain, in addition to their monthly turnover, is very small. By the time the next shipment is due to arrive from Medan, the amount of cloth in the store has very noticeably decreased.

Toko Saudara sells about 70 percent of its cloth to other traders known as clients (*langganan*). These

[3] The estimate of monthly business is based on the following information: Zulkifli said that Toko Saudara had seven customers who regularly spent from Rp.20,000 to Rp.70,000 per week in the store. The store also had about ten other smaller customers who traded on a regular basis. I estimated the amount spent monthly by regular traders at Rp.1,700,000. Zulkifli said that about 70 percent of the trade was with these regular customers, thus making the whole amount about Rp.2,430,000 per month.

traders also buy cloth elsewhere, but some of them buy most of their cloth at Toko Saudara because the store allows them more credit than they could get elsewhere. There are seven traders who have debts as high as Rp.300,000 with Toko Saudara. All of the traders come in once a week to pay part of their debt (between Rp.20,000 and Rp.70,000) and take more cloth. The new cloth they take usually has a value equal to the amount they have paid that week. Toko Saudara extends credit because without it the traders would buy elsewhere. During the period of severe inflation following the Indonesian–Malaysian crisis, Umar said that he was going to limit all credit to twenty days. He said that if clients did not pay off the full amount of their monthly purchases by that time, they would have to return the goods. Meanwhile, they could pay off their basic debt little by little. He told us that on Friday; on Saturday, the day that clients usually come in to pay and buy more cloth, he said he could not do it. His clients would just go to other shops where they could get credit. Thus, instead of shortening the amount of time in which to pay, he raised the prices and clients took less cloth.

Normally, the price of cloth is never less than 20 percent above cost for ordinary customers and 10 to 20 percent for regular clients. When a client buys cloth, the amount he takes plus the amount he pays is recorded in a ledger. A second ledger is used to record all sales, with the clerk noting the selling price as soon as the customer leaves. There is also a third book in which the prices at which the various kinds of cloth were bought are recorded. Theoretically, this book is used to determine the selling price. Actually, however, neither Umar nor Zulkifli ever needs to refer to it. In any case, the book is not useful in times of great inflation, since they figure the cost price not at what they paid for the cloth, but at what it would cost to replace it.

As I have mentioned, credit is extended because without it buyers would go elsewhere. On what basis is it given? How does the store owner know whom he can trust? There is a preference for extending credit to those to whom the store owner is not related and who come from somewhere other than his own village. According to informants, this is because kin, feeling that the store owner might be more sympathetic to them than to strangers, are likely to be slower in repaying debts. Store owners say they judge only by the customer's *gerak gerik*, his general demeanor. If questioned further about this, they say they ask whether a man is trustworthy and if he has ever defaulted on his debts. According to one debtor, it is "at first difficult to get credit. But when people know you, you can get it. They want to know if you are honest, if you have ever gambled, and, sometimes, if you fulfill *ibadat*. You have to be careful to guard your name so that you can continue to get credit." Other debtors said much the same thing. Generally, they said, you begin by buying a little at a store and gradually the store owner comes to know you. Then he might give you a little credit and perhaps later he will give you more.

Creditors were reluctant to tell me who their debtors were, so that I have very little information to substantiate these generalities about the kind of people
who get credit. In the case of Toko Saudara, however,
I do know the debtors. Of the seven large clients mentioned above, six are neither related to any of the
partners nor do they come from the partners' village.[4]
All of the clients with large debts have been buying
from Toko Saudara for at least three years, except for
one who has only been buying from them for a little
more than a year. In addition to these clients, Toko
Saudara sells large amounts of cloth to some of the
smaller stores situated between Bireuen and Takengon in the coffee-growing districts. These customers
do not come personally to the store every week; rather, they order the cloth by letter (which is brought
to Bireuen by the local bus line). These clients, however, do not have any continuous debts with Toko
Saudara as the individual traders do. They pay the
whole amount within a month.

In both Toko Makmur and Toko Saudara, apprentices operate with a minimum of control by store
owners. Apprentices are sometimes known as "store
children" (*aneuk kedè*; in Indonesian, *anak kedai*).
When they first come, they are usually about fifteen
or sixteen and are not yet considered adults. Because
of this, the store owner has a basis for authority, which
he often exercises by telling the apprentice to fetch
coffee from the coffee shop or to run some similar

---

[4] The seventh is Abdul Muis, the oldest of the three brothers;
see below.

errand. But when the apprentice has been with him for a couple of years, this ceases and the apprentice becomes a sort of junior partner.

Although the relationship between the employer and the apprentice is supposed to be one of learning, there is no formal teaching. Instead, the apprentice is supposed to watch and then practice. The apprentice in a cloth store, for instance, is not taught how to sew—rather, when the tailor is not working, he tries to learn by using the machine himself. So, too, when the owner is not present, the apprentice waits on clients. The assumption underlying this seems to be that mature people are entitled to full control over their acts. To take orders from someone is an infringement of one's control over his own destiny, and even learning does not seem to justify that. Eventually the apprentice graduates out of the store altogether and operates in the various *peukan*. Thus as soon as the rudiments of the trade are learned, the relationship between store owner and apprentice becomes one of partners, except that the apprentice does not get any of the return on capital.

Partnerships in Atjeh are peculiar in that investment does not confer any rights of control. In fact, investments are really a type of loan. (Investments do not grow, investors being entitled only to a fixed percentage of the return on capital.) Even where a partner furnishes only labor, the investor has no rights of control. We saw examples of this in the cases of the former apprentices of Toko Makmur; the situation in Toko Saudara is only slightly different.

Toko Saudara has a branch store in Takengon. This was originally established by the oldest brother, Abdul Muis, and his brother-in-law with capital from Toko Saudara in Bireuen. After a year in business, however, it became apparent that Abdul Muis' brother-in-law was taking the firm's money,[5] and the store was closed. Two years later it was reopened, this time with a man named M. Kasim in charge. M. Kasim is from the same village as the partners of Toko Saudara, but he is not related. ("He is," said Umar, "more than a relation. He is a very close friend [*Leubeh nibak sjèdara. Ngon that-that*].") All of the money for reopening the store was furnished by Toko Saudara in Bireuen, and the name Toko Saudara was retained. Gradually, M. Kasim put his profits back into the store and became a partner, although only in the Takengon store. But even when M. Kasim had no money of his own in the Takengon store, he made all the decisions concerning it. He decided how much and what kind of cloth to buy and to whom to give credit. The owners felt that they had no right to interfere in the business. The only sign of M. Kasim's relationship to the store owners was the fact that they received most of the annual profits.

Some partners confine their dealings with each other to the annual division of profits. This is usually the case with apprentices who become partners work-

[5] The incident is also interesting in that it illustrates the lack of reliance of businessmen on the police and on the government in general. Atjehnese traders explicitly state that they want to remain uninvolved with the police even when they might benefit. No one ever calls the police if a debtor absconds, for instance.

ing with their former employer's capital. They may begin as clients of their former master, but they cease trading with them when it is no longer economic. In Bireuen there are two brothers, the older of whom owns a large cloth store. The younger brother worked as his apprentice and then, using his older brother's capital, began trading in the *peukan* by himself. During this time he also was a client of his older brother. Eventually he opened his own shop and began buying cloth from Medan and Lho Seumawè because he could get it there at a lower price than he could from his brother. The older brother still had capital in the younger brother's store, although his percentage of the total capital was very small. Regardless of this, however, and despite the fact that the two men are brothers, the younger man could only buy from his older brother at the same price as any other client. Neither brother thought that this was wrong or unusual.

The lack of corporateness of Atjehnese firms is even more apparent when two partners have money in a firm and both work. Here each makes an explicit effort to isolate his activities from those of the other so that the two partners will not have to make decisions jointly. In the case of Toko Saudara, Umar, the youngest brother, runs the store itself, deciding to whom he will give credit and when to buy more cloth. Abdul Muis, the oldest, spends his time trading cloth in the *peukan*. He operates as much as possible as if he had nothing to do with the store, and, indeed, if he is there while Umar is away for a minute, he will not

wait on customers. Abdul Muis takes all of his stock
of cloth from Toko Saudara, but only in this respect
does he differ from a client. His stock consists of
about Rp.300,000 worth of cloth which he takes to
the weekly markets. When he returns to the store to
sleep, his cloth is kept wrapped up; it is never returned
to stock. Every Saturday he takes about Rp.70,000
worth of cloth and repays the same amount in cash.
He is entered in the books in the same way that other
clients are. At the end of the year he returns his profits
to the store before the profits of the entire firm are
divided.

The striking feature of Atjehnese firms, then, is
their lack of corporateness. The role of kinship and
locality in the relations of people in the market will
be discussed later, but from the examples given it is
evident that neither is used as a basis of authority.
Nor is there a structure of authority inherent in the
nature of the firms themselves. No one directs anyone else's labor in return for wages or any other re-
muneration. The role most similar to wage earner is
that of apprentice, but even here authority is minimal; in fact, effort is made to deny that it exists rather
than elaborate it. As we have seen, apprentices work
not with the knowledge that they are under the direction of someone else, but with the expectation that
they will become fully independent in a short time.
As a result, they consider themselves autonomous,
although this is, of course, a fiction. Partners operate
independently of one another, even when they exist

in what we would consider an employer-employee relationship (as in the case of M. Kasim).

The arrangements that stress the autonomy of each trader are not limited to the cloth stores. They are true of every other enterprise in the market, including manufacturing and crafts. In the barber shops, for instance, no barber works for another, even on a piece basis. If one barber owns a shop, he may rent chairs to others on a daily basis. If a barber did not own his own tools, he would rent them from someone else in return for half his earnings. However, nearly all barbers do own their own tools, the only exceptions being those who have just entered the profession.[6]

In the cloth trade and in most other trading operations it is not difficult to get enough capital to go into business for yourself. Thus apprentices only temporarily work for others. They see themselves as future independent traders, not as permanent employees, and only to a very limited extent under the control of the owners of the business. It is interesting that this fiction of autonomy exists even in those cases where the amount of capital necessary for business is so great that only a few workers can aspire to have their own businesses. The bus companies are such a case.

Atjehnese buses consist of truck chassis made in America fitted with bodies made in Medan. The gov-

[6] There is no apprentice system for barbers. A man learns by practicing on children in the village. When he is sufficiently skilled, he goes to the market to practice his trade.

ernment issues import permits for these chassis and also regulates franchises for routes between various points within Atjeh and for routes extending as far as Medan. The bus companies are really consortiums of bus owners. Each firm has a director who secures the government permits for new buses and routes, but he himself may or may not be a bus owner. The director gets 2 percent of the price of each ticket, and the firms also have agents in the towns who sell tickets for a 10-percent commission. After this, however, each bus owner operates as if he constituted a separate business. The major companies have more than one franchise—Bus National, for instance, has franchises for the Medan–Banda Atjeh (Kutaradja), Lho Seumawè–Medan, Bireuen–Medan, Sigli–Medan, Bireuen–Lho Seumawè, and Sigli–Lho Seumawè routes—but the owner of a bus can only operate on one of these franchises, even though the firm owns all of them.

The case is complicated by the fact that some people own more than one bus (and some buses are owned by partners) and so operate on more than one franchise. Also, an important route, such as Medan–Kutaradja, may be operated by more than one bus owner from the same firm. Nonetheless, the principle that each bus owner functions as a separate concern, even though he shares the same trademark with other owners, persists.

The buses themselves are outfitted with benches which run all the way across the bus. There is no aisle as such, but all of the benches have a small back-less area in the middle. This creates a narrow center aisle, and the passengers, who enter from the front and the rear, climb over this portion of the benches to reach the seats assigned them when they bought their tickets. During the journey itself, this aisle is used for seating. The top of the bus is piled high with cargo which consists both of the passengers' luggage and general freight. Freight revenues account for about half of the income of a bus.

Each bus has a crew of three or four men. These are the driver, the conductor (*tjintju*), and one or two others who load the freight. The *tjintju* makes sure that everyone who gets on has a ticket. He also sells tickets to those who flag the bus down between towns. The amount he collects for this he divides with the crew. When a passenger wants to get off, he tells the *tjintju* who then rings a bell signaling the driver to stop. When the bus is ready to go again, the *tjintju* rings the bell once more. The *tjintju* also carries letters between the towns on the route, hand-ing them over to an agent for delivery. This is a free service, and it is a good deal faster than the regular post. (One bus company offers a service to people who want to send money which is similar to registered mail. For a fee, the company guarantees that the amount sent will be safely delivered.)

The *tjintju* and the freight handlers are apprentice drivers. They work so that they can learn how to drive and repair the truck. When the bus arrives in a town,

the passengers get off for coffee and the regular driver
rests. One of the other crew men then drives the bus
to the stores to deliver freight. Mechanical skill is of
no small importance, for even new buses break down
on the unpaved, bumpy roads. Because spare parts
are extremely expensive in Indonesia, no part is replaced until it can no longer be repaired, a practice
that tends to increase the number of mechanical
breakdowns. A crew member usually works at least
two years before he is experienced enough to drive
and repair the bus.

The interesting feature of the bus companies is the
kind of contract that exists between workers and
owners. The crew is paid a small monthly salary.
This salary, however, is not really payment for work
but represents a type of option that the bus owner has
on his workers' services. It means that the workers
cannot be hired by another bus owner. It does not,
however, mean that the workers will necessarily work
for the bus owner holding their option. Each trip is
arranged separately, and each member of the crew
has the right to decline to make the trip. The rate for
the trip is fixed. Thus, the monthly salary is really an
exchange of money not for service, but for an agreement between an owner and his workers that the latter
will not work for anyone else. There is also a group of
"floating" workers who are not bound by options on
their services and who work on short notice. This
resolves the problem that arises when workers decline to make a trip.

The combination of an option on a worker's services and the worker's right to refuse to make a trip seems to be a compromise between rationalization of labor and the autonomy of the worker. On the one hand, the owner wants to be assured he has a crew for each of his scheduled trips; on the other, the crew wants to maintain control over their own actions. The resulting arrangement between them is marked by the same minimization of authority that characterizes the relationship between store owners and their apprentices, or between capital providers and their working partners in trade.

The minimization of authority in the bus companies is further marked by the complete surrender of the bus to the crew while they are actually operating it, a practice that is rather like the surrender of a ship to its captain. I once boarded a bus between stations, and, sitting next to the owner, I offered to pay him for my ticket. He said that he could not take the money since that was the duty of the *tjintju*.

The attempt to diminish the authority of owners and to increase the autonomy of the workers is carried even further in one bus company operating between Bireuen and Takengon. In addition to the usual arrangements between owners and workers, each crew member has the right to sell space on each trip for 200 kilos of freight. (If they do not sell the space, they use it themselves to transport their own trade goods.) In two other companies the crew members get a percentage of the freight revenues. In these companies, then, partial rights in the bus itself have been given over to the crew, increasing the fiction of their autonomy.

## THE SHAPE OF THE DISTRIBUTIVE SYSTEM: THE COFFEE AND TOBACCO MARKETS

If we look at the coffee and tobacco markets in a macroscopic fashion, we can see how the lack of corporateness of Atjehnese firms influences the shape of the distributive network.

Although coffee had been grown in Atjeh by Europeans before the war, only since 1945 has it been grown in significant amounts by small-scale freeholders. The postwar cultivation of coffee began in the Takengon area on an 805-hectare tea estate. The workers were former employees of the estate and of a nearby turpentine factory.[7] They were mostly Javanese, but their ranks were quickly swelled by Atjehnese men who came into the area to join in the cultivation. Before long, all of the cleared land in the area was planted, and the heavily wooded areas were cleared for more coffee plots. Just how much land around Takengon is now under cultivation is not known. The area cultivated, however, extends for about five miles back from both sides of the road to Takengon and then to the north along the trails leading out from Takengon.

Both *robusta* and *arabica* coffees are grown, de-

[7] See Jongejans ([1939]: 164). Most Atjehnese coffee in prewar times was apparently grown not in the Takengon area but in West Atjeh on larger estates (Gonggrijp, 1944).

pending upon the altitude; *arabica* needs a cooler climate than *robusta*. The *arabica* coffee is exported, while the *robusta* is consumed mostly within Atjeh. Both types require continuous hard work for four years before any berries appear. The ground must be cleared of tremendous fir trees and the stumps have to be dug out. This work alone takes a single man about four months. Then the ground has to be hoed and holes sixty centimeters deep and fifty centimeters wide have to be dug for the coffee seeds. After the planting, which must be in September or October, the grower must weed continuously and carefully or the plants will die. In the fourth year a hectare of coffee will yield about 500 kilos of berries and in the fifth year about 1,000 kilos. After that the yields alternate, one year good, the next poor. After twenty-five years, the plants have to be pruned, and then there are two fallow years. By the fifth year after pruning, the harvest is once again at the level it reached in the fifth year after planting.

The owner of a hectare of mature plants is considered to have a substantial source of income. The problem, however, is for him to obtain the means to exist for four years before the plants are ripe. To support themselves, the growers plant secondary crops on part of the cleared land. The favored crop is tobacco, since it brings the greatest income in proportion to land used. Other crops grown are kidney beans (*katjang merah*), yellow beans (*katjang kuning*), cabbage, and garlic. Usually about a quarter hectare is planted in secondary crops while the rest of the land is planted in coffee. If tobacco is grown, more land must be cleared after two years since the soil in the original plot is no longer useful for tobacco, although coffee can apparently be planted there without harmful effects.

During the time the secondary crops are growing (about seven months in the case of tobacco), the growers can get credit from the merchants in the markets along the road. When the crops are ready, these merchants will take them at the market price. A few growers have arrangements with merchants in Bireuen who visit the area regularly. Most, however, deal with the local traders.

The amount earned by a grower from his secondary crops is not sufficient to cover his expenses, especially during the first year. According to various estimates, the expenses of a coffee grower in his first year were as follows in 1964: food, Rp.54,000; hoe, Rp.2,500; ax, Rp.2,000; hut, Rp.20,000; and clothes, Rp.15,000. This makes a total of Rp.93,500. The land itself is free, some of it having been parceled out by the government while most of it is just squatted on. The hut is of thatch and its cost reflects only the materials used in building it. The estimated expenses for the first year do not include money sent back to wives or the cost of trips home; together these might add another Rp.20,000. In the second, third, and fourth years, when the grower does not have the capital expenses of the first year, his expenses will still amount to about Rp.85,000. The income from a good tobacco crop is only about Rp.60,000. The difference is usually made up by sawing wood in the lumber camps; this work is done between the harvesting and the planting of the secondary crops. The local merchants cannot afford to extend long-term credit to the growers since the former buy their goods for cash or on short-term credit.

The road to Takengon is punctuated with markets that are situated only five to ten kilometers apart. These markets service the coffee growers not only by furnishing supplies and buying their secondary crops, but also by buying their coffee. When a grower's coffee plants are ripe, he no longer needs credit from the local merchants.[8] He still sells to them, however, rather than bringing the coffee down to Bireuen himself. The growers are afraid that they will be cheated in Bireuen because they do not know the market. Also, if the price is low when they arrive, they may have to spend a long and expensive time there before it rises to meet their expectations.

The local merchants do not wait for the growers to come to them. When they need coffee, they go to the growers and buy directly. If the coffee has been dried after it is picked, it will keep up to a year. The local merchants, however, do not usually buy enough to store some because they have too little capital to do so. Rather, they buy when they hear the price is

[8] There was no way for me to estimate the ratio of coffee gardens with mature plants to those with immature plants and thus the ratio of credit to cash operations among the local merchants. I can only say that there are far more mature gardens than immature ones; this is not surprising, inasmuch as coffee growing has been going on since 1945.

right and try to sell immediately. Some merchants buy coffee for agents in Bireuen and receive a commission from them. They then use this money as capital, buying coffee that they will sell themselves.

The local merchants usually do not bring the coffee to Bireuen themselves. Like the growers, they are afraid of being cheated or of a change of price that will mean a long wait for them in Bireuen. Also, since most of the local merchants run their own stores, they would have to shut down their businesses in order to bring the coffee to Bireuen. Thus, most of them sell to agents from Bireuen.

There are several different kinds of relations between agents and the coffee buyers in Bireuen. The most numerous type of agent is the one who waits until he hears that the price of coffee in Bireuen and the price in the coffee-growing area are such that he can make a profit. A satisfactory price difference is about Rp.50 per kilo, with coffee selling for about Rp.400 in Bireuen and about Rp.350 in the coffee-growing region. The agent then goes to two or three different firms in Bireuen and buys goods in demand in the coffee-growing area, such as lamp oil, rice, salt, and matches. He gets the goods on credit for a week, paying a few rupiah more per kilo for rice, for instance, than he would if he paid cash. He then sells these goods in the Takengon area and uses the revenue to buy coffee from the local merchants. He brings the coffee back to Bireuen and sells it to the coffee merchants. He makes his profit on the coffee, of course, since he usually sells the goods he brought to

Takengon for cost plus transportation. The agent sells the coffee wherever he can in Bireuen, usually not being bound to sell to his creditor, even though the creditor is often a coffee merchant. When the demand for coffee is heavy, however, the creditor may insist, as part of his terms for extending credit, that the coffee be sold to him at the going market price. The creditors do not do this too often though, for there is no way for them to reject the coffee if the quality is not as high as they would like.[9] (Coffee is not graded in Atjeh, but it could, for instance, be damp or moldy.) Most of the trucking firms which operate between Takengon and Bireuen also act as coffee agents, but most agents are not affiliated with such businesses and use the public buses.

Some agents receive direct money loans with which to buy coffee from the Bireuen firms. This occurs when these firms receive advances from the coffee exporters. Under this arrangement, the agents buy the coffee and receive a commission of Rp.5 for each kilo. The largest firm in Bireuen operates mostly in this way.

The four agents of this firm come closest to being employees since they are paid a small monthly salary to cover their living expenses in return for not working for anyone else. These agents buy more coffee than the others. They each get about two million

[9] One concern has gotten around this by making their clients give them first choice on the coffee but retaining the right to refuse it. They have, however, been able to do this only because they sell rice and other goods at the market price, taking all their profit on coffee.

rupiah for each trip and make two trips a month during the harvest season. Since they have to buy so much coffee, they do not buy directly from the Takengon merchants. Instead, they distribute the money to a few merchants who redistribute it to local traders in various parts of the coffee-growing area. A few days later, these merchants collect the coffee for the agents.

There are twenty-three coffee-buying firms in Bireuen. The smallest of these firms buy only *robusta* coffee for distribution throughout Atjeh. They do not grant credit to agents. Some of them are partnerships in which one partner does the local buying of rice and other products, while the second acts as the sole coffee agent for the firm, going himself to the Takengon area. Others buy from agents who have just returned from Takengon. These firms sell locally for immediate consumption to the coffee shops (who roast the beans themselves) and to merchants who come from other parts of Atjeh to buy coffee. These transactions are in cash. In the small firms coffee plays a less significant role than it does in the larger businesses, since the former also act as redistributing points for the other Takengon products such as cabbage, garlic, and beans. These goods are then taken by small traders to the markets along the main road from Medan to Kutaradja.

At the other end of the spectrum are the large coffee-buying firms which often act as agents for the exporters. The largest of these buys no *robusta* at all and does not deal in rice or anything else. It buys only *arabica* coffee for export. I have described the coffee-buying operations of this firm already. The owner is Chinese, although all of the agents are Atjehnese.

Of the ten largest firms, two are partly owned by coffee-exporting firms and two others are partly owned by the owner of the largest coffee firm in Bireuen. Like all other Atjehnese partnerships, these firms operate without any control by the people who furnish the capital but who do not actually participate in running the business. The various firms are connected, however, because during times of heavy demand for coffee, the exporters advance money to those firms in which they have an interest (and, if the demand is great enough, to other firms as well). This money is then distributed to agents. In the case of the largest firm, part of the advance from the exporters is distributed to the firm's own agents, as described above, and the other part is given to its two connected firms.

Although about ten Bireuen firms get advances from coffee exporters, most of them do not wait for such advances. Rather, when they feel the price is right, they buy and then try to resell the coffee. This was particularly true during the time I was studying the market, for this was the period when Indonesia's policy of confrontation toward Malaysia led to the break in diplomatic relations between the two countries, and the Atjehnese exporters who had furnished most of the advances had stopped doing business.

Each of the ten largest firms was a client of two

or three exporters, while most exporters bought
from three or four Bireuen firms, even though two
of the exporters had money invested in Bireuen firms.
The credit arrangement was an advance of money
for seven to fifteen days.

Before confrontation, the Atjehnese exporters
were based in Lho Seumawè, only a few hours by
bus from Bireuen. They sent the coffee to Penang,
using Malay ships for the most part. When trade with
Malaysia was forbidden, these exporters moved to
Medan where other shipping was available. It was
several months before they could resume business,
however. During this time, the pattern of coffee buying between the Bireuen firms and the exporters
changed, at least temporarily. As I have noted, the
advances from Atjehnese exporters stopped, and a
subsidiary pattern which had existed before became
predominant. This pattern involves independent
agents who buy coffee from the middle-sized Bireuen
firms and take it both to Medan and Lho Seumawè.
Many of these agents have short-term credit arrangements with the Bireuen firms. Arriving in either Lho
Seumawè or Medan, these agents do not sell directly
to the exporters. Instead, they sell to agents of the
exporters who meet the buses and trucks as they come
from Bireuen. The exporters' agents buy the goods,
promising to pay the original agents within a day.
Then they resell the goods to the exporters.

The exporters' agents begin the day by going to
the exporters who tell them how much coffee they
will buy and at what price, but they do not advance

them any money. The agents, or perhaps brokers is a more accurate term, then know how much they should charge the Bireuen agents. Under this arrangement, the Bireuen agents are saved the trouble of going to the exporters, whom they may not know and of whom they are therefore unsure. Moreover, they do not have the problem of not being able to sell the goods and thus of having to pay storage for them. Finally, they also can dispose of their goods more quickly, which is important if they want to maintain their credit in Bireuen.

The brokers in Medan bought coffee not only for the Atjehnese exporters but for the Chinese as well (although the brokers themselves were Atjehnese). The Chinese were able to establish new connections abroad faster than the Atjehnese exporters could. This, apparently, was because the Atjehnese exporters had connections only in Penang, whereas the Chinese knew where to sell coffee in Hong Kong as well. By late 1964 the Atjehnese exporters were back in business, but on a smaller scale, and only a few of the Bireuen firms were receiving their usual advances to buy coffee.[10] The point I would like to make here,

[10] One effect of confrontation on the market was a decline in coffee prices, coupled with inflation, or a loss of value in the rupiah (relative to the U.S. dollar). After trade with Malaysia was forbidden, the price of coffee in Bireuen dropped from Rp.400 per kilo to Rp.200. At the same time, the exchange rate for rupiah fell from about Rp.1,000 per U.S. dollar to Rp.2,000. By the first week of July 1964, when most of the export firms had found new outlets, the price of coffee had risen to Rp.400 per kilo, but the value of the rupiah had declined even further, with the U.S. dollar now being equal to Rp.2,500.

however, is that the coffee market can, and to some extent did, operate without credit arrangements between the firms in Bireuen and the exporters in Medan and Lho Seumawè.

The Atjehnese export firms, like all Indonesian export firms, operate under government license. Under the terms of this license, a permit is necessary for each export shipment. Atjehnese firms exporting from Atjeh are allowed 70 percent of the price of the goods sold abroad to come back to them at the official rate of exchange (in 1964, Rp.83 to the Malaysian dollar) and the remaining 30 percent at the free rate (before confrontation, about Rp.360 to the Malaysian dollar). However, under this regulation it is not possible to make a profit, and if the export firms really obeyed it, they would be selling their coffee at a loss.[11] To get around this regulation, Atjehnese firms set up dummy organizations in Penang. Although these organizations were established in the name of Malay merchants, they were actually owned by consortiums of Atjehnese merchants and were run by Atjehnese in Penang. These firms bought the coffee from Atjehnese exporters at the market price. The amount of coffee sent, however, was always at least

[11] Before confrontation, for instance, Atjehnese exporters sold coffee to merchants in Penang for $2.00 (Malaysian) per kilo. In addition, they were reimbursed for the shipping costs from Lho Seumawè to Penang, which was $.20 per kilo. If this money were converted into rupiah in strict accordance with the government regulation, the Atjehnese exporters would receive Rp.293 per kilo, whereas the price of coffee in Bireuen was Rp.400 per kilo.

double the amount allowed by the permit. The revenue from the smuggled coffee was kept in Malaysian dollars in Penang until the Atjehnese exporter needed it. At that time the Atjehnese firm sent a coded telegram to Penang, and the money was changed at the free-market rate and smuggled back to Atjeh. After confrontation, the Atjehnese firms were still able to bribe the custom officials to allow extra goods out, but they had difficulty in finding firms in other parts of the world outside Malaysia who would cooperate in establishing dummy organizations. Their problem in reestablishing their businesses was further complicated by the lack of available shipping in Medan after Malaysian vessels, which had carried most of the Atjehnese coffee, were forbidden to enter Indonesian waters. Moreover, the foreign ships that were available were much larger, and the exporters had difficulty in getting enough coffee all at one time to fill them.

The fact that Atjehnese coffee was ungraded added still another dimension to the problem. Traditionally, Atjehnese coffee sent to Penang was resold to Chinese who sorted it and guaranteed the quality. After confrontation, the Atjehnese began sorting the coffee themselves, but even then merchants were unable to guarantee the quality and so had difficulty selling it directly to European firms (even to those who were willing to cooperate with them on the exchange problem). What apparently was happening when I left was that Atjehnese firms in Penang were moving to

Hong Kong, or the exporters in Atjeh were putting their goods on ships ostensibly going to Hong Kong but whose manifests were switched after leaving Medan, with the ships actually going to Penang or Singapore.

Some coffee was smuggled to Penang in speedboats. This was done not by the exporting firms but for the most part by merchants who had had experience in this type of operation since the Atjehnese rebellion began in 1953. In these operations, one man acted as entrepreneur. He obtained capital from various other merchants and sometimes put in some himself; he then bought the coffee, arranged to bribe the police, and rented a truck to transport the coffee to the river mouths where it was loaded into the speedboats. The crews of these boats were usually local fishermen. Ordinarily the entrepreneur stayed home. The crossing from Atjeh to Penang takes a speedboat eighteen hours. On arriving in Penang, the crew sold the coffee and then returned to Atjeh. The Malaysian government issued printed quotations of the day's coffee prices which the boat crew brought back as proof of the price on the day they sold the coffee. These operations ended, however, after the Indonesian landings on the Malay mainland in August 1964; from then on, the Malaysian government turned back smugglers trying to enter Penang. I never witnessed any of these operations, but traders in Penang and Atjeh estimated the number of boats at about thirty a day.

The distributive system for tobacco is similar to that for coffee. Most tobacco is grown not by the Atjehnese and Javanese coffee planters but by the Gajo living in the Takengon area. The tobacco usually ripens in June or July. After harvesting, it is dried and then shredded. Most tobacco thus comes on the market in August, at which time the price falls considerably. Tobacco which sells for about Rp.800 per kilo in May costs about Rp.250 per kilo in August. The tobacco traders who buy from the Gajo villagers are Gajo themselves, not Atjehnese. There are no credit arrangements.

Most Atjehnese tobacco, like most Atjehnese coffee, is exported. Although only one kind of tobacco is planted, there are tremendous variations in the tobacco itself. These depend upon the quality of the leaf—its size and place on the plant—and on the fineness of the shredding. The better grades of tobacco are smoked by the Atjehnese themselves, with the lower grades, which are far more abundant, being exported. There are considerable differences in prices between the various grades of tobacco, and each section of Atjeh seems to smoke a different grade from the others. The tobacco smoked in Bireuen, for instance, costs about Rp.1,200 per kilo, whereas that smoked in West Atjeh is about Rp.900 per kilo and that smoked in the capital is about Rp.700 per kilo. The exported tobacco is only about Rp.550 per kilo. It requires considerable skill to know the quality of tobacco because it is often still green when it gets to

Bireuen and the variations in quality are not readily apparent.[12]

When the buses bringing tobacco from Takengon arrive in Bireuen, the twenty or so agents who deal in tobacco of the quality smoked in Bireuen scramble to unload the cargo. Three or four of them grab a bundle of tobacco and quickly inspect it by smelling and feeling it and looking into sheets for parts of stalk embedded in the leaf. If the tobacco is of the quality smoked in Bireuen, and only a small part of each shipment is, they discuss the tobacco in low tones while the owner stands nearby. When the agents have agreed on its quality, those wishing to share in the buying of the tobacco grab hold of the mat in which it was wrapped, and one of them begins bargaining with the owner. Any of the prospective buyers can let go of the mat before the sale is consummated and thus drop out. The amount of people buying a single bale of tobacco may be as many as five, depending, of course, upon the amount of tobacco available and the prospect for selling it. Most of the transactions I witnessed involved just one buyer since I was there during the months in which tobacco is plentiful. After the sale is made, the tobacco is dragged off to be weighed on the scales in the bus company's offices. The buyer then carefully rewraps the tobacco in his own mat. Nearly all transactions

[12] Tobacco arriving in Bireuen is already dried and shredded, so that variations of quality visible in the leaf are difficult to detect.

are for cash. At best the seller will agree to wait until he is ready to return to the Takengon area in a few days, but even this is unusual.

If two or more people have bought a single bale of tobacco and one of them feels that he can sell all of it quickly, he will ask his partners to "*meulaba*" or to "figure the profit." In this transaction the partners simply figure what the profit would be if the tobacco were sold immediately, and then the one who takes all of the tobacco pays off his partners. Where there is very little tobacco available, this is often done. Frequently in this situation the price is arrived at by competitive bidding between the partners.[13]

The sharing of bales of tobacco is not a way of spreading risks as it seems to be in Java (Geertz, 1963:41). Rather, it occurs only when there is a shortage of goods. When goods are plentiful, each trader buys individually.

These tobacco traders are not store owners. They sit on the sidewalks in front of the bus company and across the street from it, waiting for customers and for buses. They have stocks of about 60 kilos of tobacco at any given moment.[14] Their customers are traders from the markets in the Bireuen area. They are brokers only for the quality of tobacco which is smoked in the Bireuen area, and they account for only a small part of the total tobacco consumed in

[13] *Meulaba* is also practiced by fish merchants when the daily catch is small.

[14] This was true during the months when tobacco was plentiful. I do not know about the other months.

Atjeh. There are no credit arrangements between these buyers and their customers.

In addition to these agents, there are about 10 retail tobacco traders in Bireuen who sit mostly along one alleyway with their wares. They cannot afford to buy in large quantities; consequently they buy from the tobacco brokers rather than from the Gajo agents who will not sell less than a single bale at a time.

The Gajo agents store their goods in the bus depot or in one of the three tobacco firms in Bireuen and wait for customers. They sell both to agents taking the tobacco to Medan and to those taking it to other places within Atjeh. Once again there are no credit arrangements between the trading parties. The Gajo agents do not go to Medan or any of the other markets themselves because they are not familiar with these markets and fear being "cheated" (*tipu*).

These Gajo agents also sell to the three tobacco firms in Bireuen. Depending on the market, they may give the store owner a couple of weeks to pay. One of these stores also has its own agents buying in the Takengon area on the same basis as the coffee agents—the store advances the money for the agent to purchase the tobacco and pays him a commission on each kilo he buys. The problem with this, however, is that the store owner cannot be sure of the quality of tobacco the agent will bring him. He therefore prefers to buy from independent agents who come to Bireuen.

These three firms deal mostly in tobacco going to

Medan and from there to Malaysia (via Chinese dealers).[15] Before confrontation they exported via the Atjehnese firms in Lho Seumawè. They do not get credit from the exporters. In fact, the arrangement works the other way around. The exporters send orders to the firms and the firms deliver the tobacco; payment is sent to them by return bus. This payment consists of the market price of the tobacco in Bireuen, plus the transportation costs and a markup for the firm owner. The owner with whom I spoke would not tell me the amount of the markup, but he said that he always gives the exporters a fair price because he is afraid of losing their business. Once again the independent agents who bring the tobacco to Medan do not sell directly to the exporters, but to other agents who then resell the tobacco to the exporters.

Looking at the system of distribution for tobacco and coffee, we might well ask why it is so elaborate. Why do the growers not sell directly to the exporters? Why is the number of middlemen between the growers and the exporters so great? The elimination of some of the points of exchanges could be done in several ways. The exporters, for instance, could open their own branches in Bireuen or in Takengon to collect the coffee. This is just what they have tried to do by investing in firms in Bireuen. But, as we have seen,

---

[15] This information comes from a store owner in Bireuen; I was not able to verify it in Medan as I could the coffee-exporting arrangements. Of the three tobacco firms in Bireuen, two of the owners are Gajo and one is Atjehnese.

these are not true extensions of the exporting operations since there is no connection between capital and
control. The exporters could also send agents directly
to the coffee-growing areas, thus bypassing the Bireu-
en firms. This has been tried several times by at least
one exporter, but the result has always been financial
loss. His agents, although they know part of the coffee-
growing area, do not know enough of it to buy really
large quantities of coffee. Moreover, the Takengon
merchants have taken advantage of them by selling
them coffee at higher prices than they would to those
agents whom they know. Sometimes the agents have
not been able to buy coffee at all, and one agent ran
off with the exporter's money. Another possibility
would be for the agents who now trade with the
Takengon and the Bireuen merchants to sell directly
to the exporters. They, however, refuse to do this, saying that they do not know the market in Medan. If
they bring the coffee there, they say, they always get
taken; no one will offer them a reasonable price, and
they do not know where to take the coffee.

Coffee and tobacco for export are accumulated
by the exporters, through a series of dealings with
middlemen agents, from a vast number of coffee and
tobacco growers. Each exchange of money for goods
results in an increase in his supply of goods. Even
without consolidating the number of small holdings,
it would be possible to shorten the collection system
by extending the buying operations of the exporters
to the growers. This, however, cannot be done be-

cause of the noncorporate nature of Atjehnese firms. Given the nature of Atjehnese firms, exporters' attempts to extend themselves into the collection system result in a process of fission. Exporters establish firms in Bireuen. These firms operate, however, not as branches but as autonomous businesses. Large Bireuen firms, wanting to increase their business, buy into or set up partnerships in other firms. But these firms, too, operate as separate establishments. This is the same thing that happens in the cloth trade—no real branches are established, only separate businesses operating with shared capital.

There are in the distributive system two problems in particular, and they are related to one another. The first is that people will deal only with those whom they know. Growers do not want to sell in the Bireuen market because they do not know the merchants there. The Takengon traders do not want to take their goods to Medan for the same reason. Given the large number of growers, there must then be a large number of traders if each transaction is to be on a personal basis. The second problem is the lack of corporateness in Atjehnese firms. If firms were truly corporate, they could shorten the lines of the distributive system, for growers and traders could then deal with a corporate personality with which they would be familiar. But the firms cannot develop into corporate entities because their members insist on acting as individuals and not as members of a corporation. The result is that a kilo of coffee may have to exchange hands six times before it is loaded onto a ship for export.

## THE MARKET AND ISLAM

Up to this point, I have spoken of the market almost without mention of Islam. It is now time to ask whether there is a relation between the market and religion in Atjeh, or whether the market has its own ethic and is thus divorced from the rest of life. If the second case is true, there are some things about the market that are difficult to understand. For instance, wealthy men are not respected. The pursuit of wealth is not considered a good in itself; rich people are not admired unless they give to Islamic causes. One of the wealthiest traders in Bireuen is seldom mentioned without being described as *kriet*, or stingy, because he gives very little to charity. Furthermore, if the market does work on its own terms, why is it impossible to shorten the lines of trade in coffee collection, even though it is more economic to do so? Why is there no corporateness in Atjehnese firms when corporateness is more efficient? The economic advantages of corporateness work not only for the economy as a whole but for workers as well. Many small traders, for example, could make more working for estates than they do in trade.[16] Yet they refuse to do so, saying that it is "uncomfortable" (*hana mangat sagai*) or "humiliating" (*teupeh perasaan*) to take orders from others.

[16] This statement takes into consideration not only wages but also the payments in cloth and rice that estates make.

Actually, Atjehnese do think of their experience in the market in terms of Islamic categories, as the comments of the apprentice Zulkifli illustrate. When I asked him whom he most admired, he said that he thought most highly of the goldsmith Kasim. When I asked why, he said that in the highly inflationary economy of Indonesia, people use gold rather than money as a standard of value. The goldsmith, who not only buys and sells gold but uses it in making gold ornaments, must, more than anyone else, "precisely calculate the selling price of gold so that he is not fooled by the fluctuating price of money. If he sells at a higher price than last week but still at less than the real value of money, he can be wiped out in no time at all; he will lose all his capital and be unable to buy more gold. Also, if the price of money should drop, he has to know whether to sell the gold he has or to wait and see what the market will be next week. Kasim can do this. He has a lot of *akal* [*le akoi*; in Indonesian, *banjak akal*]."

Zulkifli admires Kasim, then, for his rational action, the meaning of which Zulkifli elaborated in this description of an unsuccessful trader: "Mahmoed is always losing money. For instance, he always gives lower prices to girls. Actually, it is alright to talk to girls in the market, but we should always keep our mind on prices and ask more money from them because they don't know anything about it. . . . But Mahmoed just does not keep his head. He doesn't pay any attention to what he is doing. If people flatter him, he gives them a lower price and then, just as if it

were paper, he wraps their goods up in white cloth.
. . . You have to be careful in trading, you have to be
on guard." Mahmoed, according to Zulkifli, does not
lack *akal*, but he is always succumbing to *hawa nafsu*.
Because he does not restrain his impulses, he puts
himself in the hands of others, and, indeed, the great
danger in trade is that one will be manipulated by
others. The only defense is to be alert, "to be careful
. . . , to be on guard."

Mahmoed is continually being "tricked" (*tipu*) in
the way that Atjehnese traders are always afraid of
being taken. This fear is not that the other party will
deceive you by offering too low a price, for example;
one expects that. Rather, the fear is of letting down
one's guard and consequently succumbing to others
and to one's self simultaneously.[17]

The fear of submission of rationality to *hawa nafsu*
is, of course, what I have discussed in the previous
chapters. It is not something learned by the experience
of losing money in the market; it is a moral precept

[17] One should note that in these examples Zulkifli is not equat-
ing interior experience with one's standing in the market. The
goldsmith, for instance, is far from the richest man in the market.
Zulkifli would only talk about Mahmoed and the goldsmith; he
refused comment on others who were more successful and also
refused to say that success in the market was always due to *akal*
and that failure was always due to *hawa nafsu*. It is very difficult
to get anyone to comment on the actual experience of others (as
opposed to their ability to trade), and Zulkifli was exceptional in
saying as much as he did. The examples of the Javanese and of
M. Kasim which I will cite later illustrate more clearly the separation of ideas about *akal* and *hawa nafsu* from valuations about
standing in the market.

underlying all actions, even when the result of being tricked does not result in financial loss.

Rationality in the market place does not take the form that Teungku Oestman envisioned it would in a world in which everyone fulfilled *ibadah*. Rationality has not created a world in which all social relationships are perfect. It has not made a society of inherently right relations between people. One cannot look at the rights and duties of people to one another to know how to act as a Muslim. Irrationality still haunts the world, and the world is a test for man to see if he can respond to its irrationality in a rational way. It is not Teungku Oestman but T. T. who correctly predicted the state of the world. The world is not perfect; it remains a place in which each individual tries himself against it and against the forces of irrationality within him. To act properly, man cannot rely on simply following a given form of social relations; rather, he can rely only on his own faculty for being rational.

Correct relations between men are thought of as such not because they conform to an ideal image of relationship, but because they demonstrate the operation of *akal* on the part of each party. The end of each action must be chosen by the actor and must be within his control. The surrendering of control means the giving up of rationality. There is thus little basis for authority, and consequently there are no corporate firms in Atjeh.

Without objective standards of morality, men work

perhaps also because women a lack of pwr?

with a statistical theory of conduct, a kind of behavioristic theory. The question they ask of traders is not whether they are good people, good Muslims, but whether they can operate in the market. Men do not attempt to know the inner states of others but look only at the record of their past actions.

In this light we can understand the roles that kinship, locality, and friendship play in the relations between men in the market. Apprentices usually come from the same village or the same area (*mukim*) as their masters, and they are often related to them. In a survey of 12 shops, 21 of 32 apprentices were related to their employers and came from the same district (*ketjamatan*). Of those not related, 9 were from the same district as their employers. Only 2, then, were neither related to their employers nor from the same district. Men show a similar tendency in forming partnerships, although not in so pronounced a form. Out of 35 shops surveyed, 19 were partnerships. These 19 shops had a total of 48 partners, 19 of whom were related to their respective partners and 18 of whom were not related but came from the same district as their partners. Eleven partners had neither locality nor kinship in common with their respective partners. The point I wish to make here is that locality and kinship are a basis for acquaintance. They do not in themselves entitle a boy to become an apprentice, nor are they essential in this respect. However, because a boy is from the same area as his employer, the latter knows something about him. He knows, for instance, whether or not the boy can be trusted to be left alone in the store and not steal. Indeed, in the only case I ever heard of where an apprentice was accused of stealing from his employer, the boy was not related to the employer nor was he from the same locality. Common locality and kinship are found less often in partnerships, because partnerships are often formed after the traders have been in the market for a while and so know one another. The only thing that locality and kinship entitle a man to in the market is a place to sleep if a fellow villager has a store in which there is extra space.

Friendship never means intimacy or sharing those things we think of as personal. I asked Maun if he had any special friends, and he replied that everywhere he goes he has friends: in Bireuen there is Teungku Umar, as well as several others, and there are many in Medan. When I asked him if he talks to them about his problems, he said, "Yes, I talk with them about trade, the market, and, sometimes, religion." I went on to ask Maun if he ever tells his friends about his family, and he replied, "Never, not even with Teungku Umar [with whom Maun and his wife shared a house for five years]."

Friendship, then, is valued, but only as an index of man's reliability. It often involves partnership, and between two men it serves the same function that being from the same village or having been to school together serves—that is, through their common exposure to the world, it reveals the realiability of one to the other. This is what Umar meant when he said of his partner in Toko Saudara in Takengon, M.

Kasim: "He is more than a relation. He is a very close friend." He had seen his partner respond to the world and he knew him to be reliable.[18] Their relationship, however, is no different than that between Umar and other men with whom he trades. It is not intimacy that one seeks but only the certainty of reliability. It is a view from the outside because the inner, personal world is not a recognized part of social intercourse.

In this context, we can also understand the meaning of extending credit. In Atjeh, giving credit has little to do with the qualities with which we usually associate it—especially honesty. What the statements of both creditors and debtors stress as a prerequisite for extending or receiving credit is a man's capacity to trade; this has nothing to do with honesty. Credit, like the rest of the exchange system, is based on the notion that the other party will do everything he can to maximize his own interests. Thus if a debtor is slow to pay, no one accuses him of being dishonest. The debtor may be jeopardizing his own position in the market, but his failure to pay is considered to be at least as much the fault of the creditor for extending him credit in the first place as it is the fault of the

[18] M. Kasim and Umar illustrate the separation of moral judgment and behavior in another sense as well. When M. Kasim was sent to Takengon to reopen the Toko Saudara branch, he had just lost all his money. According to Umar, however, this was not his fault. M. Kasim's actions when he lost his money were those of any competent trader—the course of the market was responsible for his loss. The implication is that one can always expect a friend to act as a good trader; he is reliable, even if the market itself is not.

debtor. It is expected that debtors will pay as little as possible and only when it is in their interest to do so. That, after all, is how the debts of the cloth firm clients came into being. There was no agreement that the clients could have so much credit; they simply refused to pay and the creditor accepted the situation, knowing that if he did not he would lose their business.

In one case, the confinement of judgment to behavior, or the separation of moral considerations from business, actually makes the Atjehnese give preference to a group of Communist, nonpracticing Muslims over a group of professed Muslims. In the tobacco- and coffee-growing areas, the Gajo, who have the same reputation as the Atjehnese for being fanatical Muslims, are never extended credit.[19] On the other hand, the Javanese, whom the local Atjehnese merchants consider Communists (and therefore atheists and enemies), are given this privilege. The Atjehnese explain this by saying that the Gajo, who live in their native villages, "have the spirit of the village, not the spirit of those who have left home [*seumangat gampong, keun seumangat rantau*; in Indonesian, *semangat desa, bukan semangat rantau*]." The meaning of this is that the Gajo, who grow coffee along with rice and tobacco and other crops, put their kinship obligations first, whereas the Javanese who emigrated to Atjeh and who depend on the

[19] Actually the religion of the Gajo seems to be more of the syncretic variety that Snouck observed in nineteenth-century Atjehnese villages rather than the sort that stresses *ibadah*. This, however, is a distinction that the Atjehnese themselves would not dare to make.

market for their livelihood, have shown that they put considerations of the market first.[20]

If moral considerations are kept separate from behavior in the market, it seems that we return to thinking of the market as a place in which Islam is irrelevant. Yet the Gajo case is an indication that this is not so. The reason that Atjehnese can act apart from considerations of kinship, unlike the Gajo, is that they think in terms of *akal* and *hawa nafsu*. They have a view of human nature, given to them by Islam, which supplants other definitions of identity. No relationship is intrinsically good because rationality has not yet created a perfect world. But each person has the obligation to maintain himself in a rational state. The attempt to do so in a hostile world makes men view others not in terms of innately right categories of kinship or locality, but in terms of behavior alone. An Atjehnese may not judge others in moral terms, but he tries to act in a moral way himself. Each successful act of exchange maintains the dominance of *akal* over *hawa nafsu* and affirms the rationality of the trader. The market as a whole may appear valueless, but each person in it strives to act as a Muslim.

[20] Most of the Communist coffee growers were murdered after the 1965 coup attempt by local Atjehnese youth groups.

# 9 GHOSTLIER DEMARCATIONS, KEENER SOUNDS

In Atjeh, the idea that men have a common nature which, when properly expressed, indicates religious worth has conflicted with ideas of worthiness based on social status. So far as I can tell, the conception of human nature itself, consisting of *akal* and *hawa nafsu*, has not varied. But, from the late nineteenth century until today, tension between religious and social identity has had several modes of expression. Paradise, a new society, and, in the 1960s, the celebration of the pilgrimage have successively symbolized the distinction between the world in which men live and the possibilities inherent in their nature.

*Akal* and *hawa nafsu* have been expressed in a series of aspirations that have conceptualized the imperfections of the world. However, the Atjehnese idea of human nature has been conservative in its effects. If one looks at the institutions of Atjehnese society in the twentieth century, for instance, one can in no way account for their creation in terms of religious ideas. The new distributive system was created by the Dutch and was initially run by the Chinese, non-Atjehnese Indonesians, and the Dutch themselves. The family remains as it was, although men today think of it differently. *Akal* and *hawa nafsu* have not been the basis of new social forms, although they have been the terms by which men have conceptualized experience of their institutions, including those introduced into

Atjeh. It is in the use men have made of them to come to terms with what exists that *akal* and *hawa nafsu* have been conservative beliefs.

Although religious ideas have been socially conservative in Atjeh, they have another aspect which is radical. The shifting goals of religion have stressed the tension between man's nature and his place in the world. Aspects of man's nature have thus been illuminated that, otherwise, would have remained in the shadows. *Akal* and *hawa nafsu* have enabled men to conceptualize interior nature and social experience in the same terms. This has made Atjehnese Islam socially conservative and religiously radical. Goals are expressions of *akal* and *hawa nafsu*, of interior nature. Therefore they are conservative; they do not delineate social forms. At the same time, they raise the past and express it in such a way as to make it unacceptable as a source of moral worthiness. Men cannot make their standing in the world the source of religious value. The nonsocial, nonhistorical source of worthiness is thus stressed.

Paradise, a new society, and the pilgrimage in turn have expressed the aspirations of the Atjehnese and have shaped their views of their place in the world. I want now to trace the sources of the effectiveness of these images and the transitions between them. The religiously radical and socially conservative aspects of Islam in Atjeh, as well as the changes in aspirations, are understandable if we look at Islam as a doctrine of transition from one sphere of life to another, rather than as a program of reform of social and religious institutions. As a doctrine of transition, Atjehnese Islam has its source in Atjehnese society, as well as Islamic tradition.

Nineteenth-century Atjeh consisted of four major institutions: the sultanate, the village, the *uleebelang*-ship, and the *pesantren*. These four institutions were not organically joined together in such a way that, from any point of view, each had its own place in a total cultural universe. Three of the institutions were responses to external forces. The *uleebelang*-ship was basically a station in the export trade; the sultanate was powerful only so long as it controlled that trade, and culturally it was defined by an imported religion; the *pesantren* was a representative of that religion. Each of the four Atjehnese institutions had conceptions of the other three, but there was little agreement about the nature of Atjeh as a whole. For the most part they existed side by side not because of an overriding conception of a whole, but because the real connections between them were minimal. The only large-scale contact between members of different institutions was based not on a complementary fit of sociological distinction, such as peasant and lord, but on relinquishing these distinctions.

The *ulama*, however, had a special place in this scheme. Only they had an idea of the links that existed between men despite the institutions to which they belonged. The union of men despite their social positions rested, of course, on their common nature and

belief—on *akal* and *hawa nafsu* in the service of
Islam. The *ulama*'s belief in the overriding unity of
men had its source partly in their personal experience.

Only *ulama* were born into one institution, the village, and had to leave the village and enter a second,
the *pesantren*, in order to achieve their new status.
To become an *uleebelang* one had, in theory, to be
born into an *uleebelang* family, as was also the case
with the sultan. Only *ulama* were obliged to leave their
families behind and enter the one institution where
men lived as Muslims above all.[1] The view that they
developed of human nature explained their transition
out of the family and became the basis of their lives
as Muslims in the *pesantren*. *Akal* and *hawa nafsu* explained how it is that although men are born into institutions they can overcome the identity these institutions give them and join together. From this point of
view, the *ulama's* idea of human nature is also an expression of the limits of Atjehnese society, of the
hidden ties between family and *pesantren* which
otherwise seem to be in conflict. They picture an
awareness of both as a whole experience in a single
frame of reference.

The doctrine of reformist Islam was, in fact, more
a doctrine of passage than of reform. The *ulama* said
that what was once appropriate in the family is now
no longer so. New ties are possible on the basis of *akal*
which, as it develops, delivers men out of the family.

---

[1] It is true that many of the sons of *ulama* became *ulama* themselves, but these sons grew up in the village.

The reformist part of modernist Islam was directed not toward changing the family but toward creating new bonds between men outside of it. As a plan for the creation of a new society, reformist Islam also had a theory of what prevented that society from existing—the particularistic ties that are built on *hawa nafsu*. The *ulama*, however, envisioned not the abolition of family and kinship, but only the confinement of such ties to a place that would be secondary to the new connections between men.

## PARADISE

Looking at reformist Islam in this way, we can better understand the nature of its appeal in the nineteenth century and especially the role of the idea of paradise. In Chapter 3 I stressed the points in the life cycle at which village men felt the greatest strain and so had reason to accept the views of the *ulama*. I also pointed out the misunderstandings between *ulama* and villagers: men were attracted by paradise, not by the vision of a new society here on earth. They joined in public works projects to earn the merit that would help them gain paradise, not to create the kind of society the *ulama* wanted. They fought in the Holy War for the same reason.

Paradise is an image of *hawa nafsu* fulfilled. One remembers the scenes from the *Hikajat Prang Sabi*, for instance. Paradise is an important idea for the *ulama* not only because of its theological importance but also because, in their theory of passage, the basic hindrance was *hawa nafsu*. But because *hawa nafsu*

is a part of man's nature, one of two parts, and not
an attribute of society or of anything objective, it
needs an image to be known. Paradise is such an
image, and in it one sees the pure expression of *hawa
nafsu*, unhindered by social forms, as this description
of paradise by an Atjehnese illustrates:

"In Paradise you do whatever you feel like. Each man
has many wives, up to seventy. The women do not menstruate. There is nothing dirty. It is a place of happiness.
You are hungry so you eat. Everything there is a hundred
times more delicious than here on earth. And there are a
hundred times more pleasures than we here on earth
know. Everything is complete. The lamps don't need oil;
perhaps they are even stars suspended in air. The houses
have no screws or nails. The water is a hundred times
purer than here on earth and ten times warmer. Everyone
is young. The women are about seventeen and the men
about twenty. Whatever you do, you are happy. No one
works. [He repeated this several times.] There are no type-
writers [referring to mine]. The cars are a hundred times
better than Mercedes.

"Paradise is the answer for our deeds on earth. It is a
garden where we live and where all our desires are fulfilled. For instance, whatever you want to eat, you get
immediately. There are beautiful women. . . . Your wife
will be replaced by someone better."

The *ulama*, looking back on their own transition
out of the village into the *pesantren*, conceived of
life in the village largely as the experience of *hawa
nafsu*. *Hawa nafsu* thus referred to villagers' own experience and had a meaning for them that *akal* and its
social consequences did not have. Paradise drew its

force as an effective idea in linking *ulama* and villagers partly from the real experience of both *ulama* and villagers that it imaged.

Paradise is more than a scene of *hawa nafsu*, however. It is also an idea of passage. While God created paradise before He made the earth, man can only reenter it when the earth is destroyed. Here is an Atjehnese version of the last day: "On the day of judgment, everything will be destroyed and everyone will die. Then everyone will live again and stand by their graves naked. Each will seek out his prophet. The angels will come and ask us our deeds. Our witnesses will be our own bodies. Our feet, eyes, mouth, and hands will relate our deeds. A balance will be struck and our fate determined." Only after the earth is destroyed will paradise be filled. It is as though it is not possible to call up the force of *hawa nafsu* within man without, at the same time, thinking of the destruction of the world. One remembers the prediction of the angels that if man, with *hawa nafsu*, were given the earth, there would be only bloodshed and devastation. The total expression of *hawa nafsu*, paradise, means the destruction of the world. As we saw in the *Hikajat Prang Sabi*, from a personal point of view the attainment of paradise means necessarily the giving up of the world.

Paradise was not only a place to go to but also a place to look back from. The *ulama* looked at their past in the village from a standpoint outside it; villagers had no such standpoint. Paradise, by its contrast with the world, provided such a standpoint and made life in the village objective. In the *Hikajat Prang Sabi*, life in the world is continually juxtaposed with paradise. By being made objective, the past and the present can be evaluated. The terms of the evaluation are embodied in the idea of paradise itself. Paradise is an exaggerated ("a hundred times . . .") version of life on earth; it is *hawa nafsu* itself. The juxtapositions of the *Hikajat Prang Sabi* and the implied contrasts of all other statements concerning paradise throw life on earth into perspective.

Paradise was seen as an exaggerated form of the world, a better form; it did not make the world into an intrinsically bad place. The idea of paradise could not be a standard by which the world as a source of worth was permanently rejected. It was effective only at special moments when men were prepared to give up their identities in the world. However, not until the 1930s did men accept the *ulama*'s idea of a permanent rejection of social status as a source of moral value; only then did paradise fade into the background of consciousness.

A NEW SOCIETY

The tension between religion and society in the 1930s was expressed through the idea of creating a new world in which to express religious belief. The ability of men to cross institutional boundaries in the nineteenth century seemed to the *ulama* in the 1930s, with those institutions weakened, to be the source of a new society. Unity, the direct expression of *akal*, seemed about to be expressed in new social forms, filling the void left by the erosion of ties of kinship between men.

To some extent, Atjehnese ideas of unity and society in the 1930s expressed men's ability to come together in the POESA. These meetings were not unique in Atjehnese history. The public works projects of the Habib and the Holy War were precedents for meetings of men as Muslims overriding the identifications of kinship. What is different about the POESA meetings of the 1930s is the viewpoint from which they were seen. To men in the nineteenth century, the important thing was not that they met as Muslims but that they had left something behind. In the 1930s, however, with the erosion of kinship ties and with the dependence of men on their wives, what they left behind they left easily. Their ability to join together must thus have seemed the result of something previously untapped in their nature, of some new power, as, indeed, the *ulama* said it was. The idea of a new society conceptualized the expansion of this power throughout the world.

Like the idea of paradise, that of a new society provided a standpoint from which to view the past. Now, with *akal* and its effects a property of this world, the past could be rejected as a source of worth and one could still remain in the world. The new society and the view of personal transition it entailed at once explained and resolved men's position in the family and held forth the possibility of something beyond it.

The family was now known to be the scene of *hawa nafsu*. One's experience there need not define one's true worth.

## THE PILGRIMAGE

After World War II, Atjehnese men began entering the market as traders and growers of cash crops. Having gained a place in the economy, they regained a place of sorts in the family as well. However, the achievement of positions in the world did not mean that the new society envisioned in the 1930s had been realized. The distributive system which Atjehnese entered was the creation of the Dutch, and the family did not really change. Nonetheless, men now had a means of understanding their experience in these institutions which they lacked before the reformist movement reshaped their ideas about the world. They could not explain the forms of social ties in the world, but they were able to conceptualize the experience of these relations.

The relationship the *ulama* had created between interior experience and the world now took a new form of expression. Rather than expecting that interior states would be made concrete in the social forms of the world, the Atjehnese tried to express the faculty within them that was itself the source of awareness.[2] As we will see, this had the effect of

[2] Atjehnese still believe that interior states are expressed in the world, as the expectations of men in the family indicate. Such expectations, however, are now personal rather than social. No longer is it thought that new social forms will result from the right internal balance.

maintaining the tension between worldly status and religious worth, thus preventing men from thinking that they were measured by their status.

The situation in the 1960s has many similarities to that of the nineteenth century. Again there is the belief that unity is possible despite the social roles that separate men. The difference is that today *akal* is popularly accepted as the faculty that can unite men. The expression of the unity of men in the 1960's, the pilgrimage, is, like paradise, an image of a journey. Like paradise, it distills the experience of men in society and, in the image itself, transforms that experience into something apart from the world. And, once again like paradise, the imaging of experience is at the same time the imaging of the dissolution of social bonds. Like paradise, the pilgrimage creates a viewpoint from which the world can be seen and evaluated. The major difference between the two, however, apart from the difference of *akal* and *hawa nafsu*, is that the pilgrimage explicitly delineates an interior faculty of man and thus creates a permanent measure of the world which is not contingent upon physically leaving it.

For most Atjehnese, the local celebration of the pilgrimage is more important than actually making the journey to Mecca, which only the wealthy can afford to do. On the tenth day of the month of the pilgrimage, when the pilgrims in Arabia are making a sacrifice, there is a celebration in Atjeh. This is known as *urou raja hadji*. The actual ceremonies surrounding this holiday are nearly identical with those at the

beginning and end of the fasting month. The day before the holiday itself meat is sold at the local markets and men are expected to buy some for their families. Unlike the fasting month, however, men are not
obliged to buy cloth. Women bake for the occasion
as they did for the end of the fasting month, and
there is also visiting between neighbors and relatives.
The greeting this time is "*selamat urou raja,*" "con-
gratulations on the holiday."

The day is marked by public prayers and an address by an *ulama,* followed by the slaughtering of
water buffaloes. The meat is distributed to the poor.
Before the holiday in 1964, Daud Beureuèh had
called the *imeum* of our district together and had
given them cards which they distributed to the head-
men in the various villages. These cards were then
redistributed to the poor and entitled them to receive
meat from the slaughtered buffaloes.[3] The animals
were donated by various wealthy people from the
area. However, not all districts had such a distribution to the poor.

On the morning of the tenth, groups of men from
each village walked to the site of Daud Beureuèh's
new mosque chanting the same *ratèb* that they had
chanted on *urou raja puasa*. There, as on the holiday
at the end of the fast, they washed and lined themselves in rows in order to pray. There were about
6,000 people stretched out across the field on which
the mosque was being built. On the foundation of the

---

[3] In all, 6,000 portions of meat were distributed to over 1,000
card holders in our district.

building stood Daud Beureuèh, who led the prayers, his voice amplified through a public-address system. The address which followed the prayers concerned the story of Ibrahim, Hadjar, and Ismail, as is usual on the pilgrimage celebration. As the address sets forth the meaning of the pilgrimage, I will quote it in its entirety:

This is the end of the year. God has prolonged our life. Thanks be to God. The book is closed. We thank God if we have been true. Perhaps some have been evil. If God wills it, we will change; we will change through *ibadat* and by surrendering ourselves to God.

*Urou raja* is the end of the year. At the end of the year we figure our profits if we trade. Then, if we are ahead, we are happy; if behind, sad. So, too, with the community of Muhammed. At the end of the year, the community of Muhammed closes its books with God.

Slaves of God, listen. The close of the year, the close of the book, is the time to make connections between mankind. God closes the book and so we can make connections with each other. Don't forget, besides the relation of God to man, there is also that of man to man. We must respect and pity [*sajang*] each other. All of this is contained in *ibadat*.

The first thing God ordered is the repair of connections between God and man and then of those between man and man in the whole world, in all Islam: in Atjeh, in Indonesia, in the Arab world.

We must acknowledge God's power. We must realize that He is all knowing, all hearing, all seeing. We must acknowledge that there is nothing in the world except by grant of God. We must acknowledge that all the prophets, that Adam, Moses, Jesus, and Muhammed, existed because God willed them. We must acknowledge the pity

of God. After this acknowledgment, [literally, surrender]
Islam, God orders us to unite.

The entire community must, five times a day, face toward Mecca and, at the proper time, pray the daily
prayers. So, too, for the whole Islamic community, we
must come together.

We are with God, we face toward Mecca. When we
pray in assembly [*berdjema'ah*], we are face to face with
each other after prayer. The poor confront the rich, the
evil confront the learned [*alem*], the weak confront the
firm, and the humble confront the proud. In this way,
we know each other, as during the fast the rich can feel
hungry as do the poor. Then the rich can give to the poor.
This is *zakat*. This is the connection. When we come together to pray, we see; then, when we give *zakat*, we do.

Thus the poor have a great right to take what the rich
have a duty to give. The rich are deputies of God; they
have the duty to give God's wealth to the poor. And the
poor must take it; this is their duty. This is *ibadat*.

If this is done, the Islamic community will be strong,
peaceful, and happy. There will be no troubles, no one
will be in want. But if we waste time, if we do not do this,
the result is suffering. With the mercy of God, this will
be so, and suffering will pass.

We have come together to close the book. The people of
one village have come together with those of the next village, and the people of one mosque with those of the next
mosque. So, too, those of one nation have come with
those of the next, and all of the nations have sent representatives to Arabia.

In a short while the pilgrims [who on this day are in
Mina, a few miles from Mecca] will turn in the direction
of Mecca to give thanks and perhaps will make a sacrifice.
The pilgrims will see the places where the Koran was
given to Muhammed. Finally, they will see the place
where Ismail took leave of his mother. There is great

merit [*sunnat rajeuk*; in Indonesian, *sunnat besar*] in making a sacrifice. We are sad as we remember Hadjar's feeling at that moment. And we are sadder still as we compare our lack of belief with the strength of hers.

The pilgrims wear the special clothes of the pilgrimage [white robes]. No longer are there rich and poor, evil and learned, proud and humble people. So dressed, they look at the place of Ibrahim and Hadjar and Ismail and remember how Ibrahim obeyed God's commands even though sad. This is the pilgrimage. Thus we come together village by village, mosque by mosque, and nation by nation. The whole world comes together. The community of Islam should obey all of God's commands. But what can you do [*apa boleh buat*]? Muslims do not obey the commands of God and we live futilely. If we but lived as God commanded, all would be right.

Remember, we are thankful to God. Not for his sake, but for ours. Mankind, with *akal*, gives thanks. It is in this way that we enter the category that began with Adam. Those who give thanks and who sincerely mean it are truly human. How do we do this? Through prayer. And through the relations between us. So that we all live.

Ibrahim was old. He had been married twenty years and he had no children. He asked God for a child and God gave him one. Then God told Ibrahim to go with Hadjar and Ismail to the Holy Land. Then he told Ibrahim to go home, to leave Hadjar and Ismail in the desert. Hadjar asked, "Where can we stay if you go? There is nothing here but desert." Ibrahim answered that it was God's command that she stay. So Hadjar agreed. She left herself in God's hands. Soon, all water was gone. Water came out of the sand. This was the tears of the angels. Because there was water, a country grew up where there was none before.

God ordered Ibrahim to kill Ismail. We would have argued. But Ibrahim did not, he was that faithful to God.

Ibrahim told Ismail what he was going to do. Ismail answered [here Daud Beureuèh quoted in Arabic a line from the Koran]: "Do whatever God commands. I will do what God asks of me." Ismail was not a horse, a cow, a goat, or a sheep, but his son. But without regret, Ibrahim took up a knife, the sharpest he could find, a knife that could split hairs, it was so sharp. He was not like us. If we give a cow for slaughter, we pick the stringiest, leanest one and save the good ones, but Ibrahim took his son.

Allahu Akbar, Allahu Akbar, Allahu Akbar.

Ismail did not cry. Ibrahim did not hesitate. He took up the knife. But the knife, sharp as it was, would not cut. Fire itself will not burn without the grant of God. Then came mercy. God spoke to Ibrahim [here Daud Beureuèh quoted again from the Koran]: "That which you dreamt I ordered to those who are to come." So it is good [*sunnat*] that we sacrifice every year.

I hope that in the future you will give the very best cattle. Not those whose bones are sticking through their skin. When we sacrifice, we store our goods with God. So store the best. If we are loyal to God, we give the very best.

[Then he made an announcement about the distribution of the meat to the poor, concluding, "The poor are the guests of God."]

When we die, we leave nothing. What we take with us is charity, not our bodies or our possessions. It is charity which we take to God. So—the poor should stay and collect their meat. The others go home. Do not wait to shake hands with me since the cattle must be butchered. Otherwise we won't get through until tomorrow and the poor will have to wait. [He concluded with a short prayer in Arabic.]

"This is the end of the year" is the first sentence of the speech. The significance of this to Daud Beureuèh is that "The book is [now] closed," and the community of Muhammed can make connections with each other; unity can be reached. The reasoning here is similar to that for asking pardon after the fast. Whatever happened in the past has been noted. Regardless of what set men against each other, they can now make a new start toward unity. "God closes the book and so we can make connections with each other. . . . The first thing God ordered is the repair of the connections between God and man and then of those between man and man in the whole world, in all of Islam: in Atjeh, in Indonesia, in the Arab world."

Then Daud Beureuèh speaks of the means to achieve unity: acknowledgment of God's power and prayer. The implication of prayer is, of course, the mastery of *akal* over *hawa nafsu*. In this way the past is made insignificant compared with the possibilities of the future, particularly the possibility of unity.

Unity can come only when men recognize their commonality despite their social differences. The reasoning is explicit. "When we pray in assembly, we are face to face with each other after prayer. The poor confront the rich, the evil confront the learned (*alem*), the weak confront the firm, and the humble confront the proud. In this way, we know each other." Recognition of commonality, however, does not come from the fact that the weak and the firm, the poor and the wealthy meet physically during prayers, because, of course, they meet in daily life as well. Rather, it comes from the dominance of *akal* brought about by prayer.

The giving of the rich and the reception of the gift by the poor are not meant to emphasize the moral value of wealth or poverty, but to show the common bonds between Muslims regardless of wealth. On another occasion, during the distribution of the religious payment, the *zakat pitrah*, Daud Beureuèh made some remarks that clarify this point. The payment is collected in each village, usually by the chairman of the *meunasah* and his helpers, and most of it is then distributed to the poor. Daud Beureuèh noted that in his own village only women came to receive that portion given to the poor.[4] He became angry and, in the yard of the *meunasah*, gave a long speech explaining the meaning of the *zakat pitrah*. His point was that neither wealth nor poverty was an indication of moral worth. "Do not feel proud or arrogant because you are able to give," he told the men present. And he said that the absent poor men were committing a sinful act by being ashamed of their poverty and by not collecting their share of the payment. He said then what he said on *urou raja hadji*: "The poor have a great right to take what the rich have a duty to give. . . . And the poor must take it; this is their duty." The rich do not give to the poor because the poor need their help, at least not in the first instance. Indeed, only after talking about the duty of the rich to give and the poor to receive did Daud Beureuèh speak of the need of the poor. Giving and receiving are means of recognizing common belief and, if we

---

[4] Some of the *zakat pitrah* is given to those who collect it, and the rest of it is reserved for community use.

follow the speech, are possible because of the common state brought about in believers through prayer. Without prayer, and thus without the dominance of *akal*, wealth and poverty create sentiments that are inimical to the union of believers. With prayer they appear as obstacles to be overcome, obstacles which show how unity is achieved despite social distinctions.

The points of the speech are punctuated with images of unity. The first of these appears in Daud Beureuèh's discussion of the necessity of establishing connections between God and man and between man and man ("The first thing God ordered was the repair of connections between God and man . . ."). The second such image appears after his words on wealth and poverty and prayer. "We have come together to close the book. The people of one village have come together with those of the next village, and the people of one mosque with those of the next mosque. . . ." This image is similar to the one before it; it is a picture of people in the process of coming together, with smaller units joining to form larger ones. In the first image, we have the repair of connections "in Atjeh, in Indonesia, in the Arab world." In the second, we have the people of one village, the people of one mosque, and the people of one nation all joining with those of the next. The third such image of the speech, however, is one not of joining but of unity achieved. "The pilgrims wear the special clothes of the pilgrimage. No longer are there rich and poor, evil and learned, proud and humble people." Here men no longer have to put aside distinctions in order to join with one another—

they have joined, and there are no distinctions. It is no longer a question of the rich recognizing that the poor are Muslims. At this point, all men are Muslims.

The image of the pilgrims, of unity itself, is a critical point. Up until now there has been an objective macroscopic view. One can almost see the map as, village by village, mosque by mosque, and nation by nation, people come together. But this view, stressing linkage, neglects the other half of unity, the destruction of other kinds of bonds. This second half we see in the story of Ibrahim and Ismail. Here the viewpoint shifts. We no longer see the pilgrims crossing the map, converging on Mecca. Instead we see things through the eyes of the pilgrims themselves at the moment they achieve unity: "So dressed, they look at the place of Ibrahim and Hadjar and Ismail and remember how Ibrahim obeyed God's commands." The story of Ibrahim is told from the point of view of the pilgrims and it is meant to be an explication of the pilgrimage itself: "This is the pilgrimage" is the next sentence. The pilgrims, looking back on what Daud Beureuèh has described objectively, explain how they unite through discarding the distinctions of "rich and poor, evil and learned, proud and humble."

Ibrahim had been married twenty years and was childless when God gave him Ismail. Twice God asked him to give up his son and twice he was willing to do so. He obeyed God not with the assurance that, in the end, God would give Ismail back to him, but simply because God had commanded it. When Hadjar quavered about staying in the desert, Ibrahim did not say that God would provide for her there but only that it was God's command that she (and Ismail) stay. Ibrahim did not plead with God to spare Ismail's life, although "we would have argued." Rather, he "took up a knife, the sharpest he could find, a knife that could split hairs, it was so sharp."

"Then came mercy," but God's mercy is not the moral of the story. The narrative breaks off at this point, and there is no mention of the reunion of Ibrahim with his son. The point of the story is that Ibrahim was willing to give up everything that he most valued in the world and thought that he would have to. It is this refusal not to let worldly values be paramount, it is this willingness to sacrifice that the pilgrims think of when they unite (they "remember how Ibrahim obeyed God's commands even though sad").

The organization of the narrative makes sense only when the point of it is seen to be that true unity comes through the shedding of all worldly ties. The first reference to the story comes when the pilgrims are about to make a sacrifice and see the place where Ismail took leave of his mother. Hadjar's feelings are recalled to emphasize the greatness of her sacrifice. Then the pilgrims are seen at the climax of the pilgrimage, and Ibrahim's sacrifice is remembered. There is no need for Daud Beureuèh to intersperse the story of Ibrahim with the picture of the pilgrims except that by doing so one realizes that the unity of nations means relinquishing personal ties. "This is the pilgrimage" concludes the picture of the united pilgrims thinking of Ibrahim.

The next sentence of the speech, "Thus we come together . . . ," indicates that coming together approximates the unity of the pilgrims and stresses that unity means sacrifice. The central word is "thus" (*djadi*). In Indonesian, as in English, *djadi* or "thus" can mean "consequently," but it can also mean "in this way." That it is used here in the second sense is shown by the fact that the full story of Ibrahim is told with both the pilgrims and the audience in mind and comes only after the audience itself is added to the picture of the pilgrims. This "thus" is intended to include the audience and to set forth an example they must follow: in order to unite, they must make sacrifices. Clearly Daud Beureuèh is speaking no longer of the united pilgrims alone but also of the audience who, presumably, is striving to emulate the pilgrims.

The pilgrims, dressed in identical white robes and thinking of the sacrifice, are an image of Muslim unity. No longer are there distinctions between them, for no longer does the social world exist. The tension has been resolved not by changing the world but by eliminating it. Yet this image is not merely one of men without society. It is also an image of *akal*. In the 1930s "society" was a metaphor for the new awareness, for *akal*. The attempt to "realize" society was an attempt to know what man is by creating an image of *akal*, society itself. With the construction of a real society, however, the process was reversed. Now *akal* is revealed not by building a society but by dissolving it. Yet *akal* is not merely what is left when society no longer exists. *Akal* is one of two faculties, and it has a recognizable and characteristic function. It is the faculty by which man knows, and its function is to know God's commands and so to obey them. If we think about the construction of Daud Beureuèh's speech, we can see how the image of unity, which emerges from the destruction of social bonds, is an image of *akal*.

The final image is that of Ibrahim with his knife raised, about to kill Ismail. Yet, this is not the entire image for it also includes, as we have seen, the pilgrims thinking of Ibrahim about to kill Ismail as well as the audience thinking of the pilgrims thinking of Ibrahim. The interpolation of the final picture of coming together ("Thus we come together village by village . . .") after the story of the pilgrims looking at "the place of Ibrahim and Hadjar" adds another level to the story of Ibrahim and Ismail. Only after the audience itself is added to the picture of the pilgrims is the story of Ibrahim actually told.

The effect of this is to emphasize *akal* as a faculty, as something interior to man. The story is told as though it were reflected down a hall of mirrors, each mirror throwing back the same image. The result is that we are aware of the mirrors, of *akal* as the faculty of consciousness, as much as we are aware of the image itself. We see the story set in the minds of the people reflecting on it. By multiplying the number of minds, we become aware of the faculty of awareness itself.

Yet the awareness of the faculty of awareness pictures interior life alone with no exterior concomitant.

In the 1930s "society," we see now, was a metaphor
for *akal*. To Atjehnese at the time, however, society
was not a metaphor but a real possibility for the exte-
riorization of *akal*. The end of that hope created a
dilemma which is both posed and resolved in the celebration of the pilgrimage. The resolution is the image
of Ibrahim, knife raised to kill his son. The act, contrary to everything that Ibrahim felt, was perfect
obedience of God's command. *Akal* is seen no longer
as a faculty but as an unambiguous act.

Yet it is not a true resolution. No man after Muhammed can have direct experience of God. It is only
through *akal* that men today can approach knowledge
of God. God cannot be known apart from *akal*.
Furthermore, the destruction of the bonds of *hawa
nafsu*, symbolized by the act of sacrifice, is not possible in a world where *hawa nafsu* is a part of man's
nature. And so the image of Ibrahim remains an
image in the mind, not directly translatable into life.

Ibrahim, his knife raised, and Ismail, about to accept the blow that never falls—this is the final image.
God's mercy comes, but we see neither Ibrahim and
Ismail reunited nor even Ibrahim's arm relaxed. For
the audience, the knife remains poised. Men, stripped
of social distinctions, are united not because they have
left the world behind but because they are aware of
the tension between themselves and the world. If they
know that the world corrupts, that they act as social
beings rather than as true Muslims, they are also
aware of a part of their nature which is immune to the
world and which, when properly used, makes them

strive in another direction. And so there remains the hope that men will "bind themselves together with the rope of God, the rope which neither rots in the rain nor cracks in the sun."

# REFERENCES

# APPENDIX:
# A NOTE ON COMMUNITAS
# AND THE ROPE OF GOD

In the Morgan Lectures of 1966, Victor Turner developed the idea of communitas as the expression of "a generic human bond without which there would be no society" (p. 4). Because this idea is germane to the Atjehnese notion of the rope of God, I would like to make a few remarks about it. Liminality, the middle period in rites of passage, was the first of Turner's examples of communitas. Structural inferiority and millenarian movements are other examples.

Let me start by speaking of communitas in its setting in rites of passage. In cultures where social roles define one's being, there is necessarily a moment when, in transition between roles, men are neither what they were nor what they will be (Turner, 1967: 95). The novice or initiand necessarily experiences a time of unstructuredness. During this time men are thought of in ways that indicate that they are out of time and out of place. In Turner's words: "A society's secular definitions do not allow for the existence of a not-boy-not-man, which is what a novice in a male puberty rite is (if he can be said to be anything). A set of essentially religious definitions co-exist with these which do set out to define the structurally indefinable 'transitional being'" (1967: 95). In the Morgan Lectures, Turner listed the qualities of transition stressed in the symbolism of liminality. They include "homogeneity, equality, anonymity" (1966: 22), as well as many others. Among the initiands so described there exists "a community or comity of comrades and not a structure of hierarchically arrayed positions" (Turner 1967: 100). The implication is that the sense of linkage is derived from the common experience of unstructuredness. As Turner goes on to say: "This comradeship, with its familiarity, ease and, I would add, mutual outspokenness, is once more the product of interstructural liminality, with its scarcity of jurally sanctioned relationships and its emphasis on axiomatic values expressive of the common weal" (1967: 101).

In addition to the experience of unstructuredness and the resulting sense of belonging to a "community ... of comrades," novices also learn the basic, axiomatic ideas of their culture. It is in the liminal period that the sacra, sacred symbols, and sacerima, most sacred symbols and ideas, are displayed to the initiands. The sacra and sacerima are emblems or embodiments of "axiomatic principles of construction and certain basic building blocks that make up the cosmos" (Turner, 1967: 106). Turner says about them that "The central cluster of nonlogical sacra is then the symbolic template of the whole system of beliefs and values in a given culture, its archetypical paradigm and ultimate measure" (1967: 108). The experience of structurelessness is the source of the feeling of belonging to a "community or comity of comrades." However, the generic human bond is expressed through the symbolism of the basic nature of

the universe, which the initiands have discovered together. Men know that they are united because they
have discovered what they are and what the world is.
This explains Turner's statement that "liminality may
perhaps be regarded as the Nay to all positive structural assertions, but it is in some sense the source of
them all . . ." (1967: 97).

At no point in Atjehnese rituals can one say that
there is necessarily a moment of unstructuredness.
Nor is it correct to say that structurelessness inheres
in the nature of man himself. What is displayed in
the shift of religious goals in Atjehnese history is
not an experience of the undefined but an attempt to
make explicit a conception of man's nature which is
already known. The movement from paradise to a
new society and from a new society to the pilgrimage
demonstrates a consistent adherence to a belief. The
validity of *akal* and *hawa nafsu* is never questioned.
Rather *akal* and *hawa nafsu* are permanent points of
reference by way of which experience is conceptualized.[1]

While the meaning of *akal* and *hawa nafsu* do not

[1] It may be useful at this point to compare marginality in
America with that in Atjeh. Turner speaks of the beats and
their successors (1966: 23). He sees in these movements elements
of the sacred in their use of terms such as "angels" and "saints."
However, it may be more accurate to think of such American
movements not as attempts at communitas, which involves the
sacred, but simply as movements which try to realize generic
human bonds without sacra. Surely the exceedingly rapid change
in the symbols of these movements and their very short lives indicate an absence of belief in the sacred. In Atjeh, on the other
hand, the shift in religious goals displays a continuing belief in
*akal* and *hawa nafsu*.

change in Atjehnese history, the goals by which they are expressed do change. Furthermore there is always a discontinuity between these goals and current social states. This very discontinuity accounts for the similarities between Atjehnese ideas of the rope of God and communitas.

The shift in religious goals in Atjehnese history demonstrates the relationship of personal experience to conceptualization of that experience. Experience is, of course, prior. Only when men repeated the experience of the *ulama*, only when they had important and continuous social relationships outside the family, did they have an awareness of the *ulama*'s intent in the reform movements. The goal of a new society conceptualized that experience in the 1930s. However, this conceptualization of experience meant translating subjective states into objective modes and thus falsified those states. What was an aspect of the interior state of a person could not become a property of society without changing its meaning. The confusion was resolved when the idea of a new society was forgotten, and a clearer conception of the distinction between men and society was formulated in the celebration of the pilgrimage.

In the celebration of the pilgrimage men are aware of the difference between themselves and the world, and are therefore also aware of their commonness and their potential for union. The expression of the distinction between man and society may produce a feeling of connectedness, a genuine experience of linkage despite social bonds. But again, consciousness and social reality are not congruent. Men are aware of their separateness from society. Although this may produce a sensation of unity, men are aware not of unity but of the difficulties in achieving it. They could not turn their attention to the reality of their unity without destroying the distinction between themselves and the world and hence the basis of their sensation of unity. Men's potential for unity rests on awareness of their nature which in turn is possible only if man and society remain distinct.

There is no time in Atjeh when men are outside structure and aware of unity. Consciousness is always out of phase with current experience. But it is the very fact that consciousness is one thing and the situation of men another which is the condition for men's discovery of consciousness itself. The experience of generic human bonds, if it exists in Atjeh, rests not on the experience of structurelessness but on the shared discovery by men that they are basically alike. Turner says of the symbolism of liminality that it "gives an outward and visible form to an inward and conceptual process" (1967: 96). It is the experience of the discovery of something basic and inward in men, which in ritual is expressed in an "outward and visible form," rather than structurelessness, that produces a sense of generic human bonds. Men's experience in society has in one sense taught them about themselves. Only in ritual, however, is this teaching in a literal sense realized.

# GLOSSARY

achirat — The hereafter.

adat — Custom.

adat peutuha — The share of the yield of the pepper garden that belongs to the *peutuha seunubok* (see below).

akal — The faculty by which one knows God's commands; reason.

alem — A person with some learning in Islam, but not as learned as an *ulama*. (In Arabic, *alem* is the singular of *ulama*.)

aneuk — Child.

aneuk kedè — Term sometimes used for apprentices.

aneuk seunubok — The workers in the pepper gardens.

ashar — Afternoon; the afternoon prayer.

banta — An aide or deputy of an *uleebelang*.

Barat — West; the Western region of Atjeh.

blang — Rice fields.

bupati — The head of a regency (*kapubaten*).

chanduri — Feast.

dadap — The plant around which pepper vines twine themselves.

dja' utimo — Literally, "to go to the East." An expression that means to leave one's home area and find one's way elsewhere. Cf. *rantau*.

donja — The world; this world, as opposed to the next.

fikh — Islamic law.

gampong — Village.

geumeuklèh — The term which designates the status of a married woman whose parents are no longer responsible for her support; literally, "separated."

hariah | Official of the *uleebelang* responsible for collecting taxes in the market; a deputy of the *sjahbandar peukan*.

hawa nafsu | The part of man's nature that he shares with the animals; everything within man that arises spontaneously.

hukum | Law.

ibadah (ibadat) | Religious duty, especially the "five pillars of Islam": the confession of faith, the five daily prayers (*sembajang*), the religious payments (*zakat pitrah*), the pilgrimage, and the fasting month.

Idulfitri | See *urou raja puasa*.

imeum | An official of the *uleebelang* in charge of a subdivision of the *uleebelang's* area known as a *mukim*.

isja | Night; the prayer recited at night.

kadi (kali) | Islamic judge; an official of the *uleebelang*.

kanduri | See *chanduri*.

katjang kuning | Yellow bean.

katjang merah | Kidney bean.

ketjamatan | A subdivision of a regency headed by a *tjamat*.

kramat | Having supernatural qualities (Echols and Shadily, 1961).

kriet | Stingy.

leube | Village religious practitioner.

lueng | Channel, especially an irrigation channel.

malèkat | Angel.

mawaih | Name of the arrangement whereby the owner of a rice field rents it to a worker in return for half of the yield.

meudagang | "To study in a *pesantren*" (Snouck Hurgronje, 1906: II, 26).

| | |
|---|---|
| meunasah | Dormitory and meeting place for men. |
| mohgreb | Sunset; the prayer said at sunset. |
| mukim | A subdivision of an area ruled by an *uleebelang*. See *imeum*. |
| nanggrou | The area of an *uleebelang* (not used in all parts of Atjeh). |
| njang po rumoh | Slang expression for wife; literally, "the one who owns the house." |
| orang kaja | Officials of the sultan who worked within Bandar Atjeh; literally, "rich men." |
| padi | Unhusked rice. |
| pangkai | Capital. |
| panglima prang | Official of the *uleebelang* who led wars; also an official of the sultan with the same task. |
| pesantren | Religious boarding school. |
| peukan | Weekly market. |
| peutuha pangkai | Person who furnishes capital for a pepper garden. |
| peutuha seunubok | Person in charge of the working of a pepper garden; the person who arranges for the providing of capital and the procuring of workers in a pepper garden. |
| POESA | Persatoean Oelama Seloeroeh Atjeh (All-Atjeh Union of Religious Scholars). |
| prang sabi | Holy war. |
| puasa | To fast; the fasting month. |
| putron aneuk | Ceremony at the end of the period of the mother's seclusion following birth. |
| raka'at | Division of the ritual prayers. |
| rakan | The followers of an *uleebelang*; friend. |
| rantau | Indonesian word meaning "to leave one's home area" (Echols and Shadily, 1961). |
| ratèb | Religious chant. |

| | |
|---|---|
| rudjak | A salad of raw, unripened fruit. |
| rumbia | A kind of fern or palm used for making thatch. |
| sarakata | Letter patent issued by the sultan. |
| sawah | Wet rice field. |
| sembajang | To perform any of the five daily prayers. |
| seunubok | Pepper garden. |
| sjariat | Islamic law. |
| subuh | Daybreak; the prayer recited at daybreak. |
| sunat | Refers to practices recommended but not obligatory in Islam. |
| surah | Chapter of the Koran. |
| tarekat | A mystical order. |
| teungku | Title originally given to those learned in Islam but now used for all men. |
| teungku ineong | Title given to women in the village who teach girls about Islam. |
| teungku tjihk | Title given to the oldest man in the village who has some learning in Islam. |
| Timo | East; the Eastern region of Atjeh. |
| tipu | Cheated, taken. |
| tjamat | The head of a subdivision of a regency known as a *ketjamatan*. |
| tjintju | Bus conductor. |
| ulama | Religious scholar. (Both singular and plural, unlike its Arabic root.) |
| uleebelang | Traditional chieftain. |
| ureung | Man. |
| urou raja hadji | The celebration held locally on the tenth day of the month of the pilgrimage to commemorate the pilgrimage. |
| urou raja puasa | The holiday marking the end of the fasting month, which occurs on the first day (Idulfitri) of the month (Sjawwal) following the fast. |

| wasè | Duty, tariff. |
| wasè djalan | Duty collected by the *uleebelang* from those not living in his area in return for their passage through his area. |
| wasè lueng | Duty collected from pepper growers for use of an irrigation channel built by an *uleebelang*. |
| wasè uleebelang | Export duties collected by the *uleebelang*. |
| zakat pitrah | Religious payment obligatory for all Muslims who can afford to pay it. |
| zuhur | Noon; the prayer recited at noon. |

# LITERATURE CITED

A. So'dy
1941 "Fajdar Keinsafan menjingsing dioefoek timoer tanah Rentjong" [The Dawn of Consciousness Breaks on the Eastern Horizon of the Land of the Rentjong]. *Penjoeloeh* (October).

Aboebakar Atjeh
1962 *Pengantar Sedjarah Sufi dan Tasawwuf* [Introduction to the History of Sufi and Tasawwuf]. Bandung: Tjerdas.

Anderson, John
1840 *Acheen and the Ports on the North and East Coasts of Sumatra.* London: Wm. H. Allen.

Anonymous
1923 *De Rijkdom van Atjeh* [The Kingdom of Atjeh]. Amsterdam: De Atjeh–Instituut.

Arberry, A. J. (trans.)
1955 *The Koran Interpreted.* London: George Allen and Unwin.

Asmara Aini
1940 "Memperkokoh Tenaga moeda. Bahan-bahan Jang Penting Oentoek Menghidoepkan Semangat Pemoeda Dalam Bekerdja" [Strengthening the Power of the Young: Important Materials for Giving Life to the Spirit of the Youth in Their Work]. *Penjoeloeh* (December).

Atjeher
1939 "Atjeh Problemen" [Atjehnese Problems]. *Penjedar* (December 14).
1940 "Menanti Keadilan dari Radja" [Waiting for Justice from the Radjas]. *Penjedar* (March 14).

Benda, Harry
1958 *The Crescent and the Rising Sun.* The Hague and Bandung: W. van Hoeve.

Braddell, T. (ed. and trans.)
1850 "Ceremony Observed at the Court of Acheen." *Journal of the Indian Archipelago and Eastern Asia,* IV: 728–733.
1851a "Translations from the Majellis Ache." *Journal of the Indian Archipelago and Eastern Asia,* V: 26–32.

Braddell, T.
1851b "On the History of Acheen." *Journal of the Indian Archipelago and Eastern Asia,* V: 15–25.

Damsté, H. T. (ed. and trans.)
  1928   *Hikajat Prang Sabi* [Story of the Holy War], in *Bijdragen tot de Taal-, Land-, en Volkenkunde van Nederlandsch–Indie*, LXXXIV.

Das Gupta, A. K.
  1962   "Atjeh in the 17th-Century Asian Trade." *Bengal: Past and Present*, LXXXI (January–June).

Dept. van Economische Zaken
  1935   *Volkstelling* [Census]. Vol. IV. Batavia: Landsdrukkerij.

Dewey, Alice.
  1962   *Peasant Marketing in Java*. Glencoe, Illinois: Free Press.

Djajadiningrat, R. Hoesein
  1910   "Critisch Overzicht van de Maleische Werken Vervatte Gegevens over de Geschiedenis van het Soeltanaat van Atjeh" [Critical Review of Malay Works Containing Data on the History of the Sultanate of Atjeh]. *Bijdragen tot de Taal-, Land-, en Volkenkunde van Nederlandsch–Indie*, LXV.

Drewes, G. W. J., and P. Voorhoeve (eds.)
  1958   *Adat Atjeh*, in *Verhandelingen van het Koninklijk Instituut voor Taal-, Land-, en Volkenkunde*. The Hague: Martinus Nijhoff.

Echols, John, and Hassan Shadily
  1961   *An Indonesian–English Dictionary*. Ithaca: Cornell University Press.

Economische Vereeniging "Atjeh" (later, De Handelsvereeniging te Koeta–Radja)
  1925–1937   *Jaarverslagen over 1924–1936* [Annual Reports for 1924–1936]. Koeta–Radja: Atjeh–Drukkerij.

Encyclopaedisch Bureau
  1913   *De Pepercultuur in de Buitenbezittingen* [Pepper Cultivation in the Outer Possessions]. Batavia: Landsdrukkerij.
  1916   Bureau voor de Bestuurszaken der Buitenbezittingen. *De Buitenbezittingen: Atjeh en Onderhoorigheden* [The Outer Possessions: Atjeh and Dependencies.] Vol. II, Part 2, Weltevreden.

Geertz, Clifford
  1963   *Peddlars and Princes*. Chicago: University of Chicago Press.

Gennep, Arnold van
  1960   *Rites of Passage*. Chicago: University of Chicago Press.

Gibb, H. A. R., and J. H. Kramers (eds.)
1953 *Shorter Encyclopedia of Islam*. Ithaca: Cornell University Press.
Gonggrijp, J. R. C.
1944 *Overzicht van de Economische Ontwikkeling van Atjeh Sedert het Pacificatie*. [Outline of the Economic Development of Atjeh from the Time of the Pacification]. The Hague: W. P. Stockum.
Grunebaum, G. E. von
1955 *Islam: Essays in the Nature and Growth of a Cultural Tradition*. American Anthropological Association, LVII: 2, Part 2. Memoir No. 81.
Gullick, J. M.
1958 *Indigenous Political Systems of Western Malaya*. London: Athlone Press.
Hall, D. G. E.
1958 *A History of South-East Asia*. London: Macmillan.
Ismail Jakoeb
[1939] Typescript of a letter sent to the committee formed to establish the POESA.
1940 "Verslag Ringkas Congress POESA ke-1" [Short Report of the First POESA Congress]. *SINAR* (May).
Ismail Jakub
1960 *Tengku Tjhik di-Tiro*. 3rd. ed. Djakarta: Bulan Bintang.
Ismail Taib
1941 "Pemoeda Dan Persatoean Di Atjeh" [Youth and Unity in Atjeh]. *Penjoeloeh* (February).
Jacobs, J.
1894 *Het Familie en Gampongleven op Groot-Atjeh* [Family and Village Life in Great Atjeh]. Leiden: E. J. Brill.
Jongejans, J.
[1939] *Land en Volk van Atjeh Vroeger en Nu* [Land and People of Atjeh Formerly and Now]. Baarn: Hollandia Drukkerij.
Juynboll, Th. W.–[P. Voorhoeve]
1960 "Atjeh," in *The Encyclopaedia of Islam*. New edition. Leiden: E. J. Brill.
Khedourie, Elie
1966 *Afghani and Abduh: An Essay in Religious Unbelief and Political Activism in Modern Islam*. New York: Humanities Press.
Khoo Hock Cheng
1959 "The Trade of Penang, 1786–1823." Singapore: University of Malaya.

Kreemer, J.
1917 "Wetenschappelijk Onderzoek van Atjeh en Onderhoorigheden" [Scientific Investigation of Atjeh and
Dependencies]. *Tijdschrift van het Koninklijk Nederlandsch Aardrijkskundig Genootschap* [Journal of the
Royal Dutch Geographical Society], XXXIV: 153–168,
397–401, 738–748.
1922 *Atjeh.* 2 vols. Leiden: E. J. Brill.

Kruijt, J. A.
1877 *Atjeh en de Atjehers: Twee Jaren Blokkade op Sumatra's
Noord-Oost Kust* [Atjeh and the Atjehnese: Two-Year
Blockade of Sumatra's Northeast Coast]. Leiden:
Gualth Kolff.

Loon, F. H. van
1920 "Het Krankzinningenvraagstuk in Atjeh" [The Problem
of Lunatics in Atjeh]. *Mededeelingen van den Burger-
lijken Geneeskundigen Dienst in Nederlandsch–Indie*
[Announcements of the Civilian Medical Service in the
Dutch East Indies], X: 2–50.

Marsden, W.
1811 *History of Sumatra.* 3rd ed. London: privately printed.

Mohammed Said
1961 *Atjeh Sepandjang Abad* [Atjeh Through the Centuries].
Vol. I. [Medan?]: privately printed.

Muhd. Oetsman [Oestman] al Muhammady
1941 "Apa Sebab Kaoem Muslimin Moendoer? Dimana sal-
ahnja?—Bagaimana memperbaikinja?—adakah Islam
itoe agama kemoendoeran, agama kendoeri dan selamatan?" [What Is the Reason for the Backwardness of
the Islamic Community? What Went Wrong?—How
Can the Situation Be Improved?—Is Islam a Religion
of Backwardness, a Religion of Chanduri and Selamatan?]. *Penjoeloeh* (August).

Nadroen Adamiy [Adamy] Medan
1941 "Didikan Kebenaran" [Education in the Truth]. *Penjoeloeh* (October).

Oesman Raliby
1941 "Masjarakat Atjeh Baroe" [The New Atjehnese Society].
*Penjoeloeh* (October).

Piekaar, A. J.
1949 *Atjeh en de Oorlog met Japan* [Atjeh and the War with
Japan]. The Hague: W. van Hoeve

Poerwadarminta
1960    *Kamus Umum Bahasa Indonesia* [General Dictionary
        of the Indonesian Language]. 3rd printing. Djakarta:
        Dinas Penerbitan Balai Pustaka.

Puvanarajah, T.
1960    "Penang's Early Relations with Sumatra, 1786–1824."
        Singapore: University of Malaya.

Ritter, W. L.
1838–1839   "Korte Aanteekeningen over het Rijk van Atjeh"
            [Short Notes about the Kingdom of Atjeh]. *Tijdschrift
            voor Nederlandsch Indie* [Journal of the Dutch East
            Indies], I: 454–476; II: 1–27, 67–90.

Schrieke, B.
1955    *Indonesian Sociological Studies*. Part One. The Hague
        and Bandung: W. van Hoeve.

Snouck Hurgronje, C.
1906    *The Achehnese*. Translated by A. W. S. O'Sullivan. 2
        vols. Leiden: E. J. Brill.

1924    "Eene onbezonnen vraag" [A Rash Question]. Originally
        published in 1899; reprinted in *Verspreide Geschriften
        van C. Snouck Hurgronje* [Collected Writings of C.
        Snouck Hurgronje] (Bonn and Leipzig: Kurt Schroed-
        er), Vol. IV, Part One.

1957    *Ambtelijke Adviezen van C. Snouck Hurgronje, 1889–
        1936* [Official Advice of C. Snouck Hurgronje, 1889–
        1936]. Edited by E. Gobee and C. Adriaanse. Vol. I.
        The Hague: Martinus Nijhoff.

Swift, M. G.
1965    *Malay Peasant Society in Jelebu*. London: The Athlone
        Press.

T. T.
1942    "Nasehat Gratis: (Kata Orang Kritik) Soeatoe Toed-
        joean:" [Free Advice: (The Words of a Critic) An
        Aim:]. *Penjoeloeh* (January and February).

Tarling, N.
1963    *Piracy and Politics in the Malay World*. Singapore:
        Donald Moore Gallery.

Tolsen, G. P.
1880    "Acheh, Commonly Called Achin." *Journal of the Royal
        Asiatic Society*, Straits Branch, V: 37–50.

Victor Turner
  1966   Untitled Morgan Lectures. Mimeographed.
  1967   *The Forest of Symbols*. Ithaca: Cornell University Press.
Veth, P. J.
  1873   *Atchin en Zijne Betrekkingen tot Nederland; Topogra-
          phisch–Historische Beschrijving* [Atjeh and Its Relations
          with the Netherlands; Topographical and Historical De-
          scription]. Leiden: Gualth Kolff.

# INDEX

A. So'dy, quoted, 123–24, 125, 126

Abbas (cloth merchant): background, 202–03; store described, 203–04; apprentices, tailor, 203–04, 205–06; business profits, 204–05

Abdul Muis (cloth merchant), 212n; establishes Takengon store, 214; mode of operation, 215–16

Abdullah (tailor), 203, 204

Abyssinians, in Bandar Atjeh Dar-es-Salaam, 37

*Achirat*, 67, 74

Adam: created, 99; put on earth, 100–01

*Adat*: and Islam, 9–12; as basis for Atjehnese society, 70

*Adat Atjeh*, quoted, 39–40, 41, 47

Agriculture, Atjehnese. *See* Areco nuts; Beans; Coconuts; Cucumbers; Garlic; Ground nuts; Onions; Rice; Tobacco

*Akal*, 124, 126, 183, 198, 281; given to man by God, 100; enables man to regain paradise, 101; as control over *hawa nafsu*, 102–04; and prayer, 104, 108, 109, 114–15, 267; and *ibadah*, 119; and cyclical view of history, 120; and idea of new society, 130–31; and husband–father role, 137; and boys leaving family, 146; and indulgence of children, 149–50, 153–54; and experience in the market, 182, 243–44,

245, 250; and fasting, 191; and providing for one's family, 194; regained after *puasa*, 195, 196; within family, 197; and social conservatism, religious radicalism, 251–52; unifying nature of, 254–55; meaning for villagers, 256; and new unity in the *1930s*, 258–60; and pilgrimage, 261; and society, 272–73; as faculty interior to man, 273–74

Al Raniri, 121

Alas, 14

*Alem*, 57, 58

Ali Mughayat Shah, Sultan, 4

All-Atjeh Union of Religious Scholars. *See* POESA

Anderson, John, 15; quoted, 16

*Aneuk*, 115

Apprentices: in cloth stores, 203–04, 205–07, 208, 212–13, 217; in bus companies, 219; and masters, kinship and common locality, 246–47

Arabic, 37, 39; as mandatory language for prayers, 110

Arabs: in Bandar Atjeh Dar-es-Salaam, 37; as traders, 85

Arberry, A. J., 75n, 151

Areca nut: as export, 14, 16, 93; in Pidie, 24, 27

Asan Kambang, 204

Asmara Aini, quoted, 128–29

Atjeh, Atjehnese: history, 3–6; rebellion (*1953–1961*), 6; Japanese occupation, 6, 89, 203, 207; regions, 12–14; map, 13; trade, 14–29; ex-

# ACEH VIEWED IN 1978 AND 1999

# CURING RIGHTS, DREAMS, AND DOMESTIC POLITICS IN A SUMATRAN SOCIETY

One widespread form of curing ritual is that in which spirits in the body of the patient speak through mediums or curers. Raymond Firth has described a form of this rite in Kelantan on the west coast of Malaysia.[1] He sees the ritual as a means of expression for the patient. In it, the patient states "issues in [her] life and behavior which relate to [her] illness." However, he also points out that the language is "stereotyped and follows conventional formula while the issues mentioned are trivial."[2] Clive Kessler has discerned the political dimension of these rites and capitalized on the cryptic quality of the language.[3] He sees the rituals as a way for women to say things that

I have noted the contributions of Sandra Siegel in several places in the body of the text. Her contributions, however, exceed that. My understanding was developed partly in opposition to her own notions of Acehnese curing and dreaming. Though she has refused to be so listed, she could rightfully claim to be coauthor of this piece.

The data in the paper were collected in 1962–64 under a Ford Foundation Foreign Area Training Fellowship and in 1969–70 under an Office of Education Area Center Faculty Grant.

The orthography of Acehnese words follows that of R. Hoesein Djajadiningrat in his *Atjehsch-Nederlandsch Woordenboek* (Batavia: Lansdrukkerij, 1934).

[1] Raymond Firth, "Ritual and Drama in Malay Spirit Mediumship," *Comparative Studies in Society and History* 9 (1967).

[2] Ibid.

[3] Clive Kessler, "Conflict and Sovereignty in Kelantanese

enhance their position vis-à-vis their husbands, which if expressed in everyday language would either cause trouble or be of no avail.

I want to follow Kessler's linkage of curing rites and domestic politics in a society in the same part of the world, namely, Aceh in Sumatra. But I want to suggest that the Acehnese ritual, similar but not identical in form to the Malay one, can best be understood not by decoding the message of the patient but by looking at the relation of language and "person."[4]

Relations between Acehnese husbands and wives are governed by an unspoken contract; there are men's duties and women's duties, and it is the fulfillment of the contract rather than the emotional attachment that is the foundation of an Acehnese marriage. Men have the obligation to furnish money and market goods, while women furnish food and their labor raising children.[5] The delineation of exchange, however, does not completely describe notions of authority in the family. Men feel they

---

Malay Spirit Mediumship," in *Case Studies in Malay Spirit Possession,* ed. V. Crapanzano and V. Garrison (New York: Wiley-Interscience, 1977).

[4] The chief differences between the Acehnese and Malay rituals are noted later. It is, however, important that the Acehnese ritual lacks the metaphor of the body as a state that Kessler has brilliantly demonstrated for the Kelantanese rite.

[5] See Chandra Jayawardena, "Women and Kinship in Acheh Besar," *Ethnology* 16 (1977); and his "Achehnese Marriage Customs," *Indonesia* (April 1977); as well as chapter 7 of the current volume; and Snouck Hurgronje, *The Achehnese* (Leiden: E. J. Brill, 1906).

have the right to tell their wives what to do—how to raise children, what to cook for dinner, and whatever else—whenever they are present, not only because they live up to their part of the contract but because they feel they "know" better. It is certainly not experience that gives them this feeling. They spend very little time at home, and their suggestions are usually impractical. The reason they feel they can command is that they sense themselves to be beings of superior rationality. This is not a quality innate to them but is rather something they feel they have achieved through religion. They believe that reciting the five daily prayers and chanting the Koran put them in a state of purified rationality, one in which their energies and desires are controlled and they can find solutions to whatever might arise.[6]

They have, then, a religious basis to their feeling of being authoritative. It is important to note that this religious basis is not in itself substantive. What they learn reading the Koran does not tell them anything directly about daily life, and, in Aceh at least, there is no important body of interpretation that translates God's revelations made in seventh-century Arabia into the context of twentieth-century Indonesia. Nor do they receive inspiration from God during prayer. God does not speak to them or tell them what to do. In the daily prayers what is important is to repeat the Arabic words precisely while making the appropriate gestures with hands, trunk, head, and legs

[6] This has been described in chapters 6 and 9 of this volume.

absolutely accurately. In prayer one's mind and body, including one's mouth, move not as though one controlled them oneself but as though by so moving them one becomes the tracer of sacred commands. It is not essential to understand the words that one makes with one's mouth, though most Acehnese do know what they mean. It is important that one's mind be focused in the activities of prayer, not because one might make a mistake—after years of praying 150 times a month that is not likely—but in order to be clear of any thoughts that might result in alteration of one's gestures. Chanting the Koran is similar; most Acehnese do not understand what they read, but it is important that they chant correctly. It is as though they make the letters of the holy book speak, not in the sense of making them understood to others or themselves but simply by making themselves the audible correlate of the written words. These gestures are thought, if not to purify the Acehnese Muslim from desires that arise in him, at least to put him in control of them and to leave his mind clear to function.

It is these religious gestures that are the basis of men's right to speak. For to them, what they earn in the market (and bring home with them) is derivative of the rationality gained through prayer.

It is probably not accidental that this fits very well with traditional Acehenese notions about language. To begin with, the word for language—*basa*—refers not only to spoken language but to gestures and behavior as well. Thus one says of someone that he "has language," meaning that "he behaves well," that his manners, his demeanor are appropriate. One uses the same phrase of someone who knows, say, Malay ("he has Malay language"). If someone is crude, one says, "He has no language," which we would have to translate as "he doesn't know how to act." But this would be a mistranslation in the same way that translating the sentence about Malay as "knowing" rather than "having" Malay would be wrong. For one *has* language not when one can understand the meaning of linguistic signs or can vocalize it but rather when one "brings" or "bears," perhaps "suffers," language. There is another word for "understand," derived from Arabic, that usually means to "grasp the meaning of." The word that means to "have" a language is not to "understand" it but to "get a fix on it"—*toepeuë;* the root of the word means "what," "how," "where." It is a question of location, because linguistic signs to Acehnese are as visible as audible signs—thus behavior is included. There is even a unique verbal form of the word for "language" *(basa)* that means "to make a gesture." The correlate of this is that the word usually translated as "voice" means not "voice" but "noise" and is applied in phrases such as the "noise of the tree." A human (or animal) "voice" is "the noise of the mouth." It is the gesture of the moving mouth as well as the sound that issues from it that is involved in the relation of voice to language.[7]

[7] In traditional Acehnese literature, however, sound is privileged not because the sound of the voice contains one's ideas in

Thus one who prays "has" God's language not when he "understands" God's word (when he can put the Arabic into Acehnese) but when his own body reproduces God's words. It is essential to note that this happens in relation to writing. Mohammed is the seal of prophecy. No one alive on earth will hear God's voice or should try to do so. To pray is not to recover God's meaning but to trace or conform oneself to God's writings. One thus "becomes" the signs. These written graphs are reproduced or carried in visible or audible gestures. It is by this that men become rational, become authoritative.

When one listens to the speech of Acehnese it is easy to tell men from women and not simply by the quality of their voices. Men seldom speak. This is not because they value silence but because they think they should speak only when they have something of significance to say. Their speech expresses their rationalist nature; it must therefore be substantive. The result is that it is usually portentous in tone but banal or absurd in content. Limiting oneself to saying only what is so limits one to the obvious or nearly obvious. Conversations with men tend to be confined to subjects such as what bus passed by, prices of various commodities, and other matters of fact. When they speak to their wives men are freed from the con-

---

closest proximity to oneself but because sound is believed to be continuous and thus to obliterate all distinctions. See James T. Siegel, *Shadow and Sound: The Historical Thought of a Sumatran People* (Chicago: University of Chicago Press, 1979), chapter 1.

straints of experience, which does nothing to lighten their tone but rather allows them to utter an order for duck for dinner or to have a child washed up and make it sound highly important. Women, on the other hand, chatter continuously. Their activities are always filled with sounds, illustrating the Indonesian concept of *ramai*—or noisemaking activity. What they say is only occasionally outrageous, but they feel no constraint to be rational. However, neither do they conceive of themselves as irrational. Rather their speech to them is authority that comes from a different source. In their struggle with their husbands they win not simply by subverting men's belief in themselves as rational but by feeling no hesitation to speak. It is my contention that they find a source analogous to the Koran for the resultant authoritative tone in curing rites and dreams.

Acehnese curing rituals are similar to those of Kelantan but somewhat simpler. There is no music and no dancing. They differ also in that the curer— or medium—is always a woman, while the patients are mostly women or children and occasionally an old man (in the last case, usually someone unusual in that he has spent his life in the village farming rather than out of the village trading).

The rites themselves involve two sets of spirits: the djinns, or the spirits who have caused the illness, and the spirits who "belong" to the medium—the *pòtjoets*—who enter the body of the sick person to out the djinns.

In the curing rites themselves, the sick person usually lies on a mat on the floor while the medium sits with her legs crossed next to her. There are ordinarily one or two other women of the house present as well, and neighbors may occasionally drop in if they hear the noises of the ceremony. (I have the impression that more people than usual were present at the rites we witnessed, as people were ordinarily anxious to talk with us.) The rites begin when the medium rubs scent on her hand, neck, and face to summon the *pòtjoets*. Often in the initial stages she mumbles unintelligible verses of Acehnese. After a few minutes her knees begin to flap like wings, beating the floor, as the first *pòtjoet* enters her body. The beating increases in tempo till, when it is very rapid, the medium half rises and then collapses on the floor, usually landing on her side. She then sits up again, and the *pòtjoet* speaks through her. The sound of the voice is no longer the sound of the everyday voice of the medium. Generally what is said is similar to these words taken down at a performance in 1963:

> *Assalamualeichum.* I am Pòtjoet Gloempang Pajōng. Who are you? [Addressing the djinn.] What do you want? Where do you live? Why have you come? What do you want? Go home. Don't bother us here. Leave the body of ...

The women in the audience can ask both the djinn and the *pòtjoets* questions, and they will answer.

They usually ask the djinn how many of his friends are in the body. Sometimes the djinn will tell them why he is there. The reason is always trivial. It is often because the sick person urinated on the (invisible) spirit. As one person told my wife, "Wouldn't you be angry if someone urinated on you?" Or it may be that the patient stepped on the djinn. Sometimes too the djinn may want something simple like a glass of water, and they promise to give it to him.[8]

After the *pòtjoet* has told the djinn to go away, the djinn leaves and then also the *pòtjoet* herself. As this happens, the medium's body trembles again. The medium rubs scent on herself, and another *pòtjoet* enters through her and speaks to the djinns remaining in the sick person. The *pòtjoet* goes away, and another djinn passes through the medium on its way back to the mountains. In the course of a single session, lasting about two hours, more or less, a dozen *pòtjoets* and a dozen djinns appear. Very sick people have more djinns in them than those with minor ailments, but every patient seems to have at least a dozen. In some cases the djinns refuse to come out, and the *pòtjoets* become angry. The medium is forced to leap at the sick person as the *pòtjoet* tries to get the djinn to leave and must be restrained by those watching. At the end of the session the servants of the *pòtjoets,* who cook rice for them in the mountains, come and through the medium make

---

[8] I use "him" for djinns, but they are of indeterminate gender. *Pòtjoets,* however, are always female.

jokes and rub oil on the patient. When they have left, the medium, who from the time the first *pòtjoet* entered her has not spoken a word in her everyday voice, awakens. Before she leaves she is given a small gift of money.

Throughout the ceremony the patient lies quietly. If she is not too sick she can act like any other person watching, asking questions of the djinns and *pòtjoets,* though this is not usual, and chatting with other women. Her attention, like that of everyone else, is directed to the medium. The medium is the stage upon which the drama of the *pòtjoets* and the djinns takes place. The drama itself, however, is not elaborate. If the djinn is stubborn and does not want to leave the body of the sick person, the *pòtjoet* can become angry. But the cause of the djinn's stubbornness is never of importance to anyone. Sometimes it is just the nature of the djinn. There was one woman who was temporarily out of her wits—she had thrown her baby against the wall and had herself jumped in the well. Several different mediums had tried to drive the djinns out without success. When the djinns finally began to leave they took the form of animals—goats, dogs, snakes, and others. I did not myself witness this, but it is important that the person who told my wife about it never mentioned why the djinns had entered the woman in the first place. One never comes across stories of the guilt of the woman involved, for instance, or, for that matter, stories of social relationships in the tales told by the djinns and *pòtjoets*. Sickness is only a matter of the djinns entering the person; if there is a reason it is unimportant.

Nor is it usually the case that djinns image pain or parts of the body of the sick person, as is often the case in such rites in other cultures. The animal forms that left the body of the uncontrolled woman perhaps come closest to representing the illness itself, but the case was quite exceptional. Most rites involve persons with physical complaints where the complaint is not reflected in the story of the djinn; the djinn, who happened to be thirsty or to have been stepped on by the patient, just entered her.

Identification of the spirits does not take us much further in understanding the rite. Belief in djinns is an article of faith for Muslims, and men, therefore, do not deny that they exist. The do deny ever having experiences involving djinns, however, and they also deny that djinns make people ill, bring dreams, or in any way affect behavior. Women believe all of these things. Djinns, like the rest of the spirit-world creatures, are vague beings. They live in the mountains and forests. They can also be found in the inhabited world and particularly in the rice fields and privies. However, in Aceh there are no longer beliefs in spirits, djinns or otherwise, who regularly inhabit specific places, as is believed in many other Southeast Asian cultures.[9] Similarly, while during curing rites djinns will sometimes give their names, there are no djinns with whom people are familiar from a context

[9] This is true, at least, of Pidie, the section of Aceh where the data presented were collected.

other than curing rites.[10] They have no identifiable
shape. As one woman said, "They are like the wind;
if you can see the wind, you can see the djinns."
People's knowledge of djinns comes almost exclusively from curing rites when djinns speak through
the mediums. When people are ill and the djinns
causing the illness speak, it nearly always is the case
that they want something. Djinns are themselves
vaguely believed to be unfulfilled desires. Here is a
portion of my wife's notes:

[B. said that] her father was sick before he died, and
they called K. [a medium], who asked the djinn what it
wanted. It answered that its name was . . . from Rambòng
[a village nearby]. It said . . . that it wanted a drink and
that was why it had come. That before it died it wanted to
drink and could not because it was killed before it found
water. Now it wandered all over looking for water. [B.
said that] when she was giving birth the same djinn bothered her; she was very sick and K. came again and identified the djinn as the same one. [B. said and the others
agreed] that whatever you want when you die, that's what
you go wandering about for trying to satisfy after death.

There are no developed myths about the origin of
djinns, nor, for that matter, are there any tales or stories that explain what they are or what they do. The
pòtjoets, the other set of spirits, also live in the
mountains and are usually believed to be the spirits
of wives of nobles, though some women deny this.
Pòtjoet is, in fact, the term used to address women

[10] There is one exception, which is noted subsequently.

of the Acehnese nobility and also men of the sultan's family. Not all such women become spirits, however. Ordinarily they are women who died in childbirth without some desire being fulfilled. Each *pòtjoet* has a name, and each curer has a series of *pòtjoets* who speak through her in the curing rites. The stories about the *pòtjoets,* naturally, are not uniform, and the same stories are sometimes told about different *pòtjoets* while the same *pòtjoets* are described in conflicting ways. One such story is about the spirit often called Pòtjoet Gloempang Pajōng. She is believed to have been the wife of the ruler of a nearby place called Gloempang Pajōng and to have died in childbirth. Her husband and father argued about where to bury her, and the body remained in the house till people began to die from the smell. Finally she was buried under her own house, and the house was burned. Since that time she has gone from place to place asking for things that are hard to find—a green duck and multicolored goats, for instance. Her wants are sometimes made known during the curing rites. This story is an unusually detailed one. Most tales are confined to saying merely that the woman died in childbirth or died wanting something or other.

Insofar as spirits have identities, then, it is not as the remains of particular historical personages. Though they may be identified as being from a particular place or even as being the shade of a particular person, this is never someone known to the medium or the audience. So far as they stand for anything at all, spirits are a generalized expression of women's desires that are unfulfilled and therefore perpetually adrift. The biographies of spirits are really a means of indicating not that they were someone in particular but that they once had a body and now no longer do so, that they are now "like the wind" in being incorporeal. The source of the trouble djinns cause, in fact, is that in being incorporeal they therefore long to lodge in other people's bodies.

While spirits do not have bodies, they do, however, have voices. It would perhaps be safer to say not that they have voices but that they have language. They speak only through the medium. When she gives them voice, it is with the physical apparatus of her own body. There is no dissembling involved in this. She is not a ventriloquist and in no way hides that they speak via her larynx, her tongue, and her mouth. The sounds of their voices differ from the sound of the medium's everyday voice and from each other. This, however, is not meant to indicate that the sound is produced or controlled by the djinns. They are simply without bodies and can produce sound only through the body of the medium.

What one sees in the rite, then, is the medium giving voice to a series of creatures. What is said is always insignificant. The cause of the trouble, the reason the djinn lodged in the body of the sick person, does not reflect the intentions or the character of the sick person or, even in a coded way, her dealings with others. Firth notes that in Kelantan such an occasion is important because it furnishes the means of dealing with the spirit. That which the spirit is known to want can be given to it. What was "fate" is then "manageable." But if it is manageable, it is not because the djinn can be satisfied but because of the presence of the other spirits—the *pòtjoets,* who sometimes drive out the djinns simply by threatening or struggling with them. The desires of the spirits are thus not a means of articulating djinns with patients or curers. The spirit's intersection with the patient's experience is most tangential. The djinn's desires are important only for giving the spirits as much identity as they have—that is, as desire itself, without the body necessary to slake that desire. Though the djinns are promised whatever they ask for, no one sees any point in trying to give it to them.[11]

These desires of the spirits, though trivial or unsatisfiable, could be the basis of dramatic narration. However, what one sees watching the rite is not a drama with a moral or, indeed, with any other kind of significance but a series of entrances and exits with little connection between them. It is as though one were to go to a theater and, instead of a play, were to see twenty-six people walk across a stage, one by one. Half of them would never have been seen before; the other half would be significant only because one knew that as they left a stranger would

[11] Women say that they give djinns what they ask for during feasts. However, though we inquired on several occasions, we never saw or learned of anything being specially set out for djinns. The feasts are given for various purposes, none of which has to do with djinns. See pp. 52, 116, 159, and 161 of this volume.

appear. Whatever potential there is for developing the imaging of wishes and thus connecting it to experience is in no way developed.

The whole event is so undramatic, in fact, that one can attribute nothing cathartic to the scenes of departure. The patient is presumably cured when the last djinn is driven out. But the last is very like the first, and little different has happened between their appearances. If one were to think in such terms as "completion" or narrative development, one would have to say that the ritual ends arbitrarily. There is neither a conclusion nor change but only cessation.

In what way, then, could such a ritual image the experience of the patient as Firth and others say it does? If it does not do so, why is it believed to be effective? Is it not simply a series of practically meaningless images arranged in the skimpiest of ways? To answer these questions we have to move to the other major manifestation of spirits, that is, dreams.

Acehnese recognize three separate events that we class as dreams, two of which are said to be "brought" by djinns. There is no general word for *dream* that includes all three of these events. A *wèn-wèn* is a remembrance that occurs while one is asleep. Here is an example told to me at the time I returned to Aceh after an absence of four years by the woman in whose house my wife and I lived:

Two nights ago there was a *wèn-wèn*. It's not important. It was as though you and Sandra [my wife] came here without your child. I asked, "Why didn't you bring the baby?" "Because it was still small." That is a *wèn-wèn* because I always think of you coming back home in the afternoons.

One noted that it is not only events but memories that can be remembered in *wèn-wèn*.

A *rabeuë* is distinguished from a *wèn-wèn* in that it does not refer to anything that happened in the past in one's own experience. That is, it is not an emergence into dream of something one was aware of earlier. Another meaning of *rabeuë* is "chaotic" or "disordered." *Rabeuë* are always said to have an odd quality to them. Here is an example told by the woman to my wife:

I dreamt Djalil was selling fish on the path by the edge of the stream. Usually people put their money into a basket or a box, but he put his into a big can.

I bought a fish for fifty rupiah because the fish were still fresh. Then I went home and sat on the porch. I ate some betel. After that I didn't feel well, and my teeth were all red. My mouth didn't feel pleasant, and I did not sleep well.

What makes this a *rabeuë* is that, in addition to not really having happened, the events are odd. The facts that the man is using a can instead of a basket for his money and that she bought only one fish instead of several, even though they were fresh, make the dream odd, although the sequence of events is very much as it might have been in reality.

The third category is *loempòë* or *rahasia* (secret).

A *loempòë* also refers to events that one has not experienced, but it is distinguished from a *rabeuë* insofar
as it is "true" *(keubit)* and complete *(lengkap)*. A
*loempòë,* it turns out, has no reference at all to what is
thought to have happened any more than the other
two. It is true, however, because it contains a message. It is a sign of what will happen. Moreover, it is
sent not by djinns but by God. It is therefore coveted.
When women have to make a decision, they may
await the sending of a sign in a dream.

The connection of dreams and curing rites, aside
from the first two categories of dreams being
"brought" by djinns, is made through the attitudes of
men and women toward them. Men and women
agree about the definition of the various categories
of dreams. They agree that *loempòë,* for instance,
are "true" and that the other sorts are not. They differ, however, in what one might call their cultivation
of dreaming. During the time we did fieldwork my
wife and I went about every morning asking people
if they had dreamed, and we recorded their answers.
Women nearly always had done so but men almost
never. In four months we had hundreds of women's
dreams and only two from men. It is not surprising
that men reject their dreams. *Loempòë,* true dreams,
are brought by God, and God, they believe, no
longer speaks directly to man. Men either claim that
they do not remember their dreams or that they did
not dream. Women, on the other hand, remember not
only their true dreams but also *wèn-wèn* and *rabeuë;*
in particular they remember the latter. (We have, in

fact, only a couple of examples of "true" dreams.)

Curing rites, taken as a set of signs, are much like untrue dreams. The content of untrue dreams is dismissed. They have no "message" for women and make no "sense" to them. Insofar as they represent what happened, they are false. One is left with a set of signs devoid of content and yet remembered, even, it appears, dwelt upon. The appearance of the spirits in curing rites is likewise empty of content. The two sets of spirits may be identified as "desires," yet this is not elaborated into a narrative. Futhermore, the division of spirits into good and bad, the chasers and the chased, is unconnected with what it is that either set of spirits wants. The "content" or meaning of spirits is thus marginalized. Nor are the biographies of spirits significant. The dismissal of possible meanings of spirits, then, is similar to the dismissal of the content of dreams.

We can put all these facts together by turning back to the central figure of the ritual—the medium. A woman becomes a medium by being "summoned" by the *pòtjoets*. She falls ill, and until she agrees to "receive" the *pòtjoets* she cannot get well. Here is an account one medium gave to my wife:

I asked her how long she had been with the *pòtjoets,* and she said twenty-five years. In the beginning she was sick and ate a handful of rice during a month's time and just lay flat thinking about nothing. And her hair was down to her thighs, and there was not another person in the village who had their hair as long as hers, and it all fell out. Tjualima [an old medium] came to heal her and said that the *pòtjoets* wanted to be received by her and that until she received them she would remain very ill. She said she did not want to become a medium, and when she said that her mouth became all twisted on one side for a whole week. Everyone said to receive them. Finally she agreed, and they killed a black goat, and the men were summoned to read the Koran at night, and they had a *chanduri* (feast). She was "cooled" (a ritual) by Tjualima [the medium mentioned previously], and from that time on she has received *pòtjoets*.

On another occasion she said that the *pòtjoets* had asked for a black umbrella when she agreed to become a medium. She went to the market and bought one, and, she said, she still uses it when it rains.[12]

The initiation of the sick person as a curer depends on her willingness to let the bodyless djinns use her own body as their "voice." They are langauge without a means of expression until this happens. She, in exchange, is released from their power when she agrees to become their voice. Initially, the

[12] This may be connected with the name of the first spirit she summons, *Pòtjoet Gloempang Pajōng,* or *Pòtjoet* [a kind of large shade tree *(gloempang)*] umbrella *(Pajong)*. If so, what is involved is simply the transfer of a signifier. That place-name is Gloempang Pajōng. The "umbrella" of the title is transferred as the black umbrella used when it rains. The other association is with shadow and social position. Umbrellas are used for shade as well as for protection from rain. They were traditionally reserved for nobility, including those labeled *pòtjoet* and royalty. Shadow is associated with royal writing, while the djinn who brings dreams is also associated with shadows. See footnote 13; and Siegel, *Shadow and Sound.*

spirits chose her and occupied her body. Once she agreed to let them speak through her, however, they became her set of spirits whom she summons when she has need of them. To have their language come out through her gestures is thus not to be possessed but to escape possession and, as it turns out, to possess those whose language it initially is.

One's language is one's own, we believe, to the extent that we speak in our own voice. For Acehnese women this is not the case. For the curer in particular, all the voices are hers not because they speak in the sound of her everyday voice—they do not—but because they speak through her body, including the physical apparatus of her voice. The spirits—language without body—have found a voice in her. This does not mean that they must speak with the characteristic sound of that voice, because the curer, named "Katidjah," is identified by neither the character of her thoughts—as men would be—nor by the sound of her voice—but by her body plus that language that comes out of her. There is a voice that is "Katidjah's"—in the sense that it is her everyday voice—and there are other voices with other names—but she is the scene of all these manifestations of language that makes them "hers." She is not one voice but many; that does not make her divided, because it is not the sound of the voice that is the sign of unity but the body as it produces noises and gestures.

What the curer knows about her trance when she awakens is that there was a recent period, initiated by herself, during which spirits "entered" *(sandrōng)* her but whose sense is unknown to her. She does not know "what happened," which amounts to what she said, during that time. What she agreed to in her compact with the djinns is to be their sounding box and set of props. She has escaped illness by converting their language into her speech.

The patient sees the twitches of the curer's body and hears the messages. Nothing that she feels in her own body is an indication of what is happening there. The twitches of the curer are her only signs of what is going on within herself. But there are two ways of reading these signs. The first is that the twitches are signs of the djinn, that is, indications of what is going on within the body of the patient. In this interpretation, the signs would be produced in the body of the medium, but they would indicate what would currently be happening to the patient. It would be as though the curer were a fluoroscopic image of the patient's body. The other possibility is that the noises and gestures of the curer are the curer's own; they exist in the medium's body not merely as automatic reactions to the movements of the spirits but as a conversion of the spirits' desire into the speech of the medium. In the second case, the reading of the medium's gestures is a reading of what has already happened within the patient. For the patient to read these gestures as the curer's is thus to read them as deferred from a time inside her to a time outside, in the medium. To recognize the language of the djinn as the speech of the medium is for the patient to be released from that language. The efficacy of the rite depends on the second assumption.

We might note that just as curing rites say nothing of significance about the past of the patient, neither do they speak of her pain. To listen to the messages of the spirits is not to speak of the woman's experience or of anything substantive. The important operation in reading the signs of the spirits is not to apprehend "what they say" about anything whatsoever but rather to attribute the signs to the curer and thus to escape from their language. To think of the djinns is not to develop an image of them or of the patient but to put them out of mind.

Dreams, aside from "true" dreams *(loempòë)*, function like curing rites. It is remarkable that Acehnese divide dreams so many ways and yet have no word for "nightmare." This is because all dreams, or at least all false dreams, are unpleasant while they are being dreamed. Dreams, like illness, are thought to be brought by djinns. There is a curse that says, "May a djinn weigh you down" (by sitting on your chest), which it is customary to translate as "may a djinn bring you nightmares."[13] However the dream is known only after the djinn is gone. While the djinn sits on the chest of the dreamer he or she is simply

[13] I have myself mistranslated this phrase in "Si Meuseukin's Wedding," *Indonesia* 22 (autumn 1977). Djajadiningrat translates it the same way. See *beunò* in Djajadiningrat, *Atjehsch— Nederlandsch Woordenboek. Beunò* is the name of the particular spirit who brings dreams. It is interesting that the spirit is associated with shadows, since *shadow* is a term used by Acehnese to speak of writing. See footnote 12.

in its grasp. If one sees someone tossing about in sleep, one must not waken that person. He or she is in the possession of the djinn, who may carry the individual away. (One tries instead to scare away the djinn.) The dream itself is known only after the time that it occurs.

For women to "remember" the dream or to "put it into speech" is not to recover what occurred to them while they slept. What happened was that the djinn visited them, but they do not speak of this event. Rather, "to remember" the dream is to transform the visit of the djinn into a set of signs that are theirs since they exist in their bodies. It is thus to move out of the grip of the djinns. The djinns, language without a means of expression, do in dreams what they do in curing rites; they make women their means of speech. By accepting the demands of the djinn for expression, women, in thinking of their dreams, think not of the dream as the visitation of the djinn but of what only in retrospect is conceived to have happended at that time: the dream itself. It is not, then, the "meaning" of the dream or its phenomenological immediacy that is important to them. In remembering their dreams women give the djinns expression; but they do so in signs that, since they are women's own, celebrate not what the djinn says but their release from the djinn's grasp.

All dreams brought by djinns have unserious messages, as we have seen. We can now understand why this is so. Were the message serious, what would be celebrated would be the content and the bringer of the content. The dream would then be a *loempòë,* a message brought by God. To say that the message of a dream is trivial and yet to dwell on it is to celebrate not the dream or its occurrence but one's own possession of a set of signs. To discard content is at the same time to salute one's own control of language.

Women seldom engage in curing rituals. They seem to dream nightly, however. Their commemorations of these occasions are parallel to their husband's self-constitution in prayer and make understandable the authority of their trivial words.

# POSSESSED

History has many cunning passages,
contrived corridors. . . .
                                        —T. S. Eliot

With the fall of Suharto, Acehnese were free to react to the actions of the government against them. During the ten years when Aceh was an area of military operations (DOM) more than 3,000 Acehnese had been killed, there were well over a hundred documented cases of rape, and numerous men and women were tortured and imprisoned. It was difficult to find anyone in Aceh content with the relation between the province and the national government. The governor himself called for the replacement of central control with a federal system. Others wanted an independent Aceh. The Achehnese independence movement had its immediate impulse in changes that occurred since *The Rope of God* was published. Under Suharto's New Order, Aceh experienced development, which meant in the first place the improvement of roads and the establishment of a natural gas plant in Lho Seumawè. "Acheh Merdeka" (Independent Acheh) was a response to the displacement of peasants in the building of this plant though it had other causes as well. The movement was initiated by Hasan Mohammed di Tiro (who, refusing everything Indonesian including orthography, used the nineteenth-century English spelling *Acheh,* which we will retain in the title of the organization and which we will also use for references to his conception of the province). Di Tiro was at one time a follower of Daud Beureuèh, and he began an independence movement in 1976. It had limited support until the exactions of the army began on a wide scale in the 1980s. Its adherents were first of all injured peasants. But especially after the fall of Suharto in 1998, large numbers of university students also demanded an independent Aceh, using the same slogan as Hasan Mohammed di Tiro but knowing little about him or his program. There had been a university in Aceh when I arrived there in 1962. However under the New Order the number of students, mainly from Acehenese peasant families, had greatly expanded. Students objected first of all to the brutality of the military. Their elders were more likely to be concerned with the inequitable division of the yield from the exploitation of Aceh's natural resources, which included timber on an important scale as well as natural gas. The latter group was less interested in "Acheh Merdeka." These people were more likely to want to change Indonesia into a federation in order to guarantee the rights of the province.

Tim Kell in a monograph published in 1995 focuses on national exploitation and local needs to explain the appeal of the independence movement.[1] Agriculture, the staple of the provincial economy, was neglected by the central government, which

---

[1] Tim Kell, *The Roots of Acehnese Rebellion, 1989–1992* (Ithaca: Cornell Modern Indonesia Project, 1995).

took the vast profits from natural gas and timber for itself, hardly anything returning to Aceh.[2] At the same time, the only important local leaders, the *ulama,* were neutralized by being brought into Golkar, the government party. It was surprising to me in 1999 to find widespread political movement without religious leadership. Obviously other forces were at play. A new class of technocrats had come to power in Aceh already in the 1960s who, though Achenese themselves, were dependent on the central government and were obliged to put its demands first. One of them, Governor Ibrahim Hasan, called for more troops. Thus the introduction into Aceh of the Special Forces *(Kopassus)* led by the son-in-law of President Suharto, known for their brutality.[3]

[2] It was often repeated in Aceh that 10 percent of the national budget was furnished from Aceh while only 0.6 percent of what the government extracted from the province returned to it.

[3] There were, at the time, attacks on police stations and other forms of violence that the governor thought were out of the possibility of control of the army and police. It seems that this was the result of the disruption of trade in ganja. Ganja has been grown in Aceh since time immemorial. It is even part of Acehnese cuisine. Apparently certain elements of Acheh Merdeka were growing and exporting it with the complicity of the police. It was these arrangements that, apparently, were upset. When the Special Forces arrived, they became part not only of this trade but, according to even the highest government officials, of practically all dealings with the government, taking a 10 percent cut, even in small village matters. "Antara Ganja dan 'Aceh Merdeka,' " *Editor,* April 15, 1989, p. 16; "Hunter, Ganja, dan Atjeh Merdeka," ibid., June 3, 1989, p. 11.

The financing of the Acheh Merdeka is unclear. At present it does not seem to receive much support from Libya. The Acehnese journalist Yarmen Dinamika suggested to me in February 1999 that it is still based on the export of ganja, this, necessarily, with

Wrong was done to Aceh, and it is to right that wrong that there is widespread rebellious sentiment and even a rebellion.[4]

This notion of justice is phrased in a particular way. It is not just that wrong by any standard was done to Aceh. In Acehnese thinking, the injustice is measured against what Aceh did for the nation. Acehnese frequently repeat nearly the same words: "Aceh was the province that financed the revolution, but what has it gotten in return?"[5] Aceh was not occupied by the Dutch during the revolution; Acehnese had commercial resources and of their own volition sent large contributions to the republic. Many themselves fought. The sentence is often cited in Indonesian because it repeats the words that President Sukarno used when he thanked the province for its substantial aid. This seems to substantiate Kell's thesis: they take from us, and they

---

the cooperation of government officials. It is widely believed in Aceh that the army and the police are involved. Ganja is grown on a wide scale, particularly in the regency of southeast Aceh. From what I could learn the majority of Acheh Merdeka followers in other regencies are not directly involved.

[4] Geoffrey Robinson, "Rawan Is as Rawan Does: The Origins of Disorder in New Order Aceh," *Indonesia,* no. 66 (October 1998), updates the atrocities of the army.

[5] They frequently add that President Sukarno acknowledged Indonesia's debt for Aceh's efforts. In a speech in Bireuen, Aceh, in June 1948, he said that "[t]he People of Aceh carried the struggle to the very end; they attacked, staved off and held back Dutch imperialism from entering the province of Aceh. For this reason Aceh was the Financial Province of the Indonesian Republic." Quoted in K. H. Ramadhan and Hamid Jabbar, *Sjamaun Gaharu* (Jakarta: Pustaka Sinar Harapan, 1995), epigraph.

give us nothing back. We give and we gave to them, and we get nothing back. It is a calculation.

At the time I write, in 1999, after the general loss of confidence in the central government, Acehnese cite army violence to say, in effect, that the process of exchange between the province and the center has broken down. At this point it is assumed that there is more than simple inequity. Inequity can be compensated. Those who want a federal system assume that the government in Jakarta cannot be trusted. The central government makes promises when it is weak. When it is strong it takes back the promises. The history of Aceh since independence, when the province was temporarily dissolved into a larger entity, and again when, with the settlement of Daud Beureuèh's rebellion, the promise of autonomy in certain areas was not kept proves one cannot have confidence in the government. In this view, the system of reciprocity itself needs modification. If one wants an independent Aceh one thinks the system is irreparable. Aceh gives its resources and gets back blows and even death. It is beyond calculation; the process of exchange itself has failed.

ACHEH MERDEKA

What is called "Gerakan Acheh Merdeka" (Movement for an Independent Acheh), abbreviated as "GAM," the organization founded by Hasan Mohammed di Tiro, is comprised mainly of villagers.[6] Those I spoke with—perhaps about twenty-

[6] The question of membership is difficult to assess. If one

five—had similar stories. Either they or members of their families had been tortured or imprisoned or raped by ABRI, "ABRI" being the acronym for the Indonesian armed forces. A typical story was of a man whose father was killed by ABRI. He was fifteen at the time. His uncle took him to the mountains to join the rebels. He spent some time training in

---

means by that activists, membership until recently was probably quite small, less than 1,000. If one counts those with membership cards it is, by now, after the end of the Suharto regime, undoubtedly much more. If one counts as members those familiar with the doctrines of Hasan Mohammed di Tiro these are mainly villagers. As Kell reports, the government proceeded against Acehnese university lecturers, but it is doubtful if these had close links with the organization itself (Kell, *Roots of Acehnese Rebellion,* 69).

It was difficult for me to find people who knew Hasan Mohammed di Tiro or who had read his writings in Banda Aceh. Whereas the villagers I met were familiar with his notion of Achehnese [Atjehnese] history, this was unknown to anyone I could find in Banda Aceh. The difficulty comes because of the slogan "Acheh Merdeka." "Acheh Merdeka," Independent Acheh, is supported by many who know nothing about the organization Acheh Merdeka. Even to call these people sympathizers means only that they want independence, not that they acknowledge the authority or the views of Hasan Mohammed di Tiro, though they know his name and do not disassociate themselves from him. The violence of the army and the depredations of the central government mean that no one wants the present relation to Indonesia. This sentiment is confused with questions of membership and support of the GAM for lack of other avenues of expression. There is confusion on all sides on this issue: "Asked on one occasion about the numerical strength of the new movement, [Major-General H. R. Pramono, the regional army commander] replied: 'I've never counted. . . . Hundreds of thousands? Yes, with their followers maybe there are. The core? Perhaps there are hundreds' " ("Suara Pangdam," *Editor,* August 18, 1990, cited in Kell, *Roots of Acehnese Rebellion,* 67).

Malaysia, where he also learned English, and had returned to Aceh only a few months before I met him in February 1999, age twenty-five.

I asked these people what they did in the mountains. Unless the man had a position of leadership, the answer was always the same: "talked" *(peugah haba; ngobrol)*. Some spent five, others six, seven, eight, and even nine years in the mountains, chatting. I asked if they ever fought. Not unless they were attacked. Of course, there are exceptions to this, and I will come to them. But I asked why they did not fight, especially since each went to the mountains for the same reason: not merely to escape capture but to take vengeance.

It is important to see that there is no substitute of imaginary for real vengeance. It is not as though these people spent their time nursing rancor. They merely waited. The beginning of an explanation is given by Hasan Mohammed di Tiro, the leader of the rebellion. He wrote, in English, a diary of his time in Acheh between 1976 and 1979. In an entry for 1976 he says:

In Paradise Guns is only one of our problems that we must solve. But there are more important and more urgent problems before us that we must solve first—even before the guns: the problem of Achehnese political consciousness, the problem of the crisis of national identity, the problem of the study of Achehnese history, the status of Acheh under International Law, the problem of self-determination and international relations. . . . We cannot join international community as a people or a nation before we cured ourselves of national identity which is

now upon us. As a result of 35 years of Javanese
Indonesian colonialism, our people has been driven into
a crisis of identity: many Achehnese, especially the
younger generations are in doubt and in utter confusion
as to who they are: Achehnese or "indonesians"?...Our
first task, therefore should be to restore the national consciousness, to revive national memory, then to organize
and mobilize ourselves. Now, all these are not military
activities but political, cultural, and educational. They
are absolutely necessary to prepare before we can engage
in armed struggle. So the gun is neither the first nor the
last thing! (47-48) (grammer and capitalization as in
original in this and further quotes from the diary)[7]

It is not yet time. The delay has lasted for over
twenty years and may go on longer, even indefi-
nitely. Hasan Mohammed di Tiro assumes that once
people understand their true identity there will not
be much need to fight. Such knowledge comes, he
believes, by learning the history of Acheh since the
time of the Dutch. This history, in his version, shows
how Achehnese leadership has devolved on him.

Why do people, seeking vengeance, believe him
and wait, even risking their lives by waiting?
Perhaps because vengeance is condemned by some
who say it is counter to Islam, though this was never
said by the members of GAM whom I met. To take
vengeance one has to take it in the name of something. If people wait it is because of the way their

[7] Tengku Hasan di Tiro [sic], *The Price of Freedom: The
Unfinished Diary of Tengku Hasan di Tiro* (n.p.: National
Liberation Front of Acheh Sumatra, 1984).

injury is understood: who they think did it and who,
in turn, they, the injured, are. For them their injury
was not done, for instance, by a person but by an
agent, an agent of Indonesia. This already sets the
terms of their response. They could reply as
Indonesian citizens or as "Acehnese" or in their individual identities. Any of these would be possible.
But even given this, their willingness to delay indicates a need for someone to articulate their injury
and the response to it for them. The delay is an indication that they cannot speak for themselves. If they
wait without rancor it is because they are in a state
of suspension, holding themselves apart from daily
life but also apart from hoped for retribution. They
seem to have no choice because they are unable to
formulate their identities for themselves. They
remain in the initial stage of vengeance, aware of
wrong done them but unsure of who the "them" is.
Hasan Mohammed di Tiro promises to tell them.
Without him or a similar figure, vengeance will
never take shape.

Meanwhile, without someone to tell them properly, these stories are not yet stories. They are not yet
accounts of real events that people are eager to tell.
But these events are not forgotten. On the contrary,
the gap between experience and story is preserved
during years of idle chatter. The closure of this gap
could be violence, it could be stories, or it could be
both. Meanwhile, the urge to tell remains as with
people who approached me on the street or whom I
met only casually and who told me, "Tell them what

is happening in Aceh." They did so without specify-
ing what, precisely, was happening in Aceh or who
the "they" was.

One can compare the Acehnese view of
vengeance with the Western idea. God said,
"Vengeance is Mine," meaning that He forbade it to
His people while He reserved it for Himself. In this
view, private vengeance is still possible, but it will
be punished. In the minds of these Acehnese,
vengeance itself is not possible except if it is in the
name of something larger than themselves. To be
that, it needs the sanction of an authority.
"Vengeance is Acehnese" might be their motto, and
therefore they do not take it, not yet, being unsure
not of the existence of "Aceh" and "Acehnese" but
of the way those terms apply to them.

When I visited them, I had my camera with me. I
did not take pictures, however, fearing it would compromise their safety. Finally they asked me if I had
not brought a camera. They took out a flag of Acheh
Merdeka and asked me to take a picture of them
holding it. Then they showed me their plastic Acheh
Merdeka identification cards, complete with photograph and fingerprint, which I also photographed. If
they wait to take vengeance it is because they take it
in the name of "Acheh," but it is evident that to do so
they need confirmation that they are Achehnese.
They need identity cards and photographs of themselves with their flag. They risk their own safety to
have these items. They need representations of
themselves in order to be sure that whatever reply

they might eventually make to "Indonesia" is in their "own" name, that is, in the name of "Acheh." And for that they require someone else to articulate their representations of themselves, someone authoritative to issue identity cards.

Members of the Gerakan Aceh Merdeka showed me their wounds and asked me to photograph them. Of course I asked about the circumstances of their injuries. But their responses were, to my mind, curiously unemotional. They did not do what my refugee Algerian friends do. Each time they recount their experiences in Algeria they relive them. One can hear in their voices the emotions they felt in Algeria seeing others killed in front of them. The members of Gerakan Aceh Merdeka, by contrast, could put the moments of their injuries into words, but their words were flat, considering the drama of the events. Similarly they showed me pictures of bloody victims of the army. These too they showed me without much emotion even when they were people close to them.

If they lack emotion it is, I believe, because their memories are not attached to "them." They lack a subject, there being, at this point, no "them" who link themselves today, at the moment of their injury, and their histories before that moment. Such a subject, they feel, has to be a nationally recognized one. Their own names are insufficient. They need to have a name inscribed in "Acheh."

After I had asked five people the story of their wounds, their spokesman interrupted saying, "They [the stories] are all the same." He was not being dismissive in saying this, as though the experiences of some were not worth telling. I understood him to mean that once one hears one story of this type, one knows them all. He meant that what the army did is what is important and that each incident is merely an example of army brutality. Further, "[it is] all the same" means that the suffering of each victim is also the same. Its sense is not its uniqueness but its generality. The uniqueness of individual suffering counted for little or nothing for him but not because he was insensitive. It is rather that he could not imagine that each could tell his or her own story and have it matter. At best, it would all come out with the sense that was given to it by correct understanding. It is precisely this assumption of a need for correct understanding, meaning one that fits all cases and that is approved, that makes it necessary for them to wait for authorization to take vengeance. On the one hand, the indistinctness of individual suffering and the insufficiency of the personal name and on the other the conferring of a national, Achehnese identity that makes suffering signify.

Violence in other parts of the archipelago, though not identical to violence in Aceh, also stimulates recourse to widely recognized forms of social identity. The violence of 1999 in Ambon, for instance, started with a dispute between the conductor of a minibus and someone from a neighboring village. It became a battle between Christians and Muslims. No doubt there was encouragement to have it become so. But at the point of conflict between individuals, identity was called into question. There was then an appeal to wider, nationally known forms of social identification. In my opinion the appeal to nationally recognized identities is an attempt to make violence matter. To want vengeance, to feel violent, is also, if one is an Acehnese villager, to seek to have Hasan Mohammed di Tiro know that one acts properly in taking revenge. Merely to kill a soldier, even the very soldier who tortured one, would not do. One has to act in the name of something or someone.

Indonesian violence often stimulates a recourse to recognition outside the framework of the initial conflict. The terms of violence cannot seem to be generated out of a contest between individuals. The Hegelian idea of differences generated out of conflict, interior to the struggle itself, holds neither in Aceh nor, I think, in Indonesia. There is, in that limited sense at least, no dialectical formation of identity.

For Acehnese villagers, individual violence risks not being vengeance. That is, it would not register as their reply to "Indonesia." Indeed, the question of where such a reply would originate is the fundamental question of Acheh Merdeka. On the one hand, there is an evident need for someone else, a leader of some sort, to articulate their reply. On the other hand, there is the question of what the reply of an individual, without a spokesperson, would be. The various mass movements that followed the fall of Suharto were condemned as savagery or mere violence. This, in my opinion, is what the members of Acheh Merdeka, who chatted for so long in the mountains, feared. Why they should so fear still needs to be answered.

Their pictures of themselves are not adequate to their identities unless they are sealed in plastic, set next to their fingerprints in official documents of an organization that, in their eyes, represents Acheh itself. Otherwise, their photograph would seem to be indistinguishable from a mass of others. To reflect the full sense of who they are, the photograph needs to be supplemented, and the supplement has to be supplied from outside themselves. To act before the announcement that the time to act has come, to act individually, would be to reply vaguely, out of an identity that, photographically reproduced, would only be intelligible to the police. The police would merely compare features of one suspect with another. They might arrest the criminal, but they would learn nothing of who he is. His act, were it, for instance, undertaken for revenge, might be interpreted by the police in a number of ways that have nothing to do with vengeance. It would be merely criminal.

The situation is comparable to the time after the Acehnese War. Then the solitary killer of a Dutchman knew that, dying himself, he would awake in paradise. God would recognize him and what he did. Nothing in his simple photograph would identify him as a martyr. The Dutch thought such a person mad—that is, with no social identity at all that bore on his action—or merely a murderer. His unadorned photograph might have helped to establish his guilt.

The difference is between the photograph alone, which shows only the features of the face, and the photograph on the identity card, which reveals what these features signify. The members of Gerakan Acheh Merdeka believe that for their features to signify they require someone to identify them. The authority to do so is founded first of all on the wish of potential members, second on their feeling that they alone cannot make themselves signify but someone else can.

These bare facts are insufficient. One also has to understand that it is possible to add something to the features of the face. The identity card expresses first of all that possibility of addition. When this capacity is taken advantage of, authority comes into existence. It is thought at once to add something not there and to make something appear that, after the fact, is assumed to have been inherent in the features of the person photographed.[8] The person who belongs to the Movement for a Free Aceh is not merely a member of a political organization; he is "Acehnese" and is identifiable as such.

[8] The logic of this process was described by Jacques Derrida in speaking about Rousseau in *Of Grammatology* (Baltimore: Johns Hopkins University Press, 1974, trans. Gayatri Chakravorty Spivak); and by Freud in "From the History of an Infantile Neurosis" in *Three Case Histories* (New York: Collier Books, 1963), 187–316, and other places; and further elaborated by Jacques Lacan.

"Acehnese," without Acheh Merdeka, means to
these wounded victims of the army that they are
targets simply because they are Acehnese. As
"Acehnese" alone, they cannot speak. This failure of
speech is itself a component of trauma. But I saw
none of the compulsive repetition of the (to me) horrifying moments of their torture that would make me
think they were traumatized. However it is well possible that had they not the confidence that they were
now members of Acheh Merdeka and that someone
would speak for them, they might be traumatized.
The repetition of the traumatizing moment is the
indication that speech does not perform all its functions. For the traumatized, speech does not mark a
difference between the time of speaking and the
time of the incident recounted. But the members of
Acheh Merdeka have confidence in speech, even in
their own speech, but, of course, understood as the
speech of their spokesperson whom they await. They
are not mere targets because of who they are as they
would be if they were merely "Acehnese" without
being also members of Acheh Merdeka. They await
the restoration of a traditional mode of speech; simply awaiting such they feel themselves on the way to
being restored to normal functioning. They are thus
willing to wait.

### HASAN MOHAMMED DI TIRO

Hasan Mohammed di Tiro is a descendant of well
known religious scholars who were important in the
war against the Dutch. He was a student in the

Western-style school Daud Beureuèh founded in
1939 in Bireuen.[9] While he was studying political
science at Columbia University the Darul Islam
rebellion began. At the time he was working for the
Indonesian consulate, but he quit, declaring himself
the representative of the rebels to the United
Nations. He later became a businessman, marrying a
European woman with whom he had a son. He cultivated political connections all the while. He was
widely said to have relations with the CIA at the
time that that organization supported various rebels
against Sukarno. During the rebellion he fell out
with various followers of Daud Beureuèh, who
accused him of taking money to buy arms for them
but never delivering.[10] His own followers admit that
the GAM had aid from Libya, where some of them,
it is said, went for training. They add that relations
with Libya at the moment are not good. Hasan Tiro
now lives in Sweden. So far as I could find out, he
has not returned to Indonesia since 1979.

The young spokesman for Acheh Merdeka with
whom I spent a day often referred to Hasan
Mohammed di Tiro as "Yang di Pertuan Agung,"
(His Royal Highness). This man had spent some
time in Malaysia and doubtless picked up the phrase
from the Malay usage, Malaysians so designating
their sultans. For his part, Hasan Mohammed di Tiro

[9] M. Nur El Ibrahimy and Tgk. M. Daud Beureuèh, *Peranannya
dalam pergolakan di Aceh* (Jakarta: Gunung Agung, 1982), 139.
[10] This story was widespread in Aceh in the 1960s, where I
heard it from several people. It is told by Hasan Saleh in *Mengapa
Aceh Bergolak* (Jakarta: PT Pustaka Utama Grafiti, 1992), 326 ff.

styles himself the "forty-first head of state of Acheh Merdeka" (Kepala Negara Acheh Merdeka yang ke-41), the first forty no doubt being the sultans of Aceh, or sometimes President, National Liberation Front of Acheh Sumatra. Sometimes he calls himself the *wali,* or guardian, of the state and bases his claim on his version of Acehnese history.[11] According to him, after the Dutch deposed the sultan, the *uleebelang* took over the war. When they were defeated, leadership then passed to the *ulama,* of whom the most prominent was the Tiro family. He is the grandson of the last important leader of the war. He is therefore entitled to call himself the leader of "Free Acheh" ("Free" Aceh because Aceh never formally surrendered, having no one left to represent it).

Hasan Mohammed di Tiro proclaimed Acheh Merdeka, or Independent Aceh, or perhaps Free Aceh or Aceh Libre in 1976, as I have said. He came to Aceh for that purpose and stayed for three years. In his diary he tells his readers that he spent his time disseminating his view of Achehnese history among villagers who, according to him, had forgotten the important facts of their own past.

He begins his journal with an announcement; he has made a decision: "I have finally decided to do what I have believed all along to be my destiny in life: to lead my people and my country to freedom" (1). He decides to do what he must do, what he is, to

[11] For his various titles see for instance "Konsep-konsep kunci Ideologi Acheh Merdeka," *Suara Acheh Merdeka,* July 1996, for the first; and the title page of Di Tiro, *The Price of Freedom,* for the second.

use his word, "destined" to do. This is not exactly a decision, since destiny offers no choice. But it is a decision in the sense that he acquiesces in it. The source of his destiny is double. It is the history of Acheh that is also the history of his family. "I have to do it as a duty, an obligation put on my shoulders by my ancestors on account of future generations." He is one of a line, and as a member of that line, he has duties that he did not choose himself. The sentence continues:

a duty received and a debt that must be paid because of the past and the future of my people. I have been brought up by my family to think so, and I have seen confirmation and expectation from my people to be so. . . . As I said, my conviction about my duty in life came from my country's long history, from my education and breeding, and these being confirmed by the reaction of my people in my daily life in Acheh Sumatra. That is I have been made to feel what my family and my people expected from me. (1)

The people, it turns out, are, with his family, the source of his destiny. He is "made to feel" he should lead his people by the people themselves. They embody the expectations of him that were handed down historically. Hasan Mohammed di Tiro teaches people their history, and they learn that he is the successor to the sultan and to his ancestors. But he learns his position in the first place from those already "my people."

As I said, my conviction about my duty in life came from my country's long history, from my education and breeding, and these being confirmed by the reaction of my people in my daily life in Acheh Sumatra. That is, I have been made to feel what my family and my people expected from me. To get to the point quickly and to confine the matter to my personal history, may I tell you that since I can remember, my hand is always kissed by my people—never shaken—even when I was a little boy. I tell this not for self-indulgence but to explain my self-less actions, to give you a case history of my early experience. . . . There were times in my life when I envied to be like other boys, to be able to run around without being bothered by attention—which unfortunately I had never succeeded. I remembered once I came to complain to my mother tearfully why the people did not leave me alone because I was annoyed that when I walked to school, everybody I met along the road, especially old people, would stand up, if they were sitting, or would step down if they were on bicycles, to rush to kiss my hand. And having to do that I had never arrived on time to school. Why not everybody just leave me alone [*sic*]. My mother explained to me that the people did not mean to bother me, but to honor me, and to demonstrate their love and respect to us. She firmly added that I must show every respect and consideration for them.

I still vividly recall one day when I was already in Secondary School, age about 12, a distinguished old Achenese gentleman came to our school in Sigli, and he interrupted a lecture by asking the teacher to bring him to where I was seated in the class. When he arrived at my desk and as I stood up to shake his hand to honor him for his age, the old gentleman, whom I did not know, held my hand firmly and delivered this speech, "O Tengku, I come to find you, to remind you never to forget your heritage, and to prepare yourself to lead our people and our country to greatness again, like your ancestors had done before you." So no one let me forget about it. That little speech of his made me so embarrassed with my school mates at the time but I have never forgotten the incident or the message. I came to appreciate it later in life. Clearly my people had chipped-in in the endeavor to give me a proper education. I found out later that he was Tengku Hadji Muhammad Tahir, an ulama—Muslim spiritual leader from Teupin Raya, North Atjeh. (1–2)

These are stories of embarrassment. He remembers the mixing of realms, the intrusion of the familial into the school, and it makes him ill at ease with his classmates. One would expect a different story of school from an Indonesian nationalist, one in which modernist learning is the path out of village life. Instead these are stories, told of course in retrospect, of how an indigenous conception, wholly outside the school curriculum, is impressed on him and guides him.

During his childhood, he is not yet aware that Achehnese are "my people." When he grows up he realizes that the people taught him something earlier that he only now understands. "The people" do not exactly give themselves to him; rather they tell him who he is and what, as a result, he must do. They insist; he cannot forget. He presents this as a message transmitted at a great distance. He is in the United States, but he cannot forget what he has learned to understand. This training of himself by those who become "my people" turns into their expectation of him.

He comes to understand that he embodies the history of Aceh:

The people always expecting and waiting to receive political direction from us. This traditional and voluntary grass roots relationship between my people and my family, and presently with myself, is an important reason for what I decided to do [return to Acheh to lead a secessionist movement] and why I think I can and must do it while I am still alive. (2)

It is through a regressive movement on his part that he turns to political activity. In that sense, he is like his opponent Sukarno. In his autobiography Sukarno told how, in order to give his annual speech on independence day, he remembered the servant in the house who was herself a member of the people and who taught him to always think of the people. He spent the night before the speech united with the people, possessed, he says, by them. He then spoke as "the extension of the tongue of the people," expressing their wishes.[12] Possessed by the people, one becomes their leader. Certain contemporary Indonesian political leadership is formed out of a movement "backwards" from the higher to the underclass, which is at the same time a mental return to the family.

[12] Sukarno, *An Autobiography: As Told to Cindy Adams* (Jakarta: Gunung Agung, 1965), 18 ff. For further commentary see James T. Siegel, *A New Criminal Type in Jakarta: Counter-Revolution Now* (Durham: Duke University Press, 1998).

Hasan Mohammed di Tiro is untypical of Indonesian leaders, much less Acehnese leaders, in certain respects. Many Indonesian nationalists were exiled by the Dutch. No important leader, however, chose exile as he did. One has only to look at Daud Beureuèh, the most important Acehnese leader of the twentieth century. When he finally reached an agreement with Jakarta in 1961, Daud Beureuèh refused government offers of houses, cars, and other amenities in Jakarta and remained in Aceh, indeed, remained in Pidie, until he was kidnapped in his old age and forcibly brought to Jakarta, where he died. He is buried, however, in the yard of the mosque he built in Beureunuen, Pidie. One can read Rudolf Mrázek's magnificent biography of Sjahrir for the story of another Indonesian leader nostalgic for his origins, but, as Mrázek points out, Sjahrir always found substitute origins in, for instance, Holland to fill in for Minangkabau.[13] It is the strength of Hasan Mohammed di Tiro that in theory (his theory of the history of Acheh and himself) he refuses any substitute. Only Aceh will do. In Aceh he will in effect recreate the sultanate at the time of his grandfather. Meanwhile he lived first in the United States and now is living in Sweden and is unknown personally to anyone I met in Banda Aceh. Hasan Mohammed di Tiro is also untypical in his insistence on historical revival. This is not only a political maneuver on his part, however. It originates in the place his early

[13] Rudolf Mrázek, *Sjahrir: Politics and Exile in Indonesia* (Ithaca: Cornell University Southeast Asia Program, 1994).

experience takes in his mental life. As I have said, he is like Sukarno and Sjahrir in his insistence on the persistence of his childhood in his psyche. But unlike the latter, he finds no way to integrate his memories with his life in the present. "I never mixed my business with my politics. So very few of [his business colleagues] knew what I had in mind to do in Acheh Sumatra."[14]

Hasan is a middle class person, leading the life of a Western businessman, married to a westerner and not, for instance, feeling that his religious beliefs set him apart.[15] His personality thus contains disparate dimensions that, instead of being integrated in a political synthesis, in practice are kept separate. Here is the sentence that follows the one quoted: "This is my private affairs with my people only." For him, politics is a private affair. Politics is thus set apart, called "private" in the way that one conventionally thinks of one's early years as one's private affairs. Yet from time to time politics governs his actions, as when he returned to Acheh. It is in that sense that I call him "possessed."

Sukarno and Hasan Mohammed di Tiro both relate their biographies in English. Sukarno's biog-

[14] Di Tiro, *The Price of Freedom,* 4 f.
[15] As Erik Morris notes ("Islam and Politics in Aceh: A Study of Center-Periphery Relations in Indonesia," Ph.D. diss., Cornell University, August 1983), his lack of emphasis on Islam alienated Acehnese *ulama* and deprived him of considerable strength. Unlike Daud Beureuèh, he is not an *ulama.* His credentials rest primarily on familial descent. His followers seem to know nothing of his business activities or the source of his wealth. It seems to be enough for them that he belongs to the developed world.

raphy, however, is "as told to" an English speaker and is therefore without the stylistic awkwardnesses of Hasan Mohammed di Tiro's story. It is evident from the passages cited that Hasan Mohammed di Tiro does not inhabit the English language. He borrows from English a style of discourse that nowadays seems exaggerated and gives him self-importance, as for instance when he speaks of "a duty received and a debt that must be paid because of the past and the future of my people. I have been brought up by my family to think so, and I have seen confirmation and expectation from my people to be so." The words of this sentence would be hard to find in Indonesian rhetoric. One has the impression that Hasan Mohammed di Tiro got his ideas not only from "the people," as he claims, but from forms of expression he learned abroad.

Hasan Mohammed di Tiro's experiences may well have been as he describes them. Their persistence in his memory and their call to action, however, sit strangely in his psyche. The foreignness of his language, even its awkwardness, emphasizes the sense in which his memory is intrusive on him. Were he to speak of spirits that visited him in his childhood and that never left him, that cause him to do things today that are outside his own volition, we would better understand the nature of what he tries to tell us. He is, like the sick we have described, possessed by beings who properly belong outside himself but who find themselves interior to him. As such they cause him to act in ways contrary to his contemporary identity. In place of the successful Western businessman, he becomes again Achehnese.

Thus between villagers possessed by the taking of vengeance, moved outside their usual habitations, unable to say what they feel and Hasan Mohammed di Tiro, possessed by these villagers, real and virtual, who give him something to say, a political movement is formed. Hasan Mohammed di Tiro and the students today call repeatedly for international recognition of the situation in Aceh. They feel that not only as a matter of law but because of the sort of understanding that pervades the developed world today, Aceh, were it only to make itself known, would be understood and would be granted its independence. But Hasan Mohammed di Tiro chooses not to disclose his politics to his business colleagues. It remains "private," which I believe means in part that he feels it would be incomprehensible to them. The brutality of Indonesia would be understandable. It is the conditions of his youth with its embodiment of his version of Achehenese history, his motivation to act, that he has to keep apart. And it is his need to speak for others that is strange in the context of the "developed" world. The structure of those who suffer without the ability to articulate and those who do not suffer themselves but articulate for those who do has been left outside "modernity" insofar as it is equated with liberal politics in the West.

UNIVERSITY STUDENTS

The other important group wanting an indepen-

dent Aceh is composed of students. In February
1999, they were completely unfamiliar with Hasan
Mohammed di Tiro's ideas. For that matter, they had
no ideas about the nature of an independent Aceh.
They had had no time for reflection. Once the people
of East Timor asked for a referendum to decide their
possible independence, Acehnese students did the
same. When I told students what Hasan Mohammed
di Tiro believed about Acheh they were not interested. I asked many of them to think of an independent Aceh. Suppose they wanted to work in Medan or
in Jakarta and needed a visa and a work permit. I
made no impression. They were not worried about
getting independence, only about not getting it. And
they insisted it come via a referendum, meaning a
government sponsored vote on the possibilities of
autonomy, federation, and independence, a demand
later endorsed by some political parties. They were
convinced that independence is the wish of nearly all
Acehnese. I suggested to them that the government
was very unlikely to hold a referendum in the near
future (they thought they could have one in a few
months with independence to follow immediately)
but that they themselves could do so. Surely it would
be a major step to register the sentiments of citizens
resident in Aceh in any way possible. They thought
about it, but they were not inclined to this idea.

For them, a referendum was a way to avoid violence. Again and again they told me that the referendum was the route to a peaceful accommodation
with the government. They were afraid to hold their

own poll, they said, because they did not know what ABRI, the armed forces, would do. Unlike their elders in the middle class, they do not think first of the inequitable distribution of resources between the government and the province. Nor is their first thought of the way the army muscled itself into the lives of Acehnese for its own profit. It is rather the brutality of ABRI, which, of course, is quite real. However, in Aceh it has never been on the scale of that in East Timor, where one-third of the population, more than 200,000 people, has died as a result of the Indonesian invasion. The students, however, seemed unaware of this fact. Their knowledge of army brutality is derived almost exclusively from Aceh itself.

When students talk about army violence, they speak about what the army has done to Acehnese villagers. But they do not do so in the same way as villagers themselves. Villagers raised their shirts to show me cigarette burns, held out their hands to display broken fingers, and so on. But as I have said, they did not repeat the emotions they felt when injury was done to them. It was strange to me to hear the violence of the army described much more emotionally by students, who resembled my Algerian friends in that respect, but who were themselves untouched, than by villagers. Students have established posts in the areas of army operations to aid villagers. They speak of ameliorating villagers' "trauma," though this word, at least in its strict sense, does not seem to me to describe the state of the villagers I met myself.

For the students, the wounds of "the people" are their own injuries, no doubt in part because most of them were born themselves in Acehnese villages. But their identification is not simple. One of them explained it to me this way; I paraphrase his words: "I imagine how the mother of someone who was killed feels." Her son, of course, could be him. In his own mind he is extant only in the thoughts of his mother. He foresees two conditions. He is dead, separated from his mother. And he is in his mother's mind, existing there and only there. Both of course are bad thoughts. He has only two recourses—a peaceful way out, granted by authority, which will restore him to life, as it were, and leave him in his position of student, separated from his mother in an acceptable way and on his way to middle class existence. The other possibility is the nightmare related to me. By extrapolation, he fights against the army, and he is killed. A political victory by violent means seems forbidden to him. At least for the moment.

Students, or at least this student, picture a certain regression when they imagine their own violence as they think of opposing the army. They fall into an earlier state, one where they are children again. Children, in this Muslim society, are not what they are in Christian cultures. They are not thought to be innocent but are believed simply to be without a developed capacity to be social, and in that sense they are considered savage. These students are mainly from the countryside. They have arrived at the university and have started on a new path, one leading to the middle class, to a full place in the nation not open to their parents, who remain part of the great mass of people in need of leadership to take them out of their presumed backwardness. But these students, instead of continuing forward, feel themselves falling back. Thinking of violent opposition to the army, they imagine themselves where they began. They are again enclosed with their mothers, and they are once again in the realm of the not-yet-developed.

Students are afraid of ABRI, but that is not their only fear. They are equally afraid of what will happen to them if they themselves turn to violence. Their potential violence seems to them to originate in the underclass and to express its savagery. They lack a spokesperson, someone not merely to articulate their grievances but someone whose authority, like that of Hasan Mohammed di Tiro for the members of the Gerakan Acheh Merdeka, is such that their actions are sure not to be infantile and senseless. Failing that, they need the sanction of the authority they want to repudiate, the Indonesian government and in particular its army.

Acehnese university students, in their tastes, their manner of expression, their very status as "students" *(mahasiswa)*, are nearly indistinguishable from Indonesian students outside the province. If they nonetheless think of themselves as "Acehnese," it is not on the basis of lineage as that would be understood, for instance, in Serbia or Kosovo. Supporters

of independence include, I was told, members of
other ethnic groups, though not many. What
"Acehnese" means is not descent, common language, and common belief, though these play a part.
Rather, being born "Acehnese," one is pushed forward, out of one's family, thus out of one's ancestry,
to find a place elsewhere. To be "Acehnese" is to feel
propelled out of an original situation and to find a
resolution to the effects of that push that confers a
certain identity. At this time for these students, the
end of the trajectory finds itself in "Aceh" and no
longer in Indonesia. Finally, of course, that will
make them Acehnese where "Acehnese" refers to an
accomplished identity rather than to its origin.

Until recently there was no contradiction between
being Acehnese and being Indonesian. Rather the
contrary. For someone born in Aceh, the trajectory
of maturation, taking one through the schools especially, left one "Indonesian." Even when Daud
Beureuèh led his rebellion against the republic, he
did so in the name of Darul Islam Indonesia, not
Darul Islam or Darul Islam Aceh. This despite the
fact that material cooperation with other provinces
that were revolting was minimal. Today, for many, it
is not Indonesia but "Aceh" that is thought to provide the culmination of their trajectory.

The army is a central part of the Indonesian
nation and state. Students share the opinion of most
politically active Indonesians at present and almost
all politically active students in opposing it. Army
brutality alone does not explain why this should be.

Throughout most of the New Order the army was brutal, and yet general sentiment was in its favor. The change in judgment is the result in large part of the evolution of the myth of the New Order running to a dead end. The New Order founded itself on the idea of the danger of the underclass, identified first as Communist and later as criminal. Suharto exaggerated the power of the underclass in order to demonstrate the need for a strong military government. I have tried to show elsewhere how, for reasons embedded in Indonesian political thinking, brutal killings were intended to demonstrate that the state had a power equivalent to that of the underclass—equivalent not only in quantity but in its quality of being outside moral limitation.[16] Toward the end of the New Order, instead of finding the government a necessary counterforce to a dangerous element inherent in Indonesia itself, certain Indonesians took the government, if not the state, but certainly the army, at its word—as itself criminal. It is in this context, the truth of which was demonstrated by the atrocities of the army in Aceh itself, that student sympathies were formed.

It is misleading to think of these students, for instance, as convinced Acehnese nationalists. They are not much concerned with the ethnic identity of other Indonesians, for instance, or even with others' national identity as Indonesian as in opposition to themselves. They celebrate the myths of Acehnese

[16] See Siegel, *A New Criminal Type in Jakarta.*

history, such as the power of the ancient sultanate, to
a lesser extent then other types of Acehnese. Their
"Aceh Merdeka," independent Aceh, does not yet, at
the time I write, have a shape or a contrary, only an
enemy, the army, which for them is a metonymy for
"Indonesia." These students feel the effects of New
Order development, namely, the redefinition of the
ideas of nationalism, drawn on by Sukarno, by which
the nation was divided into *rakyat* (the people) and
their leaders. In the New Order, "the people" were
likely to be thought of as the *massa* or mass, the
feared underclass. The effect of Development
*(Pembangunan),* the motto of the New Order, was the
elaboration of the middle class as an alternative. The
Indonesian middle class, instead of having its origins
in liberation from feudal exactions, was always a
product of "development" or "enlightenment" or
"modernization." These words all indicated the
emergence of "Indonesians" out of the supposed
backwardness of regional cultures. The acceleration
of this process in the New Order as Indonesia
became richer meant in Aceh that large numbers of
youths from the countryside attended the university
and could think of themselves as new members of
this class. The silent wish of Acehnese students today
is for a middle class existence minus the violence
that, in their thinking as well as in the pronounce-
ments of the New Order and earlier, proceeds from
the savagery of the underclass when it is leaderless.
They are, if it is possible to be so, nationalists whose
nation is the middle class.

The students are not against violence on principle. And they are mentally preparing themselves, against their will, for a moment when they feel that violent opposition is all that is left to them. Violence, for them, is a phenomenon defined by its setting between the classes. But it is not class warfare they fear. They are middle class by inclination but underclass by origin and by a sentiment that they cannot rid themselves of. Students' aversion to violence does not come from a prohibition of violence any more than villagers' delay in taking vengeance comes from such a prohibition (though one can hear Muslim authorities claim that vengeance is prohibited). It comes from fear of failing to signify. I repeat this again here to point to the peculiar authority inherent in the momentary reluctance to engage in violence in these groups. It does not stem from an interdiction or a repressed impulse but from a fear of failure to matter. Thus students' horror of the army is complex. It is composed of visions of army brutality set in the assumption that to suffer such brutality is to be reduced to a state of being inarticulate.

It is impossible to decide whether this fear in turn is a fear of their own weakness or their own strength. For instance to succeed in defeating the Indonesian armed forces, a possibility that they do not allow themselves to imagine, would quite possibly be to find themselves powerful children, still unable to make themselves count. It is thus not possible to say whether these groups fear their own power or the reverse. Either way, what they anticipate if they act without spokespersons is an incomprehensible result. They are left with the contradiction that someone has to proclaim "Aceh Merdeka" for them, even if it is the Indonesian government itself, before they can appropriate their own force.

The students in Banda Aceh who call themselves "Acehnese" began their demand for independence as Indonesian students. Their model was student actions in Jakarta. They never noticed anything anomalous in this, and it certainly has many precedents in the history of nationalism. It was as Indonesian students that they satisfied a demand put on them as Acehnese just as those in earlier generations did as traders and as members of the reform movement. This demand is to answer to their origins. It is not to certify for themselves a claim to be a person from a certain village, with a certain father and a certain mother. It is rather to make these facts irrelevant in the sense that they cease to weigh on them.

Their predecessors one to two generations earlier who had university education sometimes came back to the province as university lecturers or government functionaries. Others settled elsewhere. Either way, they saw no gap between their past and their present, rather the contrary. Having succeeded in integrating themselves into the realm of "developed" Indonesia, it seemed to them that the path from an Acehnese village to the Indonesian bureaucracy was natural; the second was inherent in the first. Or so it appeared after the fact. For the students of the present generation, however, it is no longer the case. If they were, and still are, "Indonesian" by virtue of being students in a university, which is to say in a "modern" institution, this no longer means what it did to their predecessors. It seems to them, rather, that the path into "modern" life is blocked. They still assume that something about "Aceh" leads out of the village and away from their past. But they find that to be students in a university no longer satisfies their assumption. They find themselves in Indonesia, as Indonesians, and it does not suffice. On the one hand they are possessed by an Aceh they cannot leave behind, and on the other only independent Aceh will relieve them of their predicament. They are in the only apparently paradoxical situation of wanting to be "Acehnese," rather than simply being Acehnese by birth.

"Indonesia" now stands in the way of these students. It brings them back to their origins in the village and the family. It is one of the surprises of this movement that, for students at least, their past in Aceh weighs on them as a burden while they rely on the authority of a word, *merdeka* (independence), taken from the history of the country from which they wish to secede, to relieve themselves of this weight. None of this would be possible to understand unless one sees that for them, origins are merely beginnings to be left behind and that the problem for them is that it seems to them that their origins cannot be abandoned.

If students lack ideology they are merely the products of our time. They rely on the residues of

the word *merdeka,* which for them, of course, res-
onates from the time of the Revolution. At the
moment this word indicates simply a promise of
something better. In the absence of other authority, it
lends them the aura of Indonesian history as it has
continued to shine, carefully illuminated by New
Order propaganda but not less believed in for that.
Students thus rely not merely on an Indonesian word
and Indonesian experience but also on an Indonesian
authority. They know that *merdeka* is worthwhile
not because they know what it would mean practically (their Acehnese/Indonesian elders often question them about this) or even spiritually (except neg-
atively) but because of the weight of the word itself.

The lack of a program and the resurrection of one
key word of the Revolution, *merdeka,* without the
others, such as *revolusi* (revolution), indicate that
what they want is escape from the past. If they did
not feel so caught they might speak not only of
*merdeka* but also of *revolusi.* The latter could indicate
a certain freedom from social structures that comes at
the very moment one pronounces the word seriously.
They, however, saying only, "Independence," indicate
the extent to which they feel in the grip of their past.

Students borrow the injuries and even the deaths
of others the way Acehnese women take their dreams
from spirits. They thereby signal that they are in the
grip of something, that they have something to say,
that they do not know what it is and so cannot articulate it, and that until they do, they cannot rest. It
becomes a matter of finding a spokesperson, which

means a way of making whatever possesses them their own. Students want "Atjeh" to be theirs the way that dreaming women accept as their own the burden laid on them by visiting spirits.[17] Or the way that wounded village men want to be able to exorcise the injury done them. Each needs a means of articulation, and before that, each needs a word or a figure to say that they cannot speak. For women who dream, this word is *djinn,* which means a being who remains incomprehensible but holds them in its grip until they can relate their dreams. For students as for injured villagers the phrase that means "I cannot speak, but I have something to say" is "Aceh Merdeka."

One sees here the limit of the word *possession,* which in the sense we are using it refers to "spirit possession." Once one is freed of belief in spirits, the phenomenon of possession itself seems to disappear. But that is not the case in Aceh or, I think, in the rest of Indonesia. It is merely the name that has changed; the foreign thing lodged in the psyche is no longer called "spirit," and it is no longer a question of exorcism. To feel possessed is to feel that one still finds oneself in a realm of experience not yet brought into "modernity." Once fully "modern" one no longer speaks of spirits but of "experience." At that point the process we have described by which men leave their past behind is no longer possible. "Experience," by its definition, is part of oneself. Today in Indonesia, in place of curing rites, there are

[17] See "Curing Rights, Dreams, and Domestic Politics."

instead political movements that relieve Indonesians of possession by the past. In appearance such political leadership is formulated outside the village world. But in reality it draws its sustenance and even its constitution from its relation to that world.

Wherever it is institutionalized possession makes it possible to have a double personality. Where there is spirit possession those who speak for the spirit or who allow the spirit to speak for them are first possessed themselves. They are cured on the condition that they allow the spirit to speak through them. They thus become divided in their person; they have their everyday identities, and they have another, often in trance, in which they "are" the spirit.

This doubling of the person is banished from modernity. Or at least when it occurs it is thought to be a sign of illness. When it is recounted by Sukarno or by Hasan Mohammed di Tiro one is inclined to see it as metaphorical.[18] But its emergence into public life on an important scale forces one to credit these writers with a certain literalness. There is,

[18] One might think that one should at this point drop the word *possession* in favor of *obsession*. The obsessed also are in the grip of something whose name they do not know. But the repetitive gestures of the obsessed, their recurrent gestures toward an unknown authority, make them different. And as I say earlier, possession is always a question of speech, whereas obsession centers on gestures and symbols. Obsession, when it ceases to be private, is likely to become religion. See S. Freud, "Obsessive Acts and Religious Practices" in Freud, *Character and Culture* (New York: Collier Books, 1963), 17–26. Possession frequently leads to cults, but in Indonesia it often is at the commencement of political movements.

however, a difference. The spirit that causes illness is exorcised. The spirit that inhabits political movements can be assimilated to its bearer as was the case with Sukarno, with Hasan Mohammed di Tiro, and, less successfully, with students today. That is to say, they seek a unified identity to replace the division they feel. Finally, that someone else speaks for the Acehnese possessed recapitulates the history of the formation of the Indonesian nation. The *rakyat* (the people) have to be united and have to have a leader to form the nation. The people disunited are the masses. The masses are inarticulate and merely violent. The very notion of a unified Indonesian people means that the people speak with one voice and need a spokesperson to be that voice. The alternative in Indonesia is to think one is incapable of speaking at all. In that state, to obey the impulse for expression is to be merely violent. The contrast is the French Revolution, where, in the Convention for instance, there were seemingly innumerable voices, each claiming to speak for the people. The Indonesian people, in the course of their history, came to find their expression through their leaders or not at all. One sees here how the same expressions "the people," has liberal tendencies in one society and illiberal ones in another. And one sees as well the truth of Benedict Anderson's demonstration that the Indonesian Revolution was only an anticolonial revolution though a true revolution was possible.

The accomplishment of the New Order was the development of the middle class. But this class began before the New Order. It was no different than the enlightened class, composed of those who would lead the nation. The nation itself was thus assumed to be divided in two. This was not a division between segments in conflict. Both were in theory directed against colonialism and for the development of the whole. The obstacle to progress, particularly after independence, was thought to be internal division. By contrast, the European middle class developed from the bourgeoisie, the class of city dwellers, usually long distance traders, who won freedom from feudal exactions. The development of classes in Europe was via opposition, opposition that resulted in the definition of one class by reference to the other, just as personal identity took the same agonistic form. In Indonesia, as in much of the world outside Europe, history took a different course. The development of the nation and development of class were simultaneous. The goal was not the dominance of one class over another, however, but the assimilation of the whole into the "middle," or developed, class.

The consequences of this difference of historical course are numerous. Not least are the cultural effects. The French middle class, for instance, drew its culture from the aristocracy. Moreover, the awareness that culture develops out of conflict and that one can appropriate the attributes of one's opponents means that culture can be learned. To be "French" is to know "the code," which is to say, to learn mediating forms still drawn from court society.

In Indonesia, forms of etiquette are divorced from wider culture. Court society makes itself felt through mere quotation.[19] In Indonesia also one needs to learn to be middle class, but what one learns seems to appear from nowhere and thus loses its appearance as learning. The fact that the culture of the Indonesian middle class had its origins in Chinese mercantile culture and in the assimilation of Western learning, and yet led to being "Indonesian," was further reason to forget that one learns to be rather than simply becomes Indonesian. (The failure to do so is simply to be "barbarian" [biadab]). Partly for this reason the course of middle class or Indonesian culture has been not toward the development of thought but toward cultural obliviousness, leaving the dissident movements of the archipelago without much to draw on today except for the dilemma "assimilation or no assimilation" or, as students in Aceh understand it, "assimilation into Aceh or regression into the barbarous."

The people, the fundament of Indonesia, theoretically can disappear, being completely assimilated, when the course of development is complete. Indonesia would then be everything it should be. But in practice, it is unthinkable that the people should disappear. There would then be no political differentiation. The problem of leadership, even in the New Order when Suharto tried to take the power of "crim-

[19] On this complicated question see the seminal study of John Pemberton, *On the Subject of "Java"* (Ithaca: Cornell University Press, 1994).

inals," his name for the masses or for "the people," is
to reunite with the people. But it is equally the case
that the condition for this reunion is the memory of
separation. Possession, when it is a condition not of
the village sick but of members of the middle class,
is the symptom of the malfunctioning of memory;
what is chronologically in the past still operates as
though it were present. This means also that the premodern, protonational realm makes itself felt sometimes to the point of blockage of the process of
assimilation. The interior of the nation reveals its
recalcitrance to becoming part of it.

"The people" then take on different names and
multiple voices such as those of criminals, of
Communists, even of the ghosts of communists and
of ignorant secessionists. (Or, from another point of
view, of independent Acehnese.) All of these are
multiple, whereas "the people" is singular. Perhaps
there is always a moment before the people appear
in the singular when in their multiple forms they
possess whatever individual feels the necessity, as
Indonesians say, to "bear the aspirations of the
people." Possession, that is, is apparently always
possession by plural rather than singular forms.
When the people are made singular, there is a clear
difference between them and those who give them
expression. At that moment, one can speak of
"class" in Indonesia.

ANOTHER PERSPECTIVE

It seems as if possession, then, is one possibility

of the nondialectical formation of class. It is the result of an original unity now lost, not regained but resolved through political leadership on the one hand and the people who feel the lack of it on the other. But where does this lack arise? I have presented it as an effect of the historical development of the nation and as a problem of class. But does that account for the lack felt by "the people"? There is another perspective open. One might assume for a moment that there is something incomplete in Acehnese society, if not in Malay society in general, even before there were "the people."

This lack might be found in the language itself. In Acehnese, *rasi* means "to name" in the sense of "to tell the name," but it also means "to bestow a name," as for a child. In the latter case one looks for an appropriate name, one that fits the baby. One might search in a book of divinatory signs for such a name; that activity too is included in the verb *rasi*. In nineteenth-century Aceh at least, an appropriate name brought good fortune. Not everyone can bear the same fortune-bringing name; it has to be suitable to the child. Thus no particular name is a bearer of good fortune simply by its signification; it is a question of its fit. Djajadiningrat in his dictionary of Acehnese under *rasi* cites a line from an epic as an example:

Then he gave him [a newborn child] a highly appropriate *[meurasi]* name, one that fit his shining look.[20]

[20] R. A. Dr. Hoesein Djajadiningrat, *Atjèhsch-Nederlandsch Woordenboek* (Batavia: Landsdrukkerij, 1934).

When the name has to fit the child the qualities named are thought present in the infant. But to have good fortune, the child has to be given the name. The name may express qualities inherent in the child, but without the name, presumably those qualities would not develop. The possibility of a supplementary addition, like the printed name and the words *Acheh Merdeka* on an identity card, has to be assumed. The possibility of adding something and making it appear that it was already there is an attribute of Acehnese proper names.

The Acehnese language epic of the seventeenth century called the *Hikajat Malém Dagang* gives another example of naming.[21] This long poem tells of the most powerful Acehnese sultan, Iskandar Muda. Iskandar Muda, in order to raise an army, tours the Acehnese countryside. In various places, the local people and the accompanying *ulama* point to the landscape and ask the king to "give it a name." In one location, the king himself asks the *ulama* to name the place. He cannot or will not. Only the king can do so. Iskandar Muda speaks:

> What place is on this side, Teungkoe Dja, what
>     district? Name the place.

---

[21] I have dealt with this epic earlier. See Siegel, "Alexander the Great in Atjehnese: Cowardice and Historical Memory," *Archipel* 56 (1998). I have revised certain paragraphs from this piece here. Citations to the epic are from H. K. J. Cowan, *De "Hikajat Malém Dagang": Atjèhsch Heldendicht, Tekst en Toelichting* (The Hague: Koninklijk Instituut voor de Taal-, Land- en Volkenkunde van Nederl.-Indië, 1937).

Since you asked me, my lord, over here is
    Gampong Raja.
And what is over there, what would you call it?
I can't speak, as an ulama my mouth is
    ashamed.
If you are ashamed, I will speak and name it.
Know, then, that over there the place is called
    *meusé djih.*

(719–25)

The *ulama* will not say the name of the place presumably because *meusé,* according to Cowan,
means "sexual intercourse." The king, however, does
so, as we have seen.

The passage indicates an uncertain relation
between local place-names and "Aceh." Suppose, for
instance, the king did not know the names. Would
they still be securely "Acehnese"? When a place
evokes a name he knows, it is part of "Aceh"; the sultan is the authority even though he only rarely visits
the countryside. The local people, who doubtless use
the name daily, are not sure it really is the name. A
similar situation could arise if, in the midst of a conversation in English, we heard the word *mañana,* as
in fact today one easily can in New York City. To
know if the word is English, that is, recognized as
part of the language and not a foreign word, we
would consult *Webster's.* (Indeed, the name that the
*ulama* cannot pronounce might be a foreign place-
name, "Egypt."[22]) Here, it is as though if a place

---

[22] Cf. Cowan, *De "Hikajat,"* 102.

evokes a name from the king, it belongs to "Aceh."

When the king sees a place and names it, then, it is a special sort of reading. In the first place this is because it occurs across a cultural gap. The king comes from the court, whose language and culture are not Acehnese but Malay; he is from far away, culturally, socially, and geographically, and yet, seeing the landscape, the king knows the name of the place. Within the Acehnese language poem, local names are conveyed and understood across a cultural distance. The *ulama* too can read names from geographical features. But it is reserved to the king to both read the name and put it into use. The *ulama* is "ashamed." He cannot speak the name he knows. The king voices the name forbidden to the *ulama*. The *ulama* knows it, but he cannot put it into circulation. The king, however, knows it, says it, and allows it to be used by others.

One can ask what would happen if the king did not know the name. Would it remain a name? Is it possible to name inappropriately, as in giving a name to a child who lacks the qualities associated with it? In the epic, the king, in pursuit of his enemy, leaves Aceh and ventures out to sea. At that point the presentation of him is reversed. Though he is the most revered of all Acehnese rulers and known for his power, Iskandar Muda outside of Aceh is shown as a coward. Considering that his name, according to Denys Lombard, was taken from Alexander the Great's in order to assimilate him to the legend of the great conqueror, to show this powerful warrior full of fear is puzzling.[23]

When his ship is surrounded by those of his opponent and is cannonaded, Iskandar Muda retreats to his cabin. Even before this, as soon as they are out of sight of land Iskandar Muda has to be reassured that the omens are favorable to be persuaded to continue his pursuit of Si Oedjoet. The *ulama* says to him:

> Do not be fearful, do not be frightened; why are
>       you so anxious, my lord?
> I have looked into the book of signs; nowhere
>       is there calamity.
> Wait three days; we will have arrived at our
>       destination.
>
>                               (883–85)

Thus the *ulama,* among others, reassures the frightened ruler. The fear of the king is not simply fear of battle. The king is afraid well before there is any fighting. After they have put out to sea and Aceh is no longer in sight, a strong wind comes up as told in a passage that is as beautiful as it is puzzling:

> Some of the sailors were lost in thought; some
>       of the travelers prayed.
> The water fell over the bow like jasmine
>       blossoms as the ships were strewn over the
>       great sea.

[23] Denys Lombard, *Le Sultanat d'Atjéh au temps d'Iskandar Muda: 1607–1636* (Paris: École Française d'Extrême-Orient, 1967), 170–71.

Three days and three nights they sailed till land
  had entirely disappeared from sight.
As they came to the midst of the sea, the land
  was entirely covered with black.
Looking to sea one saw only the dark; looking
  for land one saw only a blank.
The water of the sea was thick like poorly risen
  apem-bread.
The country had disappeared; no one
  recognized the earth.
His majesty Meukoeta Alam [Iskandar Muda]
  felt frightened; the King was fearful and
  bathed in tears.

                                    (873–79)

Land has disappeared from sight. The king looks
for it but sees "only a blank." Whereas in Aceh when
the king looks at the landscape he speaks its name,
when Aceh is out of sight, the king looks and sees
only "black," only "a blank." He sees nothing; he
says nothing. No words come to mind. "Aceh" and
"Iskandar Muda" are bound together the way a voice,
the body in which it is located, and the language it
speaks are united when the king is within his kingdom. When Aceh has disappeared from view the king
can no longer articulate. The mighty Iskandar Muda
is fearful and weeps.

This representation of a failure to name suggests
that in Aceh, without the king, there could be the
same situation. Without the king, names might not
be names at all. Places could lack the possibility of
having a name. In order to name or in order to speak,

there needs to be something inherent in the thing that can be expressed through a word. But there needs also to be someone, some authority, who can bring the thing to expression. That authority could fail.

In the *Hikajat Malém Dagang,* there is a distinction between what is within Aceh's borders and what is outside them. Outside, language does not function. The king himself is then in the position of "the people," needing someone else (who never appears) to make words work. In Aceh, words function because someone, a supreme authority, makes them do so. The very possibility of "Aceh," given that the kingdom rarely functioned as a political unit, depended on a linguistic function united to a political office.

Times change. But the idea of a lack inherent in the landscape, or in its inhabitants, "the people," merely evolved. The very possibility of names working suggests the opposite. After the fact, the fact here being that of functioning speech, the possibility of the inability to articulate comes into view. One can transpose this horrifying possibility into the terms of the present. Something interior to Aceh or to the people calls for articulation. According to Acehnese or perhaps Malay assumptions, without a political structure it cannot be expressed. Or, to turn the proposition around, one can say that when political leadership fails, as at the end of the New Order it did, what manifested itself lacked a voice.

NORMALITY TODAY

Let us change the perspective again. This time let us look from the point of view of "the people." Not "the people" as they are already constituted but the individuals who feel they cannot articulate their own identity. They feel there is something in them that calls for recognition. When it is recognized, they are properly named. They are then "Acehnese" or "Indonesian." The other possibility, that the king will fail, so to speak, is always present.

Two girls in their twenties. They work in an outdoor restaurant during the evenings, across from the Central Mosque in Banda Aceh. They are students at Sjiahkuala University in Banda Aceh. They wear tight skirts and makeup; their hair is carefully cut. They do not wear the *jilbab,* or headscarf, even at Unsjiah, to use the common abbreviation for their university, where most women seem to wear it. But they do not feel uncomfortable. "It's perfectly all right." At the university they wear their school uniform. In any case, as it is understood in Banda Aceh, the *jilbab* does not promise modest behavior so much as it is itself a form of fashion. It is, said one lecturer at the Islamic Institute, next to Unsjiah, using English, "international influence." The elaborate makeup, the stylish shoes, even the silky *jilbab* itself with its various colors indicate a self-presentation at work that is evident also in wearers of the school uniform.

"International influence" is an ambiguous phrase.

It refers to Islamic influence, presumably on the side of modesty, but it also suggests Western influence, which works, in the minds of some, for the opposite. Even this is not certain, however. The attractiveness of these women's dress is not always an indication of immodesty but might instead signify propriety. It is another example of conformity. Were they not to present themselves attractively they would be ashamed. Once they have done so, the question of their sexual allure is confused. It is, in my opinion, certainly there. And yet the propriety of their dress is what counts in their own minds. Others, more severe in their judgment, might condemn them. It is an example of how they might be taken for one type or for another, entirely different, on the basis of the same appearance. I asked them if they would like to go to school in Java. They said it was a question of money. It was cheaper here. I said I heard life was freer in Java. They said they did not want it that way, and they clearly did not approve. Both these girls participated in the anti-Suharto demonstrations, and both were teargassed. Since then they have not been politically active. They said they were afraid. Why? One did not explain. I assumed it was because of the violence she had experienced, but she said that she was not afraid of the army. The other said it was because she looked Javanese; she thinks of herself as Acehnese and speaks Acehnese, but she believes that she looks Javanese. She was afraid of the GAM. The GAM, she knows, makes Javanese targets.

These women have two reasons to feel that they

might be misrecognized. One is sexual, the other
ethnic. This fear marks the failure of Indonesia.
When Indonesia worked, one's origins did not matter. The comparison that first comes to mind is with
the United States. But there is a difference. In the
United States many people have identities with
hyphenated names: Italian-American, African-
American, Catholic-American, Jewish-American.
The second term renders the first innocuous. A standard phrase is "we are all Americans," which means,
Tocqueville pointed out long ago, that differences
are denied. The denial of the importance of origins
in Indonesia comes about in another way. To be recognized as Indonesian means to have a place in the
nation and to think that there is an agency—the
state—that recognizes one. This is another way to
say that someone else speaks for one. Americans
assert their identity as though the assertion itself
makes it a fact. Indonesians easily say where they
were born and who their parents were. But they look
to someone else to make that an unimportant fact.
The failure of Indonesia comes when one is misrecognized, which might well mean recognized for
what one was born. The girl who fears she looks
Javanese, for instance, had a Javanese ancestor. But
the fear of misrecognition does not need to have a
basis in descent or in sexual identity. These women
feel that someone will recognize them, that, in other
words, they signify in ways that they do not control.
It is this that one sees, for instance, in the issue of
dress. To have someone speak for them, someone

authoritative, is to ensure that they do not betray themselves and are not taken for someone they do not wish to be.

Normality in Indonesia is the reassurance that recognition works as it should and that consequently differences do not matter. These women are caught in a situation where there are two competing sources of recognition. They say they fear the GAM, and no doubt they do to an extent, or at least one of them does. But they said they were afraid in such toneless voices that it is difficult to know the depths of their fear or even the truth of their assertion. In my opinion this is not the result of a lack of fear but of being uncertain of its object. It could be the GAM, it could be the army that teargassed them, even though they denied this. The most likely possibility, it seems to me, is that their fear lacks definition. This lack is the mark of the failure of Indonesia. In Aceh, for many, it is no longer the source of recognition of identity. One can imagine "Indonesia" as the king who looks and sees only blankness. Or one can imagine Indonesia as the still potent center that recognizes their disloyalty, which could take the form of being "Acehnese" or could take another form. Or it could be the GAM that sees that they are not "Acehnese." The call for recognition remains. The lack of an established agent for such and the unclarity about who one might be upset normality. Fear means here suspicion of something that arises first in oneself and that leads to being taken for someone unwelcome to oneself.

The students who want Aceh Merdeka are in the same situation as these women. Many sleep in different places every night, they told me, afraid that the army is after them. But there are not yet the kidnappings of students in Aceh that took place in Java. Perhaps they will have reason to be afraid and are merely prudent. But if one thinks that prudence means taking precautions coolly, they are not prudent. There is no realistic assessment of danger. There are, rather, the continuous nervousness and excitement that come when one feels that normality no longer prevails. They now fear being apprehended not for their actions but for their intentions, and these often enough are known only to themselves or to a few others. The success of Indonesia was simply to name a possible identity, as for instance, "Acehnese," "Batak," "Javanese," and to have it not matter. The failure of Indonesia is to make its citizens feel they are an open book and every character in it.

The name of this failure is "army violence." The army is a synecdoche for "Indonesia" in the minds of students. It was "Indonesia" who recognized them and spoke for them. Now, students fear that they are recognized for qualities that make them guilty in the eyes of the army. Their identifying term, *Acehnese,* instead of being made innocuous makes them vulnerable. The army, they fear, sees them only to murder them. The temporary relief of this unsustainable anxiety is the nightmare of the student already recounted. The army has killed him;

he exists only in his mother's memory. There at least he has his original identity, one questionable by no one since it is available to no one but the one person who knows him in his singularity.

KILLING

The failure of Indonesia, like its success, is a question of the people and their spokespersons. But "the people" metamorphose into "the masses" and into criminals while their spokespersons become themselves criminal. The pattern of violence varies accordingly. The violence in Aceh in 1999 was mainly produced by the army, and so too was the massacre in Aceh in 1965–66 of all suspected Communists. The difference comes with the public support—or not—of the army. When I was in Aceh in 1999, there had been about thirty murders known as "revenge killings" *(tueng bila)*. In most of these incidents two or three men on a motorbike rode to a village coffee shop, shot someone with a rifle, and rode off. Those killed were often identified as informers for the army. People knew that the army had forced certain villagers to identify their neighbors as members of the GAM on pain of the rape of their sisters, the kidnapping of their fathers, and so on. The government was blamed for this practice, but knowledge of it also supported the possibility that the killers were GAM members taking revenge. These killings also became known as *petrus,* an acronym for "mysterious shootings" used in 1983 when tattooed men labeled criminals were killed and their bodies left on the street. It became evident that members of the army, on the orders of President Suharto, were the murderers of these tattoed "criminals." In 1983 public opinion accepted these killings. They displayed the might of the army and relieved fears of the public about criminals. In Aceh in 1999 that no one was arrested for the killings supported the view that soldiers were doing the killing. People with this opinion did not support the army. They thought that soldiers were covering their tracks, eliminating people who could testify against them. They did not see the army as maintaining order but as culpable and as creating the disorder that marks Aceh today. Even those who felt that probably these really were revenge killings done by GAM members did not call for the suppression of GAM, which was one more indication of lack of confidence not merely in the government but in the state.

Often the same person would say about the same murder that it was the work of the police and that it was a question of vengeance. The lack of clarity is due more to lack of confidence in authority than to a paucity of facts. It could well be, they thought, that the government was killing in order that Acehnese and Indonesians elsewhere would see the need for military force. There are many examples. In the course of revising this chapter, I learned that many Acehnese suspect the GAM leader of Pidie, said to have organized sporadic attacks on the army, of being in the pay of the military. In north Aceh, the army killed a man named Ahmad Kandang, accusing him of attacks on them. But many Acehnese wanted to know how it was possible for someone who, they claimed, was so little known before the incident to suddenly emerge as an important GAM leader. They concluded that he was in the army pay and then was eliminated by the army itself. Another opinion, held sometimes by the same people, was that he was in fact a GAM leader, just as the army said. They did not necessarily approve, however, of his murder.

The contrast is with 1983, when the strong tendency was for people to believe that those killed were criminals and that the army killed them. The important difference is that in 1983, the killings were generally approved. In 1999 in Aceh the army is feared, and no one thinks that the killings maintain order. There is inquietude whose source is thought to be double and about which people are confused. Fear of disruption from within Aceh is not limited to the Acehnese middle class. Fear of the army is, it seemed to me, general. There are thus two beliefs about these killings reflecting two sources of danger: they are vengeance killings, the work of injured villagers—in the middle class version this is implied to be typical of villagers when there is no strong government; second, it is the government—it is *petrus* again but this time in the interest of disorder.

The explanation of the present killings and questions of justice are confused with one another. Older people in the urban middle class are wary of GAM,

seeing it as a source of disorder. But they have seen
the army at work in Aceh and do not approve. For
them, federation is a compromise. It is first of all
important because it means keeping the profits from
sale of natural resources for Aceh. But it also implic-
itly offers relief from army intervention. They want
order, but they do not know how, exactly, to go about
it. They feel that the republic still offers the best
chance for it. They do not speak of reprisals against
either the army or the people in the Acehnese government who called in the army.

In the countryside, the members of GAM of
course want justice even if they are willing to wait.
There have been reprisals. For instance, the house in
Pidie of Ibrahim Hasan, the governor who called for
more troops, was burned down by people from
neighboring villages who had suffered from the
army. But we have seen that, for the greater part,
those wanting vengeance have waited. The students
who are concerned with the actions of the army want
independence. But they do not know how to get it, at
least at the moment I write. To think that the government would acquiesce in a referendum is unreal-
istic. The comparison with East Timor does not hold
because Aceh is so rich and thus so important to the
center and because, though it suffers considerably
from the army, the genocidal proportions of violence
in East Timor are not yet in sight. And also because
Aceh has been part of Indonesia from Indonesia's
inception whereas Timor has not and because there is
as yet no important body of foreign opinion favor-

able to Aceh or even familiar with it. To think of independence of course means envisaging Aceh as an autonomous authority. But students at this point do not know where to find this authority. By default, which means not only by habit but by belief, they rely on the central government to furnish it.

Aceh thus finds itself in a situation where no authority holds the confidence of Acehnese. But Acehnese feel that, somewhere and somehow, such exists. Thus villagers wait over twenty years for Hasan Mohammed di Tiro to speak for them from Sweden, and students, hearing his name, want him but, as I have said, without knowing his program. One hears an eagerness in students' tone of voice when they speak of Hasan Mohammed di Tiro. One, for instance, gave me a photograph of himself to give to Hasan, telling me that, since I was going to Europe, I should tell him, "We yearn for you." If they yearn for him it is because only someone like him can normalize their situation. Add to their desire for recognition, already inherent in their "normal" transition between classes that comes with their maturation, the threat of military violence that deprives them of it and the result is a millenarian tonality as students too wait for Hasan Mohammed di Tiro.[24]

[24] This tonality manifests itself in the request frequently made to me, mentioned earlier in the chapter, that I "tell them what is happening in Aceh." The "them" of this phrase is imprecise, but the people who utter this sentence are convinced that somewhere there is an agency who will save them. The equivalent for the students when "they" is not Hasan Mohammed di Tiro is "the international community." This belief in an authority who will recog-

There is another belief in authority, whose provenience is even more vague, that has to do with killing. Murder is justified in Aceh, as I suppose almost everywhere, when it is political. Thus in 1969 Daud Beureuèh told me that the 1966 murder of Communists was justified "if they were guilty." "Guilt" meant being a Communist, which was taken to mean someone wanting to murder Muslims. But even then many were reluctant to kill. One man, the head of a school who helped organize the arrest of Communists, told me in 1969 that "it is all right to clean up the PKI [the Indonesian Communist Party], but one shouldn't mix in the killings." He was not opposed to the killings. He knew very well that the people he had had arrested were to be murdered. He meant, rather, that he would not himself kill, and he told his students the same thing. He went on to say that his brother had fought in Prang Tjumbok when Acehnese Muslim nationalists had fought *uleebelang* during the revolution. His father told him not to kill, though he felt that the *uleebelang* were supporters of the Dutch and, he implied, should be put to death. But if one killed one would die later as a consequence. It was for this reason that his brother was killed when he fought in the Darul Islam rebellion at least ten years after he fought in the revolutionary battle. One of the executioners of Communists died

nize who they are and who will help them to gain independence is partly an idea long part of Indonesian nationalism and simply assumed by some Acehnese today for the cause of Acehnese independence. It is a religious notion, but the God of this religion is not particularly Islamic.

several years after of natural causes. I was told by four or five people that his death too was taken as an effect of his having killed.

These stories of killers finding an early death resemble the fantasy of opposing the army and being killed while doing so. There is a simple fear of one's own violence and a feeling that one will pay even when such violence is thought to be justified. There is nothing rational about thinking that if one murders one's enemy and one has every available authority telling one that one is right and even heroic to do so one will be punished nonetheless. Nor is it a question of prudence. The killers in 1966 had nothing to fear in the way of reprisals; they were perfectly safe. Furthermore, the punishing agent is not a culturally defined entity. It is not the law; it is not God. It is irrational to think that a man who dies of malaria ten years after he executed political prisoners and did so, if not legally, certainly with the encouragement, the cooperation, and probably the pay of the state and the blessing of religion died because he murdered. When one believes that these prisoners ought to have been put to death and still believes that the executioner died because he killed them, the political meaning of the killing is unaffected. It was still the right thing to do. The superstitious brake put on murder is outside political and cultural life.

The interdiction does not say that murder is wrong, and, as I have said, it is held by people who think that certain murder was not only justified but desirable. It stands outside any notion of justice since, for instance, the man whose brother died fighting *uleebelang* did not merit his death any more than did the executioner from the point of view of the Acehnese who told me about them. Nor was either of these men thought a martyr. They were not considered to be men who dared to violate a prohibition in the interest of right. The man whose brother was killed, for instance, simply regretted that his brother had killed, though he approved of the cause and the act, because it led to his brother's own death. The head of the school encouraged his pupils to help in the roundup of Communists; both he and his pupils knew that those they brought in were to be executed. Remembering his brother the head of the school advised his pupils not to do the killing themselves. His words might have stopped some people from murdering. But he and his students knew of the executions, approved of them, and helped them to take place. The prohibition thus in no way prevented murder; it only stopped certain people from murdering. This superstitious belief about murder is thus useless for the prevention of killing.

Like most superstitions, the origin of the belief that if one kills one will, eventually, be killed in return is unknown. No authority for it can be quoted. Certainly it is something people hear from others, and thus it has the force of common belief. But in a culture as Islamic as Aceh, a belief without justification in Islam should not have much force. It prohibits, among other killing (and it is only killing of humans that is referred to), the taking of vengeance.

Thus one might well be tempted to repay someone for a serious aggression. But if one does so, even successfully, one will be killed oneself though probably not by the kin of the one murdered in revenge. The superstition is located in the social, but it is also partly removed from it. It is social because it says that an important social act will evoke a response. It is asocial because the source of the response is unknown, has nothing to do with ideas of justice, and serves no social end. The superstition says that a basic human gesture, killing other humans, begets a response. But this response is not itself cultural. Its source cannot be cited, and yet it is not, as I have said, religious. Were it religious its reference might not be available to humans, but they would believe it exists. The source of response to killing here remains vague.

One kills, and one is eliminated oneself. One makes a human gesture, and one is eliminated; one counts for nothing. There is a response, there is an authority that guarantees that one counts for nothing. Murder, in the light of this belief, does not signify. It falls under the same category of acts that includes the unauthorized vengeance of villagers from which they, therefore, restrain themselves. Such a superstition generates its own opposite. Against it is the belief, or the wish, that there be an authority somewhere, thus a cultural setting, that would make killing signify. Hasan Mohammed di Tiro, even though he is unknown to most members of GAM and certainly to the students, is invented to be that authority. But so too is "the international community" or even someone or somebody somewhere without a name. And so was the army in 1965, which had the ability to make the gesture count even though the killer himself had to die.

Were these killers thought martyrs one could say that they sacrificed themselves. But no one told me anything of the sort. The stories were told matter-of-factly. This superstition is an elementary form, something that is possibly protocultural rather than cultural. From this point of view, that it speaks of killing is only a way of saying that human gestures beget responses even when these responses do not signify—or do not signify according to their human intentions. It says that humans have within them the possibility of making gestures that, even when they are justified, will be recognized for some other, entirely unintended, motive. Thus the executioner of Communists thought he was behaving justly, and, from an Acehnese point of view, he was. Nonetheless he was struck down himself and this for no reason at all that can be named. It is merely that, as in the case of the women who can be seen as either modest or immodest, there is a force or an agent of recognition whose response is not entirely predictable. This agent is not culturally institutionalized. It sees in people that which few of them suspect but which nevertheless is there. The only recourse against it is an authority who can make gestures count; who can, we might say, "speak for" the people. And even then no authority can fully prevent a certain misrecognition.

It is in this light that one can look at the violence of the army. The army has not only murdered, which is the job of armies. It has also tortured and raped. These sadistic acts, at least on a wide scale, seem to be new to Indonesia. No doubt they are part of a political strategy designed to show the power of the army. They occur in a context: the state's control of the province from which it extracts natural gas and the wood from its forests. As Ruth McVey and Benedict Anderson showed early in the New Order, the Suharto regime did not depend on the mobilization of public opinion.[25] Instead it fostered fear of the underclass and the consequent need for the army plus undoubted economic progress. In Aceh, dependence on "the people" was avoided as the *ulama* were neutralized and as technocratic administrators depended on Jakarta rather than on local support.[26]

Acheh Merdeka posed no real problem until 1989, when, it seems, its export of ganja to Thailand to raise money for arms ran into difficulty.[27] It was this that led to the appeal of Governor Ibrahim Hasan for

[25] See Ruth McVey, "The Beambenstaat in Indonesia," in Benedict Anderson and Audrey Kahin, *Interpreting Indonesian Politics: Thirteen Contributions to the Debate* (Ithaca: Cornell Modern Indonesia Project, 1982); Benedict Anderson, "Old State, New Society: Indonesia's New Order in Historical Perspective," in Anderson, *Language and Power: Exploring Political Cultures in Indonesia* (Ithaca: Cornell University Press, 1990).

[26] Cf. Morris, "Islam and Politics in Aceh"; and Kell, *Roots of Acehnese Rebellion,* 47–52.

[27] See "Ganja dan Segudang Permasalahan," *Editor,* April 15, 1989, and associated articles, pp. 8–21; and "Hunter, Ganja, dan Aceh Merdeka" and associated articles, pp. 8–16.

troops and the arrival of the Special Forces. It was then that the number of killings increased greatly. It seems that the insertion of the army into the daily operations of the government and the daily lives of Acehnese required their show of force. Force thus had a strategic aim. But the odd feature of demonstrating force is that it works best when it seems as though it is limitless. The army may torture potential informers, telling them that the torture will cease if they will cooperate. The threat depends on knowing that the army will kill. To inculcate fear, it is best if people believe that the army wants to kill and that for very little or for no reason at all it is likely to do so. It is for that reason that army violence is rightly termed *sadistic,* since that word implies pleasure in the inflicting of pain. Army violence in that sense exceeds whatever strategic ends it may have had initially. Rape, new to the inventory of army tactics, can probably be placed in the same light.

It is at this point that political murder took on a new dimension in Aceh. Soldiers engaged in acts of sadism that seemed to give them pleasure. Murder too was made to seem pleasurable. Thus the most basic restraint on killing was shown to no longer apply to the army. It can act not only politically, as the arm of the state, as it were, but in an infantile fashion, for no reason, in a way that makes no sense and does not signify. It challenges the source of all restraint, even the cloudiest and most vague. It thus changes itself from a political instrument, constituted by its function and its limitations, into a criminal entity.

The army thus embodies exactly what the students and the injured villagers we have described would like to avoid for themselves. If villagers and students obey a primitive restraint on killing, waiting for the moment when it might be permissible, the army shows that it has no fear of authority. The Other that, it is feared, surveys Acehnese is blind to the army, or the army has no fear of it. Ultimately, it is the belief in this vague Other that allows students to identify themselves with villagers. They feel the possibility within themselves of being like villagers, which means that they find themselves recognizable as such by an agent that they never name. This in turn means that they believe that there is a source of recognition. The army, by its killing, shows itself to stand in no relation to this Other. It is this that creates the terror that is felt in Aceh today. Its violence asserts a sovereignty, a justification of itself that is without recourse to ulterior legitimation.

This violence may be without justification, but it has a history. The army's terror, as I have said, is the end point of the evolution of New Order legitimacy. The state was legitimated and the nation justified by the wishes of the people as articulated by their president in the Sukarno period. Suharto put an end to such populism and justified his regime by stirring the fears of resurgent Communists and later substitutes for them. By the 1980s as terror of Communists faded and fear of the underclass was consequently amorphous, Suharto gave it shape when he murdered tattooed men said to be criminals. The corpses of these men, usually punctuated with multiple bullet holes, were left in the streets and the rivers. It was, I have argued, a way of saying that the underclass was boundlessly violent and cruel but that the government took power away from the underclass and made that power its own. It could have acted against criminals through arrest and trial. But it wanted to show that it had the violence that formerly belonged to the revolutionary people as transmogrified into the masses.

State terrorism was not, then, simply a way of ensuring that Indonesians kept their place out of fear. It was, as I have said, a strange feature of the events of 1983 that most Indonesians approved of these killings, understanding as they did that they were directed against a certain class. And even members of that class approved, thinking that it was necessary to keep order. This violence was thus seen as having a purpose. The violence directed against Acehnese was similar in character. That is, it was demonstrative and part, in fact, of a contorted attempt at legitimation. It began as part of the routine involvement of the army in all transactions in which they could extract a percentage, at whatever level. Poor peasants thus paid an extra tax even on the sale of a cow. The illegality of the procedures meant that the state, once again, was criminal, while peasantry in particular was punished. There was nothing much in the way of resistance against this. The reason, in my opinion, was not only the power of the army but, more importantly, the acquiescence in that power. If Acehnese, like

Indonesians in 1983, did not seem terrified, it was because the terror of the state had become an element, and even the dominant element, of its legitimacy. Tattooed men in 1983 were shot many times, as though they were killed more than once. The violence against Acehnese was analogous. Its very surfeit was (and is) a claim that violence itself means access to a source of power and therefore the acquisition of a right. Thus the more superfluous the violence was, the more legitimate. It is easier to understand the surprising inactivity of injured peasants if we imagine that at some level in their consciousness they believe in Indonesia. They certainly feel their injuries, and they blame the army for them. But for people who have been treated with such casual violence they remain surprisingly unterrorized. It is difficult to keep in mind this lack of feeling of terror and their restraint at the same time unless one posits a belief in the legitimacy of "Indonesia" and a feeling that its violence is something more than material force.

But of course their limit is apparent in their adherence to the Gerakan Acheh Merdeka. Unlike middle class Indonesians, they cannot accept army violence, not simply because it is directed against them but because it leaves them no way to participate in the nation. Acehnese have been Indonesians since the foundation of the republic. They have proved it by their great contributions to the Revolution and, as I have said, even by their rebellion, which aimed at a reformation of the nation rather than a separate state.

But if the violence of the army may seem to them to have a plan behind it, other than the confiscation of their goods, the rape of women, and the murder and torture of men, they cannot discern it. Their adherence to Acheh Merdeka indicates that Indonesian terrorism, which originally and still, in my estimation, aims at a reinforcement of legitimacy, has become to them, and to others, incomprehensible.

In finding violence senseless peasants are like the students. I can explain this best by comparing students, in turn, with the husbands and fathers of the 1930s who became members of Daud Beureuèh's reform movement. These men, unemployed, found a place outside the village, outside their failed economic relations with their wives. This, as I described it, marked a break with the nineteenth century sociologically. But reformism was a part of nineteenth-century religious life though it had always failed to institutionalize itself. With modernist Islam, it succeeded. Before its success, men's identity, founded on meeting their familial obligations, was jeopardized. That is, they were defined by their relations to the village, but they could not maintain their part in the system of exchange that pertained between husbands and wives. Nor could they abandon their families. They were, one might say now, possessed by their failure. Modernist Islam gave them another basis for themselves. They borrowed from it an authority that I have described them exercising over their wives—or attempting to, at least.

Of course Islam merely supplemented rather than

replaced the power they regained when the economy improved. But its capacity to give men a place in the wider world, independent of where they were born, whom they were born to, or to whom they were married, cannot be doubted. "Islam," of course, means "surrender." A Muslim man surrenders himself to God. But precisely by giving up he gains. He gains the possibility of exercising religious authority. This is a trajectory like that of curers who give themselves over to the power of spirits and thus get the power of the spirits for themselves. Students, learning "modern" knowledge in national schools, go through the same process. They too surrender themselves to their studies in the sense that their experience in school, if not the content of what they learn, dictated to them by national authority, makes them into Indonesians. Like villagers whose photographs are put on GAM identification cards, they too find that there is a part of their nature, unsuspected by themselves previously, that is activated by their experience in school and that transforms a significant aspect of their identities.

It is precisely this process that has been disrupted by army terrorism. It represents Indonesia in such a way that it is impossible for certain elements of the population, those who have suffered it or those who, for reasons described, imagine it working on themselves, to find a place in the nation. Its force is now exclusively the army's. The authority that comes through the school no longer avails. The result is possession. To surrender to it means to acknowledge it without being able to assimilate it. Hence they are possessed. And hence their possession is the result of the particular evolution of nationalism itself under the New Order.

## VIOLENCE ON A LARGE SCALE

This analysis suggests that there are two ways in Indonesia to set off massive violence. Today there is a regression to the most primitive taboo on violence and then its transgression. This is violence not by the masses but by the class of leaders. No doubt it happens now in Indonesia because the army and the state reached the low point of their legitimacy toward the end of the Suharto period. What was left to them was the display of force as it was understood within the context of class relations. This path is regressive and engages the barest, most primitive cultural layers.

The second path to violence comes when "the people" are led to it by their leaders who authorize it, such as would be the case if Hasan Mohammed di Tiro gave the word that now one should seek revenge. Something of this sort happened in 1966 in Aceh when every Communist found in the province was put to death in an organized manner. The number of Communists in Aceh in 1965 was small. There were perhaps between 2,000 and 3,000, mainly transmigrants or railroad workers. These people were only murdered after army commander Isjhak Djuasa had encouraged youths to do so and let them know that they would not be punished.

Even then, there was reluctance to act. High school students took a large part in the actions. The head of a senior high school in one of the districts described their actions to me in 1969. He had helped to establish a school himself in the 1950s, then became a government official. I wrote down his words from memory just after speaking with him:

I left the DPR [the regional assembly] to return to the school. As many as ten students had already joined the PKI [the Indonesian Communist Party] youth. Some were even so fanatic that they brought rice to Thaib Adamy [the secretary of the Pidie branch of the Indonesian Communist Party, who was tried for sedition] at his trial.

My informant was the head of the school when, about a month after the presumed Communist coup attempt in Java, the local military commander called a meeting of local officials to urge an attack on the PKI. At this meeting he explained what had happened in Java. The next day there was a demonstration. The demonstrators met at the mosque in Banda Aceh, marched to PKI headquarters and tore down their signboard, then emptied the building of its contents. They then went to the PKI youth headquarters (IPPI) and did the same, taking the loot to the house of the *bupati* (regent), where they burned it. This was supposed to be the end of the affair. It had been planned by the army, the police, and youth groups. But instead of breaking up, the youths marched to a Chinese shop whose owner was the head of Baperki

(the leftist Chinese political organization) though
not himself PKI and smashed it to pieces. Then they
went to the medicine store of Kim Kie, who was the
head of GPTI (another leftist organization), and one
more shop and did the same. Neither the police nor
the army could stop them. Shortly after, a committee
was formed to smash the PKI. It consisted of representatives of the military commander, the chief of
police, the regent, and representatives of various
officials and youth organizations. They had lists of
PKI members and went out and arrested them.
Similar committees were formed in villages. Those
arrested were placed in three categories: leaders,
convinced members, and sympathizers. The first two
categories were killed. They were jailed, and then
about eleven at night youths, with trucks furnished
by the government, would take them to a place outside the city, where they were murdered. The
killings went on for three months. Without leadership, there would have been no action. But once the
movement starts, it is not always controllable. The
murders, however, were not due to "the people" acting without restraint. They were committed with the
leadership and cooperation of the police and the
army. "The people" had to be mobilized and organized. Central to this mobilization was an induced
fear. As in other places in Indonesia at the time, it
was widely believed that if one did not act against
the Communists, they would not only control the
country but kill their opponents. For the person cited
earlier this fear arose when he thought of his stu-

dents. He saw that ten teenagers were already members of the Communist youth group. He clearly thought that this was a dangerous trend. The tendency of youth was or could have been toward Communism, and the result would be catastrophic if they did not act first.

Note that there is no question in Aceh of political factions at work. There are no competing village organizations, some Communist, some Muslim, for instance. And there was no significant Communist representation in any government body. At best this fear was associated with Madiun, the battle during the Revolution between Communists and others. The military commander of Aceh told me in 1964 that ever since that battle he was vigilant out of fear of repeated Communist treachery. But Madiun, where this battle took place, was far away in Java and seldom referred to in my hearing in the early 1960s. It is not a question of remembering what "they" did to us and wanting revenge. For the head of the school fear was associated not with what certain students were but with what they might become.

In the preceding statement and, I think, in the assumption of most Acehnese at the time, there were great expectations put on the schools. It was through the school that M., the head of the school, thought he could contain the tendency toward Communism, and it was in the school that he thought he saw that movement occur. What was it in schools that made them so important? In the 1960s the Indonesian economy was in ruins. It was widely said in Aceh that teachers' wages were insufficient even to buy cigarettes. Students' parents supplemented salaries when they could, but it was quite common in Aceh for teachers to appear only once or twice a week. This did not prevent students from attending school, but it certainly affected what they learned. Nonetheless, something important happened to students; it obviously did not depend on what they learned. What was important was first being a student and then getting a diploma. The diploma, as everyone familiar with Indonesia knows, is believed to state something significant about its bearer. It is not an indication of what one knows so much as a sign of what sort of person one is. The schools could operate practically without any teachers at all, but they could not do without *ijazah* (diplomas).

The goal of the school was not to eliminate the village or the agricultural sector. Daud Beureuèh, when I knew him just after he had led the rebellion of the 1950s, spent his time, as I described, improving this sector. But he never had it in mind to make Aceh into a different sort of society altogether. The school, in his mind, was simply an instrument of enlightenment and improvement and at the same time merely brought out tendencies already present in Acehnese society. Nationalism and the local, to change the terms of the discussion, were complementary, not antagonistic. The effect of the school was to recognize village youths as nationalists and to deliver them out of the family and the village. The latter remained in place, the school being, one can say, an agent not of transformation but of recognition. When one became a student in a national school, the possibility of adding something to oneself that was not evident before was revealed. One was "a student" and as such a nationalist. It was not really necessary to learn the subjects teachers taught to find it out, membership in the school and the moral knowledge one gained there being sufficient. School was a ritual institution that revealed the bond, not otherwise evident, between family and countryside on the one hand and nation on the other.

Four years before the killings, when teachers were already not coming to work, no one feared the failure of the school. The school, meaning the junior and senior high school, was an instrument of moral change, making villagers into Muslim nationalists. Daud Beureuèh's reform movement in the 1930s had established the same sort of school; his own school in fact became part of the public school system. If these schools made new social types, it was of course because there was already a desire for such. The school was not in the first place a teaching institution. It was a place where the desire to be a nationalist was recognized or one can say brought out. It was part of a national system, but it was thought to be needed, which is to say, also, compatible with Aceh as it was. Only when a few students began to join Communist organizations and when this was seen in the light of events reported from Java was the work of the school thought to be threatened.

The people killed in Aceh in 1965–66 were mainly

railroad workers and transmigrant farmers, as I have said. But the fear of Communism was not from these people. Nor, for that matter, could it be said that there was a fear of Communists on an important scale before 1965. There had been contention, and there had been action, principally the trial of Thaib Adamy, an official of the party, for sedition, but people did not much discuss Communists, and they were certainly not trembling in fear. When such fear arose in 1965, it had little to do with the Communists known to reside in Aceh. It was a much less locatable fear, as people reported seeing lights at sea imagined to be Communist signals and, as elsewhere in Indonesia, rumors circulated of lists made by the Communists designating their future victims. The fear of Communists was a fear of a fundamental process of development gone wrong. "Communists" designated an anxiety about something amiss in the very heart of Acehnese society, that part of it that linked it to Indonesia and, long before there was an Indonesia, made it possible for there to be an "Aceh" at all.[28]

[28] By this I refer to the system of villages and trade along diverse river routes, each self-contained and only seldom linked into a functioning unit, which, nonetheless, constituted a symbolic political entity, all Acehnese recognizing the same sultan, the sultan being the figure of supplementarity much later taken by the school.

Ever since Snouck the boundaries of Aceh posed a problem to analysts. Snouck repeatedly pointed out that except for a few rulers the sultan had no power in the interior. Control of the interior depended on control of trade up the rivers. The sultan seldom had naval forces sufficient to maintain an effective presence. Real political power passed into the hands of the *uleebelang*. And yet Aceh remained a unity. It was of course a cultural or symbolic

What is involved is a fantasy, though a serious fantasy, of identity. In this century this fantasy is set on the national scene. Those who feared Communists did not envision them as workers or farmers or Javanese or Acehnese or villagers or descendants of *uleebelang*. Rather, as expressed by M., the school head quoted earlier, Communist students were feared, because "student" was a transitional type, one that led to being a full member of the Indonesian nation. For M. membership in a Communist youth organization did not merely reflect a political opinion. He called these youth *fanatik* (fanatical). To say someone is *fanatik* means, in English as in Acehnese, that the individual is not open to the opinions of others and has restricted horizons. The word comes into Acehnese from Indonesian through Dutch and was used by Dutch in the Indies in particular for Muslims and especially for Acehnese. It expressed the Dutch view of Acehnese as closed in their thinking and enclosed in a world set apart. For M., Communist students were a monstrosity. The school should produce modernists, Indonesians in the developed sense of the

---

unity that centered on the sultan. The Acehnese War destroyed the sultanate, but it did not end Aceh as a symbolic entity. Institutions changed radically as Aceh reconstituted itself around Islamic reformism, which was, of course, an educational project. But the underlying symbolic processes, the notion of the incompleteness of the local that called for another force, did not change. What gave Aceh its unity was not its external boundaries but the focus on a single figure or agent of supplementarity, whether the sultan or the school. Aceh, in this view, constituted itself from below.

term; instead, it was turning out persons whom one could not recognize. The world they belonged to was not open to him. And yet he knew that he, as a teacher and the head of a school and a modernist, should know them. It was, for him, the fear not merely of boys born in Aceh turning to Communism but of such boys doing so through the (mis)working of the institution that was supposed to ensure a path from village to nation. When that institution was thought not to work, a phantasm arose that the New Order drew on for thirty-two years: the inassimilable "masses," incapable of being made part of the Indonesian people. Events on the national scene, the presumed Communist coup attempt of 1965, were thus localized in Aceh. The menace of something resurgent from within the heart of the nation and of Aceh but nonetheless in his view foreign to it justified the massacre that followed.

In the complicated relations between the Indonesian state and its people there are two main strands of development since the beginning of the New Order in 1966. There is the fear of the underclass that existed before the New Order but which was deliberately accentuated after the massacres of 1965–66. And there is the criminalization of the state in conjunction with this. It created a situation where it was easier than ever, given the weakness of response in Aceh and the lack of representation possible for Acehnese, to extract wealth from Aceh and elsewhere without much return to the province. But there was also much development in Aceh under the technocrats. No one can doubt the good brought by enormous improvement in the transportation system or the growth of the university though there were many other less important projects done mainly for the 10 percent that went to government officials. The result of these developments was in Aceh as elsewhere the growth of a national middle class.[29]

I have called the present students who advocate Acheh Merdeka nationalists whose nation is the middle class. But it is a different middle class than we know from Europe because it was not formed through liberation from feudalism and explicit class antagonism. We see how the boundaries between classes are erected in Aceh when we see students possessed by a past that they cannot put behind them. It is this unwanted possibility that shows them the immense difference between life in the middle class and life in their place of origin. Class boundaries in Indonesia are not formed through conflict but through the supersession of the past as the middle class is formed out of the underclass.

In the difference between the massacres that bracket the New Order one sees the political developments of the Suharto period. When that period began, unless they were Communists, no Acehnese seemed to doubt the danger in the interior of Aceh. When it ended students identified themselves with that dangerous element and felt themselves victims.

[29] Fachry Ali, "Aceh Baru, Politik Baru," *Tempo,* May 9, 1987, p. 86.

Were they not to feel threatened in this way they might have been like their predecessors, ready for the most extreme action against Indonesia's enemies, this time, of course, not Communists but the Gerakan Acheh Merdeka. Such an evolution depends on loss of confidence not merely in the state but in the nation. With it class formation is also blocked. And with that blockage comes possession. Possession, I have said, is an effect of the past. It is the past that cannot be made into history. Possession reveals the process of class distinction precisely when the process is blocked. With that, Indonesia itself is thrown into doubt. One sees the dependence of the Indonesian nation on the continued presence of what preceded it.

Normally, this past is superseded. Abnormally, today, for some Indonesians, holding on to it, or, rather, having it hold on to them, is nearly the only recourse against becoming part of New Order savagery. In effect, many Acehnese find themselves caught in the original process of the production of the nation, unable to go forward and threatened with death. The result, which at first seems odd, is their restraint of violence. Seeing the poverty of thinking and the terror practiced in Aceh today one sees how the New Order destroyed culture as its barbarity developed. The resistance in Aceh today is very far from what was termed *fanatik* during the Acehnese War. It is equally removed from revolution. Students merely borrow a term, *merdeka,* which does more to express their fear than to designate a political goal.

Hasan Mohammed di Tiro, rather than being the continuation of his *ulama* predecessors, is a Western businessman who has alienated Acehnese *ulama* by his lack of emphasis on religion. His followers are scarcely *fanatik* even if, as I write at the moment, they perhaps have been provoked into retaliation against the army.

When one sees the unwillingness of Acehnese to retaliate violently, an unwillingness that may soon enough give way to the impulses of revenge in answer to army provocations, one wonders finally at the source. There are the protonational impulse, the need for a spokesperson and thus the reconstitution of unity. This repeats the history of the nation and perhaps later the history of its revolution. But there is also the superstition against killing. One finds this when all established cultural authority either works against it or, as today, scarcely works at all. And there is the identification of students and injured villagers with its dependence on a vague power of recognition, now no longer an element of the Indonesian nation. It is not much to depend upon, but it points to the possibility of another authority, one not yet institutionalized, that arises with the destruction of cultures. It is a vague hope, but, it seems to me, if the impasse that Aceh and, I believe, Indonesia are caught in today is to be surpassed, perhaps it is not worthless.

In any case, were I to rewrite *The Rope of God* today, I would pay attention to the forces within Aceh and within other Indonesian societies that generate a call for recognition. From such a perspective, the unsuspected depths of personality, for lack of a more precise term, called out by photographs would be placed alongside premodern and precolonial elements that we have seen in the Acehnese epic. It is not merely "Islam" and not merely "Aceh" that draws these forth. It was also "Indonesia." But all of it depends on the source of recognition being potentially undefinable, as, I believe, is the case today. It is against this indefiniteness that authority asserts its claim. Against the incomprehensible violence of the army, there is a wild call for help to anyone at all from its victims, past and potential. This appeal is directed to a force that, even if embedded only in superstition, or only in wishfulness, precisely because it lacks definition, can conjure up other paths than the ones we have seen to date. Such an approach would show a less linear development of identity than appears in the book now.

"What's thought can be dispensed with/Till the refusal propagates a fear," to continue with the thinking of T. S. Eliot, with which this piece began. Had Acehnese thought before murdering Communists, the course of their history would have been different. What would have been the result if release from possession was allowed plural ends? The pressure for such release in 1966, however, dispensed with thinking and propagated fear. Nothing in the situation at the time in Aceh showed this to be a necessity. But it happened, and it led to the support of a regime that gained power through murder and retained it by propagating fear of the same sort. "Virtues/Are forced upon us by our impudent crimes," Eliot tells us, but it will take something more for the wish for tolerance that one finds embedded in much of Indonesian everyday life, including Aceh, and that infuses Indonesia with a deceptively reassuring tonality to find a basis in national identities. For this to happen, the unexpected fears that course through "cunning passages" and "contrived corridors" have to be somehow accommodated.

New Order violence continues past the New Order. It is founded on fear of what might emerge from the people. It builds on fears consolidated in 1965 that were, in Aceh at least, present as a condition of the region's relation to the nation. Fears generated from the logic of possession today govern the opposition to that violence just as they governed support of it thirty-four years earlier. What makes the difference between the periods is the violence of the army directed against Indonesians on the one hand and, on the other, the silencing of "the people." Recall the description in *The Rope of God* of the resistance to the Dutch after Aceh was "pacified." Then the Holy War was continued by individuals the Dutch authorities considered not merely fanatical but mad. Their ability to act was also a form of speech; their text was the *Hikajat Prang Sabi* (the Story of the Holy War). Though this text is referred to by GAM members, the Holy War no longer is continued by individuals acting alone, nor, as we have seen, have individual Acehnese, at least on any scale, found a reason to take revenge. What has intervened is the Revolution, the time when individuals formed themselves into small groups and acted without waiting for their leaders. From the testimony of certain revolutionaries, it is evident that the Revolution was a time when something beyond the voice manifested itself. It was a time, for some at least, of violent action that needed no "leadership," no one to speak for these revolutionaries. This expression of something outside speech never found and could never find an institutional expression when Indonesia began to construct itself as an independent country. But it leaves its trace in the fear of the people and in the attempt of the army to recoup that power for itself. It finds its further trace, I believe, in the silence of the people today, in their willingness to wait for authorization before unleashing a possibly blind violence they do not consciously admit to, even now.[30]

June 1999

[30] At this point I want to suggest the value of a comparative study of possession in its political and cultural dimensions. Such work would draw on the quite different and quite comparable place of possession in Thailand and the Philippines as described in the excellent work of Rosalind Morris, *In the Place of Origins: Modernity and Its Mediums in Northern Thailand* (Durham: Duke University Press, 2000); and by Fenella Cannell in *Power and Intimacy in the Christian Philippines* (Cambridge: Cambridge University Press, 1999), parts II–IV.

*Author's Note:* At the time this book was being published, I received word that five bodies had been discovered in Medan. Amongst them was that of a student active in exposing Army violence in Aceh, Jafar Siddiq Hamzah. Jafar had been abducted; all five were tortured before being murdered. The other corpses are presently unidentified.

## Ann Arbor Paperbacks